MY EARLY LIFE

A ROVING COMMISSION

MY EARLY LIFE

A ROVING COMMISSION

by

WINSTON S. CHURCHILL

A CHARLES SCRIBNER'S SONS BOOK
MACMILLAN PUBLISHING COMPANY
NEW YORK

First published in the United States under the title *A Roving Commission:
My Early Life*

Charles Scribner's Sons
Macmillan Publishing Company
866 Third Avenue, New York, N.Y. 10022

Library of Congress Cataloging-in-Publication Data

Churchill, Winston, Sir, 1874–1965.
   My early life.

   1. Churchill, Winston, Sir, 1874–1965.
   2. Prime ministers—Great Britain—Biography.
   3. War correspondents—Great Britain—Biography.
   4. Great Britain. Army—Biography. I. Title.
   DA566.9.C5A3 1987   941.082′092′4 [B]   87-4782
   ISBN 0-684-18803-1

Macmillan books are available at special discounts for bulk purchases for sales
promotions, premiums, fund-raising, or educational use. For details, contact:

Special Sales Director
Macmillan Publishing Company
866 Third Avenue
New York, N.Y. 10022

Scribner Paperback Edition, 1987

10 9 8 7 6 5 4

Printed in the United States of America

TO

A NEW GENERATION

AUTHOR'S PREFACE

VARIOUS accounts having appeared from time to time of my early life and adventures, and I myself having published thirty years ago stories of the several campaigns in which I took part, and having written later about particular episodes, I have thought it right to bring the whole together in a single complete story; and to tell the tale, such as it is, anew. I have therefore not only searched my memory, but have most carefully verified my facts from the records which I possess. I have tried, in each part of the quarter-century in which this tale lies, to show the point of view appropriate to my years, whether as a child, a schoolboy, a cadet, a subaltern, a war-correspondent or a youthful politician. If these opinions conflict with those now generally accepted, they must be taken merely as representing a phase in my early life, and not in any respect, except where the context warrants, as modern pronouncements.

When I survey this work as a whole I find I have drawn a picture of a vanished age. The character of society, the foundations of politics, the methods of war, the outlook of youth, the scale of values, are all changed, and changed to an extent I should not have believed possible in so short a space without any violent domestic revolution. I cannot pretend to feel that they are in all respects changed for the better. I was a child of the Victorian era, when the structure of our country seemed firmly set, when its position in trade and on the seas was unrivalled, and when the realisation of the greatness of our Empire and of our duty to preserve it was ever growing stronger. In those days the dominant forces in Great Britain were very sure of themselves and of their doctrines. They thought they could teach the world the art of government, and the science of economics. They were sure they were supreme at sea and consequently safe at home. They rested therefore sedately under the convictions of power and security. Very different is the aspect of these anxious and dubious times. Full allowance for such changes should be made by friendly readers.

I have thought that it might be of interest to the new generation to read a story of youthful endeavour, and I have set down candidly and with as much simplicity as possible my personal fortunes.

It seems specially appropriate to this new American edition that I should give some further account of my American forbears. My mother was a Jerome. Timothy Jerome sailed from England in 1717 and settled in the village of Pompey, not far from the town of Syracuse in the colony of New York. His son, Samuel, and four of his grandsons fought in Washington's armies during the revolutionary war. The Jeromes continued to dwell at Pompey for four or five generations. In the early part of the nineteenth century my grandfather, Leonard Jerome, and one of his brothers, Larry, after graduating at Princeton College, having become more prosperous, moved to Rochester. Here they married two sisters, the Miss Halls. They built two small houses side by side in what was then the best quarter of the city, and connected them by a bridge. My grandfather had four daughters and his brother had four sons. My mother, the second of Leonard Jerome's daughters, was born in Rochester in the year 1854. Meanwhile the family had been gathering prosperity in the general advance of the United States, and in 1856 they moved to New York. Here my grandfather built two houses in Madison Square, one of which was the Manhattan Club House and in the other he lived for the rest of his life. At Rochester he had founded a new paper which was the organ of what was in those days called the "Know Nothing Party." This paper survives today as the *Rochester Democrat and Chronicle*.

In New York he embarked upon much larger ventures,

both in newspaper ownership and in real estate business, and at the outbreak of the Civil War he was already a wealthy man and a leading citizen. He was an ardent supporter of the Union cause throughout the struggle, though he never meddled much with politics. His main interests apart from his business were Sport and Music. He was a magnificent looking man with long flowing moustachios, a rather aquiline nose, and very bright eyes. All these I remember. He was accustomed to drive about New York on important occasions in a coach with a team of six horses of which he was an expert Whip. He has good claims to be regarded as the father of the American Turf, and Jerome Park, the old racecourse now built over, was named after him. He formed the Jockey Club and was long its Vice-President. He owned the famous racehorse, Kentucky, who never knew defeat. He was one of the original founders of the Academy of Music in New York, helped to start opera, befriended Jenny Lind and Patti, and educated Miss Minnie Hauk, the creator of the role of Carmen.

His wife took her daughters to Paris just before the outbreak of the Franco-German War. Driven from the French capital by the German advance they lived for a time in England and made many friends there. In the summer of 1873 while on a visit to Cowes, Miss Jennie Jerome met my father Lord Randolph Churchill. She was at that time widely known in New York, Paris and London Society as one of the most beautiful girls of the day. Lord Randolph Churchill fell in love with her at first sight, and in a few months they were man and wife.

WINSTON S. CHURCHILL.

CONTENTS

CONTENTS

CHAPTER I

CHILDHOOD

WHEN does one first begin to remember? When do the waving lights and shadows of dawning consciousness cast their print upon the mind of a child? My earliest memories are Ireland. I can recall scenes and events in Ireland quite well, and sometimes dimly even, people. Yet I was born on November 30, 1874, and I left Ireland early in the year 1879. My father had gone to Ireland as secretary to his father, the Duke of Marlborough, appointed Lord-Lieutenant by Mr. Disraeli in 1876. We lived in a house called 'The Little Lodge,' about a stone's throw from the Viceregal. Here I spent nearly three years of childhood. I have clear and vivid impressions of some events. I remember my grandfather, the Viceroy, unveiling the Lord Gough statue in 1878. A great black crowd, scarlet soldiers on horseback, strings pulling away a brown shiny sheet, the old Duke, the formidable grandpapa, talking loudly to the crowd. I recall even a phrase he used: 'and with a withering volley he shattered the enemy's line.' I quite understood that he was speaking about war and fighting and that a 'volley' meant what the black-coated soldiers (Riflemen) used to do with loud bangs so often in the Phœnix Park where I was taken for my morning walks. This, I think, is my first coherent memory.

Other events stand out more distinctly. We were to go to a pantomime. There was great excitement about it. The long-looked-for afternoon arrived. We started from the Viceregal and drove to the Castle where other children were no doubt to be picked up. Inside the Castle was a great square space paved with small oblong stones. It rained. It nearly always rained—just as it does now. People came out of the doors of the Castle, and there seemed to be much stir. Then we were told we could not go to the pantomime because the theatre had been burned down. All that was found of the manager was the keys that had been in his pocket. We were promised as a consolation for not going to the pantomime to go next day and see the ruins of the building. I wanted very much to see the keys, but this request does not seem to have been well received.

In one of these years we paid a visit to Emo Park, the seat of Lord Portarlington, who was explained to me as a sort of uncle. Of this place I can give very clear descriptions, though I have never been there since I was four or four and a half. The central point in my memory is a tall white stone tower which we reached after a considerable drive. I was told it had been blown up by Oliver Cromwell. I understood definitely that he had blown up all sorts of things and was therefore a very great man.

My nurse, Mrs. Everest, was nervous about the Fenians. I gathered these were wicked people and there was no end to what they would do if they had their way. On one occasion when I was out riding on my donkey, we thought we saw a long dark procession of Fenians approaching. I am sure now it must have been the Rifle Brigade out for a route march. But we were all very much alarmed, particularly the donkey, who expressed his anxiety by kicking. I was thrown off and had concussion of the brain. This was my first introduction to Irish politics!

In the Phœnix Park there was a great round clump of trees with a house inside it. In this house there lived a personage styled the Chief Secretary or the Under Secretary, I am not clear which. But at any rate from this house there came a man called Mr. Burke. He gave me a drum. I cannot remember what he looked like, but I remember the drum. Two years afterwards when we were back in Eng-

2

land, they told me he had been murdered by the Fenians in this same Phœnix Park we used to walk about in every day. Everyone round me seemed much upset about it, and I thought how lucky it was the Fenians had not got me when I fell off the donkey.

It was at 'The Little Lodge' I was first menaced with Education. The approach of a sinister figure described as 'the Governess' was announced. Her arrival was fixed for a certain day. In order to prepare for this day Mrs. Everest produced a book called *Reading without Tears*. It certainly did not justify its title in my case. I was made aware that before the Governess arrived I must be able to read without tears. We toiled each day. My nurse pointed with a pen at the different letters. I thought it all very tiresome. Our preparations were by no means completed when the fateful hour struck and the Governess was due to arrive. I did what so many oppressed peoples have done in similar circumstances: I took to the woods. I hid in the extensive shrubberies—forests they seemed—which surrounded 'The Little Lodge.' Hours passed before I was retrieved and handed over to 'the Governess.' We continued to toil every day, not only at letters but at words, and also at what was much worse, figures. Letters after all had only got to be known, and when they stood together in a certain way one recognised their formation and that it meant a certain sound or word which one uttered when pressed sufficiently. But the figures were tied into all sorts of tangles and did things to one another which it was extremely difficult to forecast with complete accuracy. You had to say what they did each time they were tied up together, and the Governess apparently attached enormous importance to the answer being exact. If it was not right, it was wrong. It was not any use being 'nearly right.' In some cases these figures got into debt with one another: you had to borrow one or carry one, and afterwards you had to pay back the one you had borrowed. These complications cast a steadily gathering shadow over my daily life. They took one away from all the interesting things one wanted to do in the nursery or in the garden. They made increasing inroads upon one's leisure. One could hardly get time to do any of the things one wanted to do. They became a general worry and preoccupation. More especially was this true when we descended into a dismal bog called 'sums.' There appeared to be no limit to these. When one sum was done, there was always another. Just as soon as I managed to tackle a particular class of these afflictions, some other much more variegated type was thrust upon me.

My mother took no part in these impositions, but she gave me to understand that she approved of them and she sided with the Governess almost always. My picture of her in Ireland is in a riding habit, fitting like a skin and often beautifully spotted with mud. She and my father hunted continually on their large horses; and sometimes there were great scares because one or the other did not come back for many hours after they were expected.

My mother always seemed to me a fairy princess: a radiant being possessed of limitless riches and power. Lord D'Abernon has described her as she was in these Irish days in words for which I am grateful.

. . . 'I have the clearest recollection of seeing her for the first time. It was at the Vice-Regal Lodge at Dublin. She stood on one side to the left of the entrance. The Viceroy was on a dais at the farther end of the room surrounded by a brilliant staff, but eyes were not turned on him or on his consort, but on a dark, lithe figure, standing somewhat apart and appearing to be of another texture to those around her, radiant, translucent, intense. A diamond star in her hair, her favourite ornament—its lustre dimmed by the flashing glory of her eyes. More of the panther than of the woman in her look, but with a cultivated intelligence unknown to the jungle. Her courage not less great than that of her husband —fit mother for descendants of the great Duke. With all these attributes of brilliancy, such kindliness and high spirits that she was universally popular. Her desire to please, her delight in life, and the genuine wish that all should share her joyous faith in it, made her the centre of a devoted circle.'

My mother made the same brilliant impression upon my childhood's eye. She shone for me like the Evening Star. I loved her dearly—but at a distance. My nurse was my confidante. Mrs. Everest it was who looked after me and tended all my wants. It was to her I poured out my many troubles, both now and in my schooldays. Before she came to us, she had brought up for twelve years a little girl called Ella, the daughter of a clergyman who lived in Cumberland. 'Little Ella,' though I never saw her, became a feature in my early life. I knew all about her; what she liked to eat; how she used to say her prayers; in what ways she was naughty and in what ways good. I had a vivid picture in my mind of her home in the North country. I was also taught to be very fond of Kent. It was, Mrs. Everest said, 'the garden of England.' She had been born at Chatham, and was immensely proud of Kent. No county could compare with Kent, any more than any other country could compare with England. Ireland, for instance, was nothing like so good. As for France, Mrs. Everest who had at one time wheeled me in my perambulator up and down what she called the 'Shams Elizzie' thought very little of it. Kent was the place. Its capital was Maidstone, and all round Maidstone there grew strawberries, cherries, raspberries and plums. Lovely! I always wanted to live in Kent.

I revisited 'The Little Lodge' when lecturing on the Boer War in Dublin in the winter of 1900. I remembered well that it was a long low white building with green shutters and verandahs, and that there was a lawn around it about as big as Trafalgar Square and entirely surrounded by forests. I thought it must have been at least a mile from the Viceregal. When I saw it again, I was astonished to find that the lawn was only about sixty yards across, that the forests were little more than bushes, and that it only took a minute to ride to it from the Viceregal where I was staying.

My next foothold of memory is Ventnor. I loved Ventnor. Mrs. Everest had a sister who lived at Ventnor. Her husband had been nearly thirty years a prison warder. Both then and in later years he used to take me for long walks over the Downs or through the Landslip. He told me many stories of mutinies in the prisons and how he had been attacked and injured on several occasions by the convicts. When I first stayed at Ventnor we were fighting a war with the Zulus. There were pictures in the papers of these Zulus. They were black and naked, with spears called 'assegais' which they threw very cleverly. They killed a great many of our soldiers, but judging from the pictures, not nearly so many as our soldiers killed of them. I was very angry with the Zulus, and glad to hear they were being killed; and so was my friend, the old prison warder. After a while it seemed that they were all killed, because this particular war came to an end and there were no more pictures of Zulus in the papers and nobody worried any more about them.

One day when we were out on the cliffs near Ventnor, we saw a great splendid ship with all her sails set, passing the shore only a mile or two away. 'That is a troopship,' they said, 'bringing the men back from the war.' But it may have been from India, I cannot remember.[1] Then all of a sudden there were black clouds and wind and the first drops of a storm, and we just scrambled home without getting wet through. The next time I went out on those cliffs there was no splendid ship in full sail, but three black masts were pointed out to me, sticking up out of the water in a stark way. She was the *Eurydice*.[2] She had capsized in this very

[1] In fact she was a training ship.
[2] Pronounced by us in two syllables.

squall and gone to the bottom with three hundred soldiers on board. The divers went down to bring up the corpses. I was told—and it made a scar on my mind—that some of the divers had fainted with terror at seeing the fish eating the bodies of the poor soldiers who had been drowned just as they were coming back home after all their hard work and danger in fighting savages. I seem to have seen some of these corpses towed very slowly by boats one sunny day. There were many people on the cliffs to watch, and we all took off our hats in sorrow.

Just about this time also there happened the 'Tay Bridge Disaster.' A whole bridge tumbled down while a train was running on it in a great storm, and all the passengers were drowned. I supposed they could not get out of the carriage windows in time. It would be very hard to open one of those windows where you have to pull up a long strap before you can let it down. No wonder they were all drowned. All my world was very angry that the Government should have allowed a bridge like this to tumble down. It seemed to me they had been very careless, and I did not wonder at all that the people said they would vote against them for being so lazy and neglectful as to let such a shocking thing happen.

In 1880 we were all thrown out of office by Mr. Gladstone. Mr. Gladstone was a very dangerous man who went about rousing people up, lashing them into fury so that they voted against the Conservatives and turned my grandfather out of his place as Lord-Lieutenant of Ireland. He liked this place much less than his old office of Lord President of the Council, which he had held in Lord Beaconsfield's previous government. When he was Lord-Lieutenant he had to spend all his money on giving entertainments to the Irish in Dublin; and my grandmother had also got up a great subscription called 'The Famine Fund.' However, it was borne in upon me that the Irish were a very ungrateful people: they did not say so much as 'Thank you' for the entertainments, nor even for 'The Famine Fund.' The Duke would much rather have stayed in England where he could live in his own home at Blenheim and regularly attend the Cabinet. But he always did whatever Lord Beaconsfield told him to do. Lord Beaconsfield was the great enemy of Mr. Gladstone, and everybody called him 'Dizzy.' However, this time 'Dizzy' had been thoroughly beaten by Mr. Gladstone, so we were all flung out into Opposition and the country began to be ruined very rapidly. Everyone said it was 'going to the dogs.' And then on top of all this Lord Beaconsfield got very ill. He had a long illness; and as he was also very old, it killed him. I followed his illness from day to day with great anxiety, because everyone said what a loss he would be to his country and how no one else could stop Mr. Gladstone from working his wicked will upon us all. I was always sure Lord Beaconsfield was going to die, and at last the day came when all the people I saw went about with very sad faces because, as they said, a great and splendid Statesman, who loved our country and defied the Russians, had died of a broken heart because of the ingratitude with which he had been treated by the Radicals.

I have already described the dreaded apparition in my world of 'The Governess.' But now a much worse peril began to threaten. I was to go to school. I was now seven years old, and I was what grown-up people in their offhand way called 'a troublesome boy.' It appeared that I was to go away from home for many weeks at a stretch in order to do lessons under masters. The term had already begun, but still I should have to stay seven weeks before I could come home for Christmas. Although much that I had heard about school had made a distinctly disagreeable impression on my mind, an impression, I may add, thoroughly borne out by the actual experience, I was also excited and agitated by this great change in my life. I thought in spite of the lessons, it would be fun living with so many other boys, and that we should make friends together and have great adventures. Also I was told that 'school days were the happiest time in one's life.' Several grown-up people added that in their day, when they were young, schools were very rough: there was bullying, they didn't get enough to eat, they had 'to break the ice in their pitchers' each morning (a thing I have never seen done in my life). But now it was all changed. School life nowadays was one long treat. All the boys enjoyed it. Some of my cousins who were a little older had been quite sorry—I was told—to come home for the holidays. Cross-examined the cousins did not confirm this; they only grinned. Anyhow I was perfectly helpless. Irresistible tides drew me swiftly forward. I was no more consulted about leaving home than I had been about coming into the world.

It was very interesting buying all the things one had to have for going to school. No less than fourteen pairs of socks were on the list. Mrs. Everest thought this was very extravagant. She said that with care ten pairs would do quite well. Still it was a good thing to have some to spare, as one could then make sure of avoiding the very great dangers inseparable from 'sitting in wet feet.'

The fateful day arrived. My mother took me to the station in a hansom cab. She gave me three half-crowns which I dropped on to the floor of the cab, and we had to scramble about in the straw to find them again. We only just caught the train. If we had missed it, it would have been the end of the world. However, we didn't, and the world went on.

The school my parents had selected for my education was one of the most fashionable and expensive in the country. It modelled itself upon Eton and aimed at being preparatory for that Public School above all others. It was supposed to be the very last thing in schools. Only ten boys in a class; electric light (then a wonder); a swimming pond; spacious football and cricket grounds; two or three school treats, or 'expeditions' as they were called, every term; the masters all M.A.'s in gowns and mortar-boards; a chapel of its own;

no hampers allowed; everything provided by the authorities. It was a dark November afternoon when we arrived at this establishment. We had tea with the Headmaster, with whom my mother conversed in the most easy manner. I was preoccupied with the fear of spilling my cup and so making 'a bad start.' I was also miserable at the idea of being left alone among all these strangers in this great, fierce, formidable place. After all I was only seven, and I had been so happy in my nursery with all my toys. I had such wonderful toys: a real steam engine, a magic lantern, and a collection of soldiers already nearly a thousand strong. Now it was to be all lessons. Seven or eight hours of lessons every day except half-holidays, and football or cricket in addition.

When the last sound of my mother's departing wheels had died away, the Headmaster invited me to hand over any money I had in my possession. I produced my three half-crowns which were duly entered in a book, and I was told that from time to time there would be a 'shop' at the school with all sorts of things which one would like to have, and that I could choose what I liked up to the limit of the seven and sixpence. Then we quitted the Headmaster's parlour and the comfortable private side of the house, and entered the more bleak apartments reserved for the instruction and accommodation of the pupils. I was taken into a Form Room and told to sit at a desk. All the other boys were out of doors, and I was alone with the Form Master. He produced a thin greeny-brown-covered book filled with words in different types of print.

'You have never done any Latin before, have you?' he said.

'No, sir.'

'This is a Latin grammar.' He opened it at a well-thumbed page. 'You must learn this,' he said, pointing to a number of words in a frame of lines. 'I will come back in half an hour and see what you know.'

Behold me then on a gloomy evening, with an aching heart, seated in front of the First Declension.

Mensa	a table
Mensa	O table
Mensam	a table
Mensae	of a table
Mensae	to or for a table
Mensa	by, with or from a table

What on earth did it mean? Where was the sense of it? It seemed absolute rigmarole to me. However, there was one thing I could always do: I could learn by heart. And I thereupon proceeded, as far as my private sorrows would allow, to memorise the acrostic-looking task which had been set me.

In due course the Master returned.

'Have you learnt it?' he asked.

'I think I can *say* it, sir,' I replied; and I gabbled it off.

He seemed so satisfied with this that I was emboldened to ask a question.

'What does it mean, sir?'

'It means what it says. Mensa, a table. Mensa is a noun of the First Declension. There are five declensions. You have learnt the singular of the First Declension.'

'But,' I repeated, 'what does it mean?'

'Mensa means a table,' he answered.

'Then why does mensa also mean O table,' I enquired, 'and what does O table mean?'

'Mensa, O table, is the vocative case,' he replied.

'But why O table?' I persisted in genuine curiosity.

'O table,—you would use that in addressing a table, in invoking a table.' And then seeing he was not carrying me with him, 'You would use it in speaking to a table.'

'But I never do,' I blurted out in honest amazement.

'If you are impertinent, you will be punished, and punished, let me tell you, very severely,' was his conclusive rejoinder.

Such was my first introduction to the classics from which,

I have been told, many of our cleverest men have derived so much solace and profit.

The Form Master's observations about punishment were by no means without their warrant at St. James's School. Flogging with the birch in accordance with the Eton fashion was a great feature in its curriculum. But I am sure no Eton boy, and certainly no Harrow boy of my day, ever received such a cruel flogging as this Headmaster was accustomed to inflict upon the little boys who were in his care and power. They exceeded in severity anything that would be tolerated in any of the Reformatories under the Home Office. My reading in later life has supplied me with some possible explanations of his temperament. Two or three times a month the whole school was marshalled in the Library, and one or more delinquents were haled off to an adjoining apartment by the two head boys, and there flogged until they bled freely, while the rest sat quaking, listening to their screams. This form of correction was strongly reinforced by frequent religious services of a somewhat High Church character in the chapel. Mrs. Everest was very much against the Pope. If the truth were known, she said, he was behind the Fenians. She was herself Low Church, and her dislike of ornaments and ritual, and generally her extremely unfavourable opinion of the Supreme Pontiff, had prejudiced me strongly against that personage and all religious practices supposed to be associated with him. I therefore did not derive much comfort from the spiritual side of my education at this juncture. On the other hand, I experienced the fullest applications of the secular arm.

How I hated this school, and what a life of anxiety I lived there for more than two years. I made very little progress at my lessons, and none at all at games. I counted the days and the hours to the end of every term, when I should return home from this hateful servitude and range my soldiers in line of battle on the nursery floor. The greatest pleasure I had in those days was reading. When I was nine and a half my father gave me *Treasure Island*, and I remember the delight with which I devoured it. My teachers saw me at once backward and precocious, reading books beyond my years and yet at the bottom of the Form. They were offended. They had large resources of compulsion at their disposal, but I was stubborn. Where my reason, imagination or interest were not engaged, I would not or I could not learn. In all the twelve years I was at school no one ever succeeded in making me write a Latin verse or learn any Greek except the alphabet. I do not at all excuse myself for this foolish neglect of opportunities procured at so much expense by my parents and brought so forcibly to my attention by my Preceptors. Perhaps if I had been introduced to the ancients through their history and customs, instead of through their grammar and syntax, I might have had a better record.

I fell into a low state of health at St. James's School, and finally after a serious illness my parents took me away. Our family doctor, the celebrated Robson Roose, then practised at Brighton; and as I was now supposed to be very delicate, it was thought desirable that I should be under his constant care. I was accordingly, in 1883, transferred to a school at Brighton kept by two ladies. This was a smaller school than the one I had left. It was also cheaper and less pretentious. But there was an element of kindness and of sympathy which I had found conspicuously lacking in my first experiences. Here I remained for three years; and though I very nearly died from an attack of double pneumonia, I got gradually much stronger in that bracing air and gentle surroundings. At this school I was allowed to learn things which interested me: French, History, lots of Poetry by heart, and above all Riding and Swimming. The impression of those years makes a pleasant picture in my mind, in strong contrast to my earlier schoolday memories.

My partiality for Low Church principles which I had acquired from Mrs. Everest led me into one embarrassment.

We often attended the service in the Chapel Royal at Brighton. Here the school was accommodated in pews which ran North and South. In consequence, when the Apostles' Creed was recited, everyone turned to the East. I was sure Mrs. Everest would have considered this practice Popish, and I conceived it my duty to testify against it. I therefore stood stolidly to my front. I was conscious of having created a 'sensation.' I prepared myself for martyrdom. However, when we got home no comment of any kind was made upon my behaviour. I was almost disappointed, and looked forward to the next occasion for a further demonstration of my faith. But when it came, the school was shown into different pews in the Chapel Royal facing East, and no action was called for from any one of us when the Creed was said. I was puzzled to find my true course and duty. It seemed excessive to turn away from the East. Indeed I could not feel that such a step would be justified. I therefore became willy-nilly a passive conformist.

It was thoughtful and ingenious of these old ladies to have treated my scruples so tenderly. The results repaid their care. Never again have I caused or felt trouble on such a point. Not being resisted or ill-treated, I yielded myself complacently to a broad-minded tolerance and orthodoxy.

CHAPTER II

HARROW

I HAD scarcely passed my twelfth birthday when I entered the inhospitable regions of examinations, through which for the next seven years I was destined to journey. These examinations were a great trial to me. The subjects which were dearest to the examiners were almost invariably those I fancied least. I would have liked to have been examined in history, poetry and writing essays. The examiners, on the other hand, were partial to Latin and mathematics. And their will prevailed. Moreover, the questions which they asked on both these subjects were almost invariably those to which I was unable to suggest a satisfactory answer. I should have liked to be asked to say what I knew. They always tried to ask what I did not know. When I would have willingly displayed my knowledge, they sought to expose my ignorance. This sort of treatment had only one result: I did not do well in examinations.

This was especially true of my Entrance Examination to Harrow. The Headmaster, Dr. Welldon, however, took a broad-minded view of my Latin prose: he showed discernment in judging my general ability. This was the more remarkable, because I was found unable to answer a single question in the Latin paper. I wrote my name at the top of the page. I wrote down the number of the question 'I'. After much reflection I put a bracket round it thus '(I)'. But thereafter I could not think of anything connected with it that was either relevant or true. Incidentally there arrived from nowhere in particular a blot and several smudges. I gazed for two whole hours at this sad spectacle: and then merciful ushers collected my piece of foolscap with all the others and carried it up to the Headmaster's table. It was

15

from these slender indications of scholarship that Dr. Well-don drew the conclusion that I was worthy to pass into Harrow. It is very much to his credit. It showed that he was a man capable of looking beneath the surface of things: a man not dependent upon paper manifestations. I have always had the greatest regard for him.

In consequence of his decision, I was in due course placed in the third, or lowest, division of the Fourth, or bottom, Form. The names of the new boys were printed in the School List in alphabetical order; and as my correct name, Spencer-Churchill, began with an 'S,' I gained no more advantage from the alphabet than from the wider sphere of letters. I was in fact only two from the bottom of the whole school; and these two, I regret to say, disappeared almost immediately through illness or some other cause.

The Harrow custom of calling the roll is different from that of Eton. At Eton the boys stand in a cluster and lift their hats when their names are called. At Harrow they file past a Master in the school yard and answer one by one. My position was therefore revealed in its somewhat invidi-ous humility. It was the year 1887. Lord Randolph Church-ill had only just resigned his position as Leader of the House of Commons and Chancellor of the Exchequer, and he still towered in the forefront of politics. In consequence large numbers of visitors of both sexes used to wait on the school steps, in order to see me march by; and I frequently heard the irreverent comment, 'Why, he's last of all!'

I continued in this unpretentious situation for nearly a year. However, by being so long in the lowest form I gained an immense advantage over the cleverer boys. They all went on to learn Latin and Greek and splendid things like that. But I was taught English. We were considered such dunces that we could learn only English. Mr. Somervell—a most delightful man, to whom my debt is great—was charged with the duty of teaching the stupidest boys the most dis-regarded thing—namely, to write mere English. He knew how to do it. He taught it as no one else has ever taught it. Not only did we learn English parsing thoroughly, but we also practised continually English analysis. Mr. Somervell had a system of his own. He took a fairly long sentence and broke it up into its components by means of black, red, blue and green inks. Subject, verb, object: Relative Clauses, Conditional Clauses, Conjunctive and Disjunctive Clauses! Each had its colour and its bracket. It was a kind of drill. We did it almost daily. As I remained in the Third Fourth (β) three times as long as anyone else, I had three times as much of it. I learned it thoroughly. Thus I got into my bones the essential structure of the ordinary British sentence—which is a noble thing. And when in after years my schoolfellows who had won prizes and distinction for writing such beautiful Latin poetry and pithy Greek epigrams had to come down again to common English, to earn their living or make their way, I did not feel myself at any disadvantage. Naturally I am biassed in favour of boys learning English. I would make them all learn English: and then I would let the clever ones learn Latin as an honour, and Greek as a treat. But the only thing I would whip them for would be for not knowing English. I would whip them hard for that.

I first went to Harrow in the summer term. The school possessed the biggest swimming-bath I had ever seen. It was more like the bend of a river than a bath, and it had two bridges across it. Thither we used to repair for hours at a time and bask between our dips eating enormous buns on the hot asphalt margin. Naturally it was a good joke to come up behind some naked friend, or even enemy, and push him in. I made quite a habit of this with boys of my own size or less. One day when I had been no more than a month in the school, I saw a boy standing in a meditative posture wrapped in a towel on the very brink. He was no bigger than I was, so I thought him fair game. Coming stealthily behind I pushed him in, holding on to his towel out of humanity, so that it should not get wet. I was startled to see a furious face emerge from the foam, and a being evidently of enormous strength making its way by fierce strokes to the shore. I fled, but in vain. Swift as the wind my pursuer overtook me, seized me in a ferocious grip and hurled me into the deepest part of the pool. I soon scrambled out on the other side, and found myself surrounded by an agitated crowd of younger boys. 'You're in for it,' they said. 'Do you know what you have done? It's Amery, he's in the Sixth Form. He is Head of his House; he is champion at Gym; he has got his football colours.' They continued to recount his many titles to fame and reverence and to dilate upon the awful retribution that would fall upon me. I was convulsed not only with terror, but with the guilt of sacrilege. How could I tell his rank when he was in a bath-towel and so small? I determined to apologise immediately. I approached the potentate in lively trepidation. 'I am very sorry,' I said. 'I mistook you for a Fourth Form boy. You are so small.' He did not seem at all placated by this; so I added in a most brilliant recovery, 'My father, who is a great man, is also small.' At this he laughed, and after some general remarks about my 'cheek' and how I had better be careful in the future, signified that the incident was closed.

I have been fortunate to see a good deal more of him, in times when three years' difference in age is not so important as it is at school. We were afterwards to be Cabinet colleagues for a good many years.

It was thought incongruous that while I apparently stagnated in the lowest form, I should gain a prize open to the whole school for reciting to the Headmaster twelve hundred lines of Macaulay's 'Lays of Ancient Rome' without making a single mistake. I also succeeded in passing the preliminary examination for the Army while still almost at the bottom of the school. This examination seemed to have called forth a very special effort on my part, for many boys far above me in the school failed in it. I also had a piece of good luck. We knew that among other questions we should be asked to draw from memory a map of some country or other. The night before by way of final preparation I put the names of all the maps in the atlas into a hat and drew out New Zealand. I applied my good memory to the geography of that Dominion. Sure enough the first question in the paper was: 'Draw a map of New Zealand.' This was what is called at Monte Carlo an *en plein*, and I ought to have been paid thirty-five times my stake. However, I certainly got paid very high marks for my paper.

I was now embarked on a military career. This orientation was entirely due to my collection of soldiers. I had ultimately nearly fifteen hundred. They were all of one size, all British, and organised as an infantry division with a cavalry brigade. My brother Jack commanded the hostile army. But by a Treaty for the Limitation of Armaments he was only allowed to have coloured troops, and they were not allowed to have artillery. Very important! I could muster myself only eighteen field-guns—besides fortress pieces. But all the other services were complete—except one. It is what every army is always short of—transport. My father's old friend, Sir Henry Drummond Wolff, admiring my array, noticed this deficiency and provided a fund from which it was to some extent supplied.

The day came when my father himself paid a formal visit of inspection. All the troops were arranged in the correct formation of attack. He spent twenty minutes studying the scene—which was really impressive—with a keen eye and captivating smile. At the end he asked me if I would like to go into the Army. I thought it would be splendid to command an Army, so I said 'Yes' at once: and immediately I was taken at my word. For years I thought my father with his experience and flair had discerned in me the qualities of military genius. But I was told later that he had only come to the conclusion that I was not clever enough to go to the Bar. However that may be, the toy soldiers turned the current of my life. Henceforward all my education was directed to passing into Sandhurst, and afterwards to the technical details of the profession of arms. Anything else I had to pick up for myself.

*　　*　　*　　*　　*

I spent nearly four and a half years at Harrow, of which three were in the Army class. To this I was admitted in consequence of having passed the preliminary examination. It consisted of boys of the middle and higher forms of the school and of very different ages, all of whom were being prepared either for the Sandhurst or the Woolwich examination. We were withdrawn from the ordinary movement of the school from form to form. In consequence I got no promotion or very little and remained quite low down upon the school list, though working alongside of boys nearly all in the Fifth Form. Officially I never got out of the Lower School, so I never had the privilege of having a fag of my own. When in the passage of time I became what was called 'a three-yearer' I ceased to have to fag myself, and as I was older than other boys of my standing, I was appointed in my House to the position of Head of the Fags. This was my first responsible office, and the duties, which were honorary, consisted in keeping the roster of all the fags, making out the lists of their duties and dates and placing copies of these lists in the rooms of the monitors, football and cricket champions and other members of our aristocracy. I discharged these functions for upwards of a year, and on the whole I was resigned to my lot.

Meanwhile I found an admirable method of learning my Latin translations. I was always very slow at using a dictionary: it was just like using a telephone directory. It is easy to open it more or less at the right letter, but then you have to turn backwards and forwards and peer up and down the columns and very often find yourself three or four pages the wrong side of the word you want. In short I found it most laborious, while to other boys it seemed no trouble.

But now I formed an alliance with a boy in the Sixth Form. He was very clever and could read Latin as easily as English. Caesar, Ovid, Virgil, Horace and even Martial's epigrams were all the same to him. My daily task was perhaps ten or fifteen lines. This would ordinarily have taken me an hour or an hour and a half to decipher, and then it would probably have been wrong. But my friend could in five minutes construe it for me word by word, and once I had seen it exposed, I remembered it firmly. My Sixth-Form friend for his part was almost as much troubled by the English essays he had to write for the Headmaster as I was by these Latin cross-word puzzles. We agreed together that he should tell me my Latin translations and that I should do his essays. The arrangement worked admirably. The Latin master seemed quite satisfied with my work, and I had more time to myself in the mornings. On the other hand once a week or so I had to compose the essays of my Sixth-Form friend. I used to walk up and down the room dictating—just as I do now—and he sat in the corner and wrote it down in long-hand. For several months no difficulty arose; but once we were nearly caught out. One of these essays was thought to have merit. It was 'sent up' to the Headmaster who summoned my friend, commended him on his work and proceeded to discuss the topic with him in a lively spirit. 'I was interested in this point you make here. You might I think have gone even further. Tell me exactly what you had in your mind.' Dr. Welldon in spite of very chilling responses continued in this way for some time to the deep consternation of my confederate. However the Headmaster, not wishing to turn an occasion of praise into one of cavilling, finally let him go with the remark 'You seem to be better at written than at oral work.' He came back to me like a man who has had a very narrow squeak, and I was most careful ever afterwards to keep to the beaten track in essay-writing.

Dr. Welldon took a friendly interest in me, and knowing that I was weak in the Classics, determined to help me himself. His daily routine was heavy; but he added three times a week a quarter of an hour before evening prayers in which to give me personal tuition. This was a great condescension for the Headmaster, who of course never taught anyone but the monitors and the highest scholars. I was proud of the honour: I shrank from the ordeal. If the reader has ever learned any Latin prose he will know that at quite an early stage one comes across the Ablative Absolute with its apparently somewhat despised alternative 'Quum with the pluperfect subjunctive.' I always preferred 'Quum.' True he was a little longer to write, thus lacking the much admired terseness and pith of the Latin language. On the other hand he avoided a number of pitfalls. I was often uncertain whether the Ablative Absolute should end in 'e' or 'i' or 'o' or 'is' or 'ibus,' to the correct selection of which great importance was attached. Dr. Welldon seemed to be physically pained by a mistake being made in any of these letters. I remember that later on Mr. Asquith used to have just the same sort of look on his face when I sometimes adorned a Cabinet discussion by bringing out one of my few but faithful Latin quotations. It was more than annoyance, it was a pang. Moreover Headmasters have powers at their disposal with which Prime Ministers have never yet been invested. So these evening quarters of an hour with Dr. Welldon added considerably to the anxieties of my life. I was much relieved when after nearly a whole term of patient endeavour he desisted from his well-meant but unavailing efforts.

I will here make some general observations about Latin which probably have their application to Greek as well. In a sensible language like English important words are connected and related to one another by other little words. The Romans in that stern antiquity considered such a method weak and unworthy. Nothing would satisfy them but that the structure of every word should be reacted on by its neighbours in accordance with elaborate rules to meet the different conditions in which it might be used. There is no doubt that this method both sounds and looks more impressive than our own. The sentence fits together like a piece of polished machinery. Every phrase can be tensely charged with meaning. It must have been very laborious, even if you were brought up to it; but no doubt it gave the Romans, and the Greeks too, a fine and easy way of establishing their posthumous fame. They were the first comers in the fields of thought and literature. When they arrived at fairly obvious reflections upon life and love, upon war, fate or manners, they coined them into the slogans or epigrams for which their language was so well adapted, and thus preserved the patent rights for all time. Hence their reputation. Nobody ever told me this at school. I have thought it all out in later life.

But even as a schoolboy I questioned the aptness of the Classics for the prime structure of our education. So they told me how Mr. Gladstone read Homer for fun, which I thought served him right; and that it would be a great pleasure to me in after life. When I seemed incredulous, they added that classics would be a help in writing or speaking English. They then pointed out the number of our modern words which are derived from the Latin or Greek. Apparently one could use these words much better, if one knew the exact source from which they had sprung. I was fain to admit a practical value. But now even this has been swept away. The foreigners and the Scotch have joined together to introduce a pronunciation of Latin which divorces it finally from the English tongue. They tell us to pronounce 'audience' 'owdience'; and 'civil' 'keyweel.' They have distorted one of my most serviceable and impressive quotations into the ridiculous booby 'Wainy, Weedy, Weeky.' Punishment should be reserved for those who have spread this evil.

We shall see another instance of perverted pedantry when we reach the Indian chapters of this book. When I was a boy everyone wrote and said 'Punjaub,' 'pundit,' 'Umbala,' etc. But then some learned notables came along saying 'No, you must spell them correctly.' So the Englishman now refers to the 'Panjab,' to the 'pandit so and so,' or to 'the troubles at Ambala or Amritsar.' When Indians hear him they are astonished at his outlandish speech: and that is the sole reward of his superior erudition. I am very conservative in all these things. I always spell the Czar, 'Czar.' As for the Revised version of the Bible and the alterations in the Prayer Book and especially the Marriage service, they are grievous.

CHAPTER III

EXAMINATIONS

IT took me three tries to pass into Sandhurst. There were five subjects, of which Mathematics, Latin and English were obligatory, and I chose in addition French and Chemistry. In this hand I held only a pair of Kings—English and Chemistry. Nothing less than three would open the jackpot. I had to find another useful card. Latin I could not learn. I had a rooted prejudice which seemed to close my mind against it. Two thousand marks were given for Latin. I might perhaps get 400! French was interesting but rather tricky, and difficult to learn in England. So there remained only Mathematics. After the first Examination was over, when one surveyed the battlefield, it was evident that the war could not be won without another army being brought into the line. Mathematics was the only resource available. I turned to them—I turned on them—in desperation. All my life from time to time I have had to get up disagreeable subjects at short notice, but I consider my triumph, moral and technical, was in learning Mathematics in six months. At the first of these three ordeals I got no more than 500 marks out of 2,500 for Mathematics. At the second I got nearly 2,000. I owe this achievement not only to my own 'back-to-the-wall' resolution—for which no credit is too great; but to the very kindly interest taken in my case by a much respected Harrow master, Mr. C. H. P. Mayo. He convinced me that Mathematics was not a hopeless bog of nonsense, and that there were meanings and rhythms behind the comical hieroglyphics; and that I was not incapable of catching glimpses of some of these.

Of course what I call Mathematics is only what the Civil Service Commissioners expected you to know to pass a very rudimentary examination. I suppose that to those who enjoy this peculiar gift, Senior Wranglers and the like, the waters in which I swam must seem only a duck-puddle compared to the Atlantic Ocean. Nevertheless, when I plunged in, I was soon out of my depth. When I look back upon those care-laden months, their prominent features rise from the abyss of memory. Of course I had progressed far beyond Vulgar Fractions and the Decimal System. We were arrived in an 'Alice-in-Wonderland' world, at the portals of which stood 'A Quadratic Equation.' This with a strange grimace pointed the way to the Theory of Indices, which again handed on the intruder to the full rigours of the Binomial Theorem. Further dim chambers lighted by sullen, sulphurous fires were reputed to contain a dragon called the 'Differential Calculus.' But this monster was beyond the bounds appointed by the Civil Service Commissioners who regulated this stage of Pilgrim's heavy journey. We turned aside, not indeed to the uplands of the Delectable Mountains, but into a strange corridor of things like anagrams and acrostics called Sines, Cosines and Tangents. Apparently they were very important, especially when multiplied by each other, or by themselves! They had also this merit— you could learn many of their evolutions off by heart. There was a question in my third and last Examination about these Cosines and Tangents in a highly square-rooted condition which must have been decisive upon the whole of my after life. It was a problem. But luckily I had seen its ugly face only a few days before and recognised it at first sight.

I have never met any of these creatures since. With my third and successful examination they passed away like the phantasmagoria of a fevered dream. I am assured that they are most helpful in engineering, astronomy and things like that. It is very important to build bridges and canals and to comprehend all the stresses and potentialities of matter, to say nothing of counting all the stars and even universes and measuring how far off they are, and foretelling eclipses, the arrival of comets and such like. I am very glad there are quite a number of people born with a gift and a liking for all of this; like great chess-players who play sixteen games at once blindfold and die quite soon of epilepsy. Serve them right! I hope the Mathematicians, however, are well rewarded. I promise never to blackleg their profession nor take the bread out of their mouths.

I had a feeling once about Mathematics, that I saw it all—Depth beyond depth was revealed to me—the Byss and the Abyss. I saw, as one might see the transit of Venus —or even the Lord Mayor's Show, a quantity passing through infinity and changing its sign from plus to minus. I saw exactly how it happened and why the tergiversation was inevitable: and how the one step involved all the others. It was like politics. But it was after dinner and I let it go!

The practical point is that if this aged, weary-souled Civil Service Commissioner had not asked this particular question about these Cosines or Tangents in their squared or even cubed condition, which I happened to have learned scarcely a week before, not one of the subsequent chapters of this book would ever have been written. I might have gone into the Church and preached orthodox sermons in a spirit of audacious contradiction to the age. I might have gone into the City and made a fortune. I might have resorted to the Colonies, or 'Dominions' as they are now called, in the hopes of pleasing, or at least placating them; and thus had, à la Lindsay Gordon or Cecil Rhodes, a lurid career. I might even have gravitated to the Bar, and persons might have been hanged through my defence who now nurse their guilty secrets with complacency. Anyhow the whole of *my* life would have been altered, and that I suppose would have altered a great many other lives, which in their turn, and so on. . . .

But here we seem to be getting back to mathematics, which I quitted for ever in the year 1894. Let it suffice that this Civil Service Commissioner putting this particular question in routine or caprice deflected, so far as I was concerned, the entire sequence of events. I have seen Civil Service Commissioners since. I have seen them in the flesh. I have even appointed their Chief. I admire them. I honour them. We all do. But no one, least of all themselves, would suppose they could play so decisive and cardinal a part in human affairs. Which brings me to my conclusion upon Free Will and Predestination; namely—let the reader mark it—that they are identical.

I have always loved butterflies. In Uganda I saw glorious butterflies the colour of whose wings changed from the deepest russet brown to the most brilliant blue, according to the angle from which you saw them. In Brazil as everyone knows there are butterflies of this kind even larger and more vivid. The contrast is extreme. You could not conceive colour effects more violently opposed; but it is the same butterfly. The butterfly is the Fact—gleaming, fluttering, settling for an instant with wings fully spread to the sun, then vanishing in the shades of the forest. Whether you believe in Free Will or Predestination, all depends on the slanting glimpse you had of the colour of his wings—which are in fact at least two colours at the same time. But I have not quitted and renounced the Mathematick to fall into the Metaphysick. Let us return to the pathway of narrative.

When I failed for the second time to pass into Sandhurst, I bade farewell to Harrow and was relegated as a forlorn hope to a 'crammer.' Captain James and his highly competent partners kept an establishment in the Cromwell Road. It was said that no one who was not a congenital idiot could avoid passing thence into the Army. The Firm had made a scientific study of the mentality of the Civil Service Commissioners. They knew with almost Papal infallibility the sort of questions which that sort of person would be bound on the average to ask on any of the selected subjects. They specialised on these questions and on the answering of them. They fired a large number of efficient shot-guns into the brown of the covey, and they claimed a high and steady average of birds. Captain James—if he had known it—was really the ingenious forerunner of the inventors of the artillery barrages of the Great War. He fired from carefully selected positions upon the areas which he knew must be tenanted by large bodies of enemy troops. He had only to fire a given number of shells per acre per hour to get his bag. He did not need to see the enemy soldiers. Drill was all he had to teach his gunners. Thus year by year for at least two decades he held the Blue Ribbon among the Crammers. He was like one of those people who have a sure system for breaking the Bank at Monte Carlo, with the important difference that in a great majority of cases his system produced success. Even the very hardest cases could be handled. No absolute guarantee was given, but there would always be far more than a sporting chance.

However, just as I was about to enjoy the advantage of this renowned system of intensive poultry-farming, I met with a very serious accident.

My aunt, Lady Wimborne, had lent us her comfortable estate at Bournemouth for the winter. Forty or fifty acres of pine forest descended by sandy undulations terminating in cliffs to the smooth beach of the English Channel. It was a small, wild place and through the middle there fell to the sea level a deep cleft called a 'chine.' Across this 'chine' a rustic bridge nearly 50 yards long had been thrown. I was just 18 and on my holidays. My younger brother aged 12, and a cousin aged 14, proposed to chase me. After I had been hunted for twenty minutes and was rather short of breath, I decided to cross the bridge. Arrived at its centre I saw to my consternation that the pursuers had divided their forces. One stood at each end of the bridge; capture seemed certain. But in a flash there came across me a great project. The chine which the bridge spanned was full of young fir trees. Their slender tops reached to the level of the footway. 'Would it not,' I asked myself, 'be possible to leap on to one of them and slip down the pole-like stem, breaking off each tier of branches as one descended, until the fall was broken?' I looked at it. I computed it. I meditated. Meanwhile I climbed over the balustrade. My young pursuers stood wonder-struck at either end of the bridge. To plunge or not to plunge, that was the question! In a second I had plunged, throwing out my arms to embrace the summit of the fir tree. The argument was correct; the data were absolutely wrong. It was three days before I regained consciousness and more than three months before I crawled from my bed. The measured fall was 29 feet on to hard ground. But no doubt the branches helped. My mother, summoned by the alarming message of the children, 'He jumped over the bridge and he won't speak to us,' hurried down with energetic aid and inopportune brandy. It was an axiom with my parents that in serious accident or illness the highest medical aid should be invoked, regardless of cost. Eminent specialists stood about my bed. Later on when I could understand again, I was shocked and also flattered to hear of the enormous fees they had been paid. My father travelled over at full express from Dublin where he had been spending his Christmas at one of old Lord Fitzgibbon's once-celebrated parties. He brought the greatest of London surgeons with him. I had among other injuries a ruptured kidney. It is to the surgeon's art and to my own pronounced will-to-live that the reader is indebted for this story. But for a year I looked at life round a corner. They made a joke about it in those days at the Carlton Club, 'I hear Randolph's son met with a serious accident.' 'Yes? Playing a game of Follow my Leader,'— 'Well, Randolph is not likely to come to grief in that way!'

*　　*　　*　　*　　*

The Unionist Government had been beaten, though only by forty, in the Summer Election of 1892 and Mr. Gladstone had taken office with the help of the Irish Nationalists. The new Parliament, having met to change the Administration, was in accordance with the wise and happy practice of those days prorogued for a six months' holiday. The Session of 1893 and the inevitable re-opening of the Home Rule struggle were eagerly and anxiously awaited. Naturally our household had not been much grieved at the defeat of what my father had described as 'a Government and party which for five years have boycotted and slandered me.' In fact our whole family with its many powerful branches and all his friends looked forward to the new situation with lively hope. It was thought that he would in Opposition swiftly regain the ascendancy in Parliament and in his party which had been destroyed by his resignation six years before.

No one cherished these hopes more ardently than I. Although in the past little had been said in my hearing, one could not grow up in my father's house, and still less among his mother and sisters, without understanding that there had been a great political disaster. Dignity and reticence upon this subject were invariably preserved before strangers, children and servants. Only once do I remember my father having breathed a word of complaint about his fortunes to me, and that for a passing moment. Only once did he lift his visor in my sight. This was at our house at Newmarket in the autumn of 1892. He had reproved me for startling him by firing off a double-barrelled gun at a rabbit which had appeared on the lawn beneath his windows. He had been very angry and disturbed. Understanding at once that I was distressed, he took occasion to reassure me. I then had one of the three or four long intimate conversations with him which are all I can boast. He explained how old people were not always very considerate towards young people, that they were absorbed in their own affairs and might well speak roughly in sudden annoyance. He said he was glad I liked shooting, and that he had arranged for me to shoot on September 1st (this was the end of August) such partridges as our small property contained. Then he proceeded to talk to me in the most wonderful and captivating manner about school and going into the Army and the grown-up life which lay beyond. I listened spellbound to this sudden complete departure from his usual reserve, amazed at his intimate comprehension of all my affairs. Then at the end he said, 'Do remember things do not always go right with me. My every action is misjudged and every word distorted. . . . So make some allowances.'

Of course I was his vehement partisan and so in her mild way was Mrs. Everest, who had now become housekeeper in my grandmother's house, 50, Grosvenor Square, where we had all gone to live to save expense. When after twenty years of faithful service she retired upon a pension, she entrusted her savings to my father, who drove down to the city in his private hansom to a special luncheon with Lord Rothschild at New Court for the purpose of investing them with the utmost security and advantage. I knew quite well that the 'Old Gang' of the Conservative Party owed their long reign to his personal fighting, and to his revival of Tory democracy, and that at his first slip—a grave one— they had shown themselves utterly destitute of generosity or gratitude. We all of course looked forward to his reconquest of power. We saw as children the passers-by take off their hats in the streets and the workmen grin when they saw his big moustache. For years I had read every word he spoke and what the newspapers said about him. Although he was only a private member and quite isolated, everything he said even at the tiniest bazaar was reported verbatim in all the newspapers, and every phrase was scrutinized and weighed. Now it seemed that his chance had come again.

I had been carried to London, and from my bed I followed with keen interest the political events of 1893. For this I was well circumstanced. My mother gave me full accounts of what she heard, and Mr. Edward Marjoribanks, afterwards Lord Tweedmouth, Mr. Gladstone's Chief Whip, was married to my father's sister Fanny. We thus shared in a detached way the satisfaction of the Liberals at coming back to power after their long banishment. We heard some at least of their hopes and fears. Politics seemed very important and vivid to my eyes in those days. They were directed by statesmen of commanding intellect and personality. The upper classes in their various stations took part in them as a habit and as a duty. The working men whether they had votes or not followed them as a sport. They took as much interest in national affairs and were as good judges of form in public men, as is now the case about cricket or football. The newspapers catered obediently for what was at once an educated and a popular taste.

Favoured at first by the indulgences accorded to an invalid, I became an absorbed spectator of Mr. Gladstone's last great Parliamentary battle. Indeed it far outweighed in my mind the dreaded Examination—the last shot—which impended in August. As time wore on I could not help feeling that my father's speeches were not as good as they used to be. There were some brilliant successes: yet on the whole he seemed to be hardly holding his own. I hoped of course that I should grow up in time to come to his aid. I knew that he would have received such a suggestion with unaffected amusement; but I thought of Austen Chamberlain who was allowed to fight at his father's side, and Herbert Gladstone who had helped the Grand Old Man to cut down the oak trees and went everywhere with him, and I dreamed of days to come when Tory democracy would dismiss the 'Old Gang' with one hand and defeat the Radicals with the other.

During this year I met at my father's house many of the leading figures of the Parliamentary conflict, and was often at luncheon or dinner when across his table not only colleagues, but opponents, amicably interchanged opinions on the burning topics of the hour. It was then that I first met

Mr. Balfour, Mr. Chamberlain, Mr. Edward Carson and also Lord Rosebery, Mr. Asquith, Mr. John Morley and other fascinating ministerial figures. It seemed a very great world in which these men lived; a world where high rules reigned and every trifle in public conduct counted: a duelling-ground where although the business might be ruthless, and the weapons loaded with ball, there was ceremonious personal courtesy and mutual respect. But of course I saw this social side only when my father had either intimate friends or persons of high political consequence as his guests. I have heard that on neutral ground he was incredibly fierce, and affronted people by saying the most blunt or even savage things. Certainly those who did not know him well approached him with caution or heavily armed.

So soon as I was convalescent I began to go to the House of Commons and listen to the great debates. I even managed to squeeze in to the Distinguished Strangers' Gallery when Mr. Gladstone wound up the second reading of the Home Rule Bill. Well do I remember the scene and some of its incidents. The Grand Old Man looked like a great white eagle at once fierce and splendid. His sentences rolled forth majestically and everyone hung upon his lips and gestures, eager to cheer or deride. He was at the climax of a tremendous passage about how the Liberal Party had always carried every cause it had espoused to victory. He made a slip, 'And there is no cause,' he exclaimed (Home Rule), 'for which the Liberal Party has suffered so much or *descended so low*.' How the Tories leapt and roared with delight! But Mr. Gladstone, shaking his right hand with fingers spread clawlike, quelled the tumult and resumed 'But we have risen again. . . .'

I was also a witness of his celebrated tribute to Mr. Chamberlain on his son Austen's maiden speech. 'I will not enter upon any elaborate eulogy of that speech. I will endeavour to sum up in a few words what I desire to say of it. It was a speech which must have been dear and refreshing to a father's heart.' From where I crouched on the floor of the Gallery peering through the balustrade I could see the effect these words instantaneously produced on Mr. Chamberlain. He was hit as if a bullet had struck him. His pale almost sallow countenance turned pink with emotion he could not, or did not care to restrain. He half rose and made a little bow, and then hunched himself up with lowered head. There does not seem to be much in these words however well chosen, when they are written down. It was the way the thing was done that swept aside for a moment the irreparable enmities of years.

On another occasion when I was in the Gallery I heard my father and Sir William Harcourt have some very fierce and rough interchanges. Sir William seemed to be quite furious and most unfair in his reply, and I was astonished when only a few minutes later, he made his way up to where I sat and with a beaming smile introduced himself to me, and asked me what I thought of it all.

*   *   *   *   *

What with the after-weakness of my accident and these political excitements Captain James hardly had a fair chance in preparing me for my examination. Nevertheless my third attempt achieved a modified success. I qualified for a cavalry cadetship at Sandhurst. The competition for the infantry was keener, as life in the cavalry was so much more expensive. Those who were at the bottom of the list were accordingly offered the easier entry into the cavalry. I was delighted at having passed the examination and even more at the prospect of soldiering on horseback. I had already formed a definite opinion upon the relative advantages of riding and walking. What fun it would be having a horse! Also the uniforms of the cavalry were far more magnificent than those of the Foot. It was therefore in an expansive spirit that I wrote to my father. I found to my surprise that he took a contrary view. He thought it very discreditable that I had not qualified for the infantry. He had proposed that I should enter the 60th Rifles, a famous four-battalion regiment which although habited in black had a red flash on cuffs and collar. 'By going into the 60th Rifles,' he had said, 'you will be able to serve two or three years in a Mediterranean fortress, and thus be fully matured before you begin your service in India.' He had, it seemed, already written to the Duke of Cambridge who was the Colonel-in-Chief of the 60th, suggesting that I should ultimately enter his regiment, and had received a gracious response. Now all these plans were upset, and upset in the most inconvenient and expensive manner. The Duke would never have a chance of welcoming me: and cavalry are not required in Mediterranean fortresses. 'In the infantry,' my father had remarked, 'one has to keep a man; in the cavalry a man and a horse as well.' This was not only true, but even an understatement. Little did he foresee not only one horse, but two official chargers and one or two hunters besides—to say nothing of the indispensable string of polo ponies! Nevertheless he was extremely dissatisfied and in due course I received from him a long and very severe letter expressing the bleakest view of my educational career, showing a marked lack of appreciation at my success in the examination, which he suggested I had only scraped through, and warning me of the danger in which I plainly lay of becoming a 'social wastrel!' I was pained and startled by this communication, and made haste to promise better results in the future. All the same I rejoiced at going to Sandhurst, and at the prospect of becoming a real live cavalry officer in no more than 18 months: and I busied myself in ordering the considerable necessary outfit of a gentleman-cadet.

*　　　*　　　*　　　*　　　*

My brother and I were sent this summer by our parents for a so-called walking-tour in Switzerland, with a tutor.

I need hardly say we travelled by train so far as the money lasted. The tutor and I climbed mountains. We climbed the Wetterhorn and Monte Rosa. The spectacle of the sunrise striking the peaks of the Bernese Oberland is a marvel of light and colour unsurpassed in my experience. I longed to climb the Matterhorn, but this was not only too expensive but held by the tutor to be too dangerous. All this prudence however might easily have been upset by an incident which happened to me in the lake of Lausanne. I record this incident that it may be a warning to others. I went for a row with another boy a little younger than myself. When we were more than a mile from the shore, we decided to have a swim, pulled off our clothes, jumped into the water and swam about in great delight. When we had had enough, the boat was perhaps 100 yards away. A breeze had begun to stir the waters. The boat had a small red awning over its stern seats. This awning acted as a sail by catching the breeze. As we swam towards the boat, it drifted farther off. After this had happened several times we had perhaps halved the distance. But meanwhile the breeze was freshening and we both, especially my companion, began to be tired. Up to this point no idea of danger had crossed my mind. The sun played upon the sparkling blue waters; the wonderful panorama of mountains and valleys, the gay hotels and villas still smiled. But I now saw Death as near as I believe I have ever seen Him. He was swimming in the water at our side, whispering from time to time in the rising wind which continued to carry the boat away from us at about the same speed we could swim. No help was near. Unaided we could never reach the shore. I was not only an easy, but a fast swimmer, having represented my House at Harrow, when our team defeated all comers. I now swam for life. Twice I reached within a yard of the boat and each time a gust carried it just beyond my reach; but by a supreme effort I caught hold of its side in the nick of time before a still stronger gust bulged the red awning again. I scrambled in, and rowed back for my companion who, though tired, had not apparently realised the dull yellow glare of mortal peril that had so suddenly played around us. I said nothing to the tutor about this serious experience; but I have never forgotten it; and perhaps some of my readers will remember it too.

My stay at the Royal Military College formed an intermediate period in my life. It brought to a close nearly 12 years of school. Thirty-six terms each of many weeks (interspersed with all-too-short holidays) during the whole of which I had enjoyed few gleams of success, in which I had hardly ever been asked to learn anything which seemed of the slightest use or interest, or allowed to play any game which was amusing. In retrospect these years form not only the least agreeable, but the only barren and unhappy period of my life. I was happy as a child with my toys in my nursery. I have been happier every year since I became a man. But this interlude of school makes a sombre grey patch upon the chart of my journey. It was an unending spell of worries that did not then seem petty, and of toil uncheered by fruition; a time of discomfort, restriction and purposeless monotony.

This train of thought must not lead me to exaggerate the character of my schooldays. Actually no doubt they were buoyed up by the laughter and high spirits of youth. Harrow was a very good school, and a high standard of personal service prevailed among its masters. Most of the boys were very happy, and many found in its classrooms and upon its playing-fields the greatest distinction they have ever known in life. I can only record the fact that, no doubt through my own shortcomings, I was an exception. I would far rather have been apprenticed as a bricklayer's mate, or run errands as a messenger boy, or helped my father to dress the front windows of a grocer's shop. It would have been real; it would have been natural; it would have taught me more; and I should have done it much better. Also I should have got to know my father, which would have been a joy to me.

Certainly the prolonged education indispensable to the progress of Society is not natural to mankind. It cuts against the grain. A boy would like to follow his father in pursuit of food or prey. He would like to be doing serviceable things so far as his utmost strength allowed. He would like to be earning wages however small to help to keep up the home. He would like to have some leisure of his own to use or misuse as he pleased. He would ask little more than the right to work or starve. And then perhaps in the evenings a real love of learning would come to those who were worthy—and why try to stuff it into those who are not?—and knowledge and thought would open the 'magic casements' of the mind.

I was on the whole considerably discouraged by my school days. Except in Fencing, in which I had won the Public School Championship, I had achieved no distinction. All my contemporaries and even younger boys seemed in every way better adapted to the conditions of our little world. They were far better both at the games and at the lessons. It is not pleasant to feel oneself so completely outclassed and left behind at the very beginning of the race. I had been surprised on taking leave of Dr. Welldon to hear him predict, with a confidence for which I could see no foundation, that I should be able to make my way all right. I have always been very grateful to him for this.

I am all for the Public Schools but I do not want to go there again.

My greatest friend at Harrow was Jack Milbanke. He was nearly two years my senior. He was the son of an old baronet whose family had lived at Chichester for many generations. He was not remarkable either at games or lessons. In these spheres he was only slightly above the average of his contemporaries. But he had a style and distinction of manner which were exceptional, and a mature outlook and

conversation the like of which I never saw in any other
Harrow boy. He was always the great gentleman, self-
composed, cool, sedate, spick and span and faultlessly
dressed. When my father came down to see me, he used to
take us both to luncheon at the King's Head Hotel. I was
thrilled to hear them talk, as if they were equals, with the
easy assurance of one man of the world to another. I envied
him so much. How I should have loved to have that sort
of relationship with my father! But alas I was only a backward schoolboy and my incursions into the conversation were
nearly always awkward or foolish.

Milbanke and I embarked upon one adventure together.
We discovered that by an old custom there should be
no compulsory football in trial week. This rule had fallen
into desuetude for some years. We therefore refused to
play, citing the custom and alleging that we must concentrate upon our studies. By so doing we courted a severe
caning from the monitors. Nevertheless it could not be denied that we 'had the law of them.' The issue was gravely
debated in the highest circles. For three or four days we did
not know what our fate would be. Our case was prejudiced
by the suspicion that we were not wearing ourselves out by
study, but on the contrary might even have been called
idle. However in the end it was decided that we must have
our way, and I trust the precedent thus boldly established
has not been lost in later generations.

Milbanke was destined for the Army and had set his
heart upon the 10th Hussars. His father allowed him to go
in through the Militia, a course which though slightly
longer, avoided most of the examinations. He therefore
left Harrow a year before I did and soon blossomed out
into a Militia subaltern. We kept up a regular correspondence and often saw each other in the holidays. We shall
meet him again in these pages. He was destined to the
highest military honours. He gained the Victoria Cross in
the South African War for rescuing, when he was already

grievously wounded, one of his troopers under a deadly fire. He fell in the Gallipoli Peninsula, leading a forlorn attack in the awful battle of Suvla Bay.

* * * * *

I enjoyed the Harrow songs. They have an incomparable book of school songs. At intervals we used to gather in the Speech Room or even in our own Houses, and sing these splendid and famous choruses. I believe these songs are the greatest treasure that Harrow possesses. There is certainly nothing like them at Eton. There they have only got one song and that about Rowing, which though good exercise is poor sport and poorer poetry. We used also to have lectures from eminent persons on scientific or historical subjects. These made a great impression on me. To have an exciting story told you by someone who is a great authority, especially if he has a magic lantern, is for me the best way of learning. Once I had heard the lecture and had listened with great attention, I could have made a very fair show of delivering it myself. I remember five lectures particularly to this day. The first by Mr. Bowen, the most celebrated of Harrow masters and the author of many of our finest songs, gave us a thrilling account in popular form of the battle of Waterloo. He gave another lecture on the battle of Sedan which I greatly enjoyed. Some years afterwards I found that he had taken it almost literally from Hooper's *Sedan*—one of my colonel's favourite books. It was none the worse for that. There was a lecture on climbing the Alps by the great Mr. Whymper with wonderful pictures of guides and tourists hanging on by their eyelids or standing with their backs to precipices which even in photographs made one squirm. There was a lecture about how butterflies protect themselves by their colouring. A nasty tasting butterfly has gaudy colouring to warn the bird not to eat it. A succulent, juicy-tasting butterfly protects himself by making himself exactly like his usual branch or leaf.

But this takes them millions of years to do; and in the meanwhile the more backward ones get eaten and die out. That is why the survivors are marked and coloured as they are. Lastly we had a lecture from Mr. Parkin on Imperial Federation. He told us how at Trafalgar Nelson's signal—'England expects that every man this day will do his duty'—ran down the line of battle, and how if we and our Colonies all held together, a day would come when such a signal would run not merely along a line of ships, but along a line of nations. We lived to see this come true, and I was able to remind the aged Mr. Parkin of it, when in the last year of his life he attended some great banquet in celebration of our victorious emergence from the Great War.

I wonder they do not have these lectures more often. They might well have one every fortnight, and afterwards all the boys should be set to work to write first what they could remember about it, and secondly what they could think about it. Then the masters would soon begin to find out who could pick things up as they went along and make them into something new, and who were the dullards; and the classes of the school would soon get sorted out accordingly.

Thus Harrow would not have stultified itself by keeping me at the bottom of the school, and I should have had a much jollier time.

CHAPTER IV

SANDHURST

A^T Sandhurst I had a new start. I was no longer handi-
capped by past neglect of Latin, French or Mathematics. We had now to learn fresh things and we all started
equal. Tactics, Fortification, Topography (mapmaking),
Military Law and Military Administration formed the
whole curriculum. In addition were Drill, Gymnastics and
Riding. No one need play any game unless he wanted to.
Discipline was strict and the hours of study and parade were
long. One was very tired at the end of the day. I was
deeply interested in my work, especially Tactics and Fortification. My father instructed his bookseller Mr. Bain to
send me any books I might require for my studies. So I
ordered Hamley's *Operations of War*, Prince Kraft's *Letters on Infantry, Cavalry and Artillery*, Maine's *Infantry
Fire Tactics*, together with a number of histories dealing
with the American Civil, Franco-German and Russo-Turkish wars, which were then our latest and best specimens
of wars. I soon had a small military library which invested
the regular instruction with some sort of background. I did
not much like the drill and indeed figured for several
months in the 'Awkward Squad,' formed from those who
required special smartening up. But the practical work in
field fortification was most exciting. We dug trenches, constructed breastworks, revetted parapets with sandbags, with
heather, with fascines, or with 'Jones' iron band gabion.' We
put up *chevaux de frises* and made *fougasses* (a kind of
primitive land mine). We cut railway lines with slabs of
guncotton, and learned how to blow up masonry bridges, or
make substitutes out of pontoons or timber. We drew con-
toured maps of all the hills round Camberley, made road

reconnaissances in every direction, and set out picket lines and paper plans for advanced guards or rear guards, and even did some very simple tactical schemes. We were never taught anything about bombs or hand-grenades, because of course these weapons were known to be long obsolete. They had gone out of use in the eighteenth century, and would be quite useless in modern war.

All this was no doubt very elementary, and our minds were not allowed to roam in working hours beyond a subaltern's range of vision. But sometimes I was invited to dine at the Staff College, less than a mile away, where all the cleverest officers in the Army were being trained for the High Command. Here the study was of divisions, army corps and even whole armies; of bases, of supplies, and lines of communication and railway strategy. This was thrilling. It did seem such a pity that it all had to be make-believe, and that the age of wars between civilized nations had come to an end for ever. If it had only been 100 years earlier what splendid times we should have had! Fancy being nineteen in 1793 with more than twenty years of war against Napoleon in front of one! However, all that was finished. The British Army had never fired on white troops since the Crimea, and now that the world was growing so sensible and pacific—and so democratic too—the great days were over. Luckily, however, there were still savages and barbarous peoples. There were Zulus and Afghans, also the Dervishes of the Soudan. Some of these might, if they were well-disposed, 'put up a show' some day. There might even be a mutiny or a revolt in India. At that time the natives had adopted a mysterious practice of smearing the mango trees, and we all fastened hopefully upon an article in the *Spectator* which declared that perhaps in a few months we might have India to reconquer. We wondered about all this. Of course we should all get our commissions so much earlier and march about the plains of India and win medals and distinction, and perhaps rise to very high command like Clive

when quite young! These thoughts were only partially con-
soling, for after all fighting the poor Indians, compared with
taking part in a real European war, was only like riding in
a paper-chase instead of in the Grand National. Still one
must make the best one can of the opportunities of the age.

I enjoyed the riding-school thoroughly, and got on—
and off—as well as most. My father arranged in my holidays, or vacations as it was now proper to call them, for me
to go through an additional course of riding-school at
Knightsbridge Barracks with the Royal Horse Guards. I bit
the tan there on numerous occasions. Afterwards when I
joined my regiment I had another full five months' course,
and taking them altogether, I think I was pretty well trained
to sit and manage a horse. This is one of the most important
things in the world.

Horses were the greatest of my pleasures at Sandhurst.
I and the group in which I moved spent all our money on
hiring horses from the very excellent local livery stables.
We ran up bills on the strength of our future commissions.
We organized point-to-points and even a steeplechase in
the park of a friendly grandee, and bucketted gaily about
the countryside. And here I say to parents, especially to
wealthy parents, 'Don't give your son money. As far as you
can afford it, give him horses.' No one ever came to grief—
except honourable grief—through riding horses. No hour of
life is lost that is spent in the saddle. Young men have
often been ruined through owning horses, or through back-
ing horses, but never through riding them; unless of course
they break their necks, which, taken at a gallop, is a very
good death to die.

Once I became a gentleman cadet I acquired a new status
in my father's eyes. I was entitled when on leave to go
about with him, if it was not inconvenient. He was always
amused by acrobats, jugglers, and performing animals; and
it was with him that I first visited the Empire Theatre. He
took me also to important political parties at Lord Roth-

schild's house at Tring, where most of the leaders and a selection of the rising men of the Conservative Party were often assembled. He began to take me also to stay with his racing friends; and here we had a different company and new topics of conversation which proved equally entertaining. In fact to me he seemed to own the key to everything or almost everything worth having. But if ever I began to show the slightest idea of comradeship, he was immediately offended; and when once I suggested that I might help his private secretary to write some of his letters, he froze me into stone. I know now that this would have been only a passing phase. Had he lived another four or five years, he could not have done without me. But there were no four or five years! Just as friendly relations were ripening into an Entente, and an alliance or at least a military agreement seemed to my mind not beyond the bounds of reasonable endeavour, he vanished for ever.

In the spring of 1894 it became clear to all of us that my father was gravely ill. He still persisted in his political work. Almost every week he delivered a speech at some important centre. No one could fail to see that these efforts were increasingly unsuccessful. The verbatim reports dropped from three to two columns and then to one and a half. On one occasion *The Times* mentioned that the hall was not filled. Finally I heard my mother and the old Duchess—who so often disagreed—both urging him to take a rest, while he persisted that he was all right and that everything was going well. I knew that these two who were so near and devoted to him would never have pressed him thus without the gravest need.

I can see my father now in a somewhat different light from the days when I wrote his biography. I have long passed the age at which he died. I understand only too plainly the fatal character of his act of resignation. He was 'the daring pilot in extremity.' That was his hour. But conditions changed with the Unionist victory of 1886. Quiet times were required and political repose. Lord Salisbury represented to the nation what it needed and desired. He settled down heavily to a long steady reign. Naturally he was glad to have the whole power in his own hands, instead of dividing it with a restless rival, entrenched in the leadership of the House of Commons and the control of the public purse. It is never possible for a man to recover his lost position. He may recover another position in the fifties or sixties, but not the one he lost in the thirties or forties. To hold the leadership of a party or nation with dignity and authority requires that the leader's qualities and message shall meet not only the need but the mood of both.

Moreover from the moment Lord Randolph Churchill became Chancellor of the Exchequer responsible in large measure for the affairs of the nation, he ceased in vital matters to be a Tory. He adopted with increasing zest the Gladstonian outlook, with the single exception of Irish Home Rule; and in all social and labour questions he was far beyond what the Whig or middle-class Liberal of that epoch could have tolerated. Even on Ireland his convictions were unusually independent. The Conservative Party would not have relished any of this. Indeed I think if he had lived to keep his health, it is more than likely that he would have resisted the South African War to an extent that would have exposed him to odium with the very working-class elements of whose good-will he was so proud. His only real card of re-entry would have been to have forestalled Mr. Chamberlain's Protection campaign. Everything that I know suggests to me that he would far more likely have been one of its chief opponents. He was not the man to take his decisions from party caucuses. When he was faction-fighting he fought to win, seizing anything that came along. But when responsible, his contribution to public affairs was faithful and original. He never sat down to play a cold, calculated game. He said what he thought. It was better so.

Mr. Gladstone's reputation as an orator depends less upon

his published speeches than upon the effect they produced at the time upon the audience. Lord Randolph Churchill's place in our political history is measured not by his words and actions, but by the impression which his personality made upon his contemporaries. This was intense, and had circumstances continued favourable, might well have manifested itself in decisive episodes. He embodied that force, caprice and charm which so often springs from genius.

Now that I have been reading over all the letters which he wrote to me laboriously with his own hand after the fashion of those days, I feel that I did not at the time appreciate how much he thought and cared for me. More than ever do I regret that we did not live long enough in company to know each other. I used to go to see Lord Rosebery in the later years of his life because, apart from the respect I bore this distinguished man, I loved to hear him talk about my father. I had a feeling of getting nearer to my father when I talked with his intimate and illustrious friend. The last time I saw Lord Rosebery I said how much I should have liked to roll back the years, and talk about things with my father on even terms. The aged statesman said in a wonderful way: 'Ah! he'd have understood.'

*　　　*　　　*　　　*　　　*

I was making a road map on Chobham Common in June, 1894, when a cyclist messenger brought me the college adjutant's order to proceed at once to London. My father was setting out the next day on a journey round the world. An ordinary application to the college authorities for my being granted special leave of absence had been refused as a matter of routine. He had telegraphed to the Secretary of State for War, Sir Henry Campbell Bannerman, 'My last day in England' . . . and no time had been lost in setting me on my way to London.

We drove to the station the next morning—my mother, my younger brother and I. In spite of the great beard which he had grown during his South African journey four years before, his face looked terribly haggard and worn with mental pain. He patted me on the knee in a gesture which however simple was perfectly informing.

There followed his long journey round the world. I never saw him again, except as a swiftly-fading shadow.

*   *   *   *   *

I learned several things at Sandhurst which showed me how to behave and how officers of different ranks were expected to treat one another in the life and discipline of a regiment. My company commander, Major Ball, of the Welsh regiment, was a very strict and peppery martinet. Formal, reserved, frigidly courteous, punctilious, impeccable, severe, he was held in the greatest awe. It had never been his fortune to go on active service, but we were none the less sure that he would have had to be killed to be beaten.

The rule was, that if you went outside the college bounds, you first of all wrote your name in the company leave-book, and might then assume that your request was sanctioned. One day I drove a tandem (hired) over to Aldershot to see a friend in a militia battalion then training there. As I drove down the Marlborough lines, whom should I meet but Major Ball himself driving a spanking dog-cart home to Sandhurst. As I took off my hat to him, I remembered with a flash of anxiety that I had been too lazy or careless to write my name in the leave-book. However, I thought, 'there is still a chance. He may not look at it until Mess; and I will write my name down as soon as I get back.' I curtailed my visit to the militia battalion and hastened back to the college as fast as the ponies could trot. It was six o'clock when I got in. I ran along the passage to the desk where the leave-book lay, and the first thing that caught my eyes was the Major's initials, 'O.B.' at the foot of the leaves granted for the day. I was too late. He had seen me in Aldershot and had seen that my name was not in the book. Then I looked again, and there to my astonishment was my own name written in the Major's hand-writing and duly approved by his initials.

This opened my eyes to the kind of life which existed in the old British army and how the very strictest discipline could be maintained among officers without the slightest departure from the standards of a courteous and easy society. Naturally after such a rebuke I never was so neglectful again.

Very much the same thing happened one day in the winter of 1915 when I was serving with the Grenadier Guards in front of Laventie. Our Colonel, then the well-known 'Ma' Jeffreys a super-martinet, and a splendid officer utterly unaffected by sixteen months of the brunt, deprecated the use of alcohol (apart from the regular rum ration) on duty, even under the shocking winter weather and in the front line. It was his wish, though not his actual order, that it should not be taken into the trenches. In a dark and dripping dug-out a bottle of port was being consumed, when the cry 'Commanding officer,' was heard and Colonel Jeffreys began to descend the steps. A young officer in whom there evidently lay the germs of military genius instinctively stuck the guttering candle which lighted the dug-out into the mouth of the bottle. Such candlesticks were common. Everything passed off perfectly. However, six months later this young officer found himself on leave in the Guards' Club, and there met Colonel Jeffreys. 'Have a glass of port wine?' said the Colonel. The subaltern accepted. The bottle was brought and the glasses emptied: 'Does it taste of candle grease?' said the Colonel; and they both laughed together.

*　　*　　*　　*　　*

In my last term at Sandhurst—if the reader will permit a digression—my indignation was excited by the Purity Campaign of Mrs. Ormiston Chant. This lady was a member of the London County Council and in the summer of

1894 she started an active movement to purge our music-halls. Her attention was particularly directed to the promenade of the Empire Theatre. This large space behind the dress circle was frequently crowded during the evening performances, and especially on Saturdays, with young people of both sexes, who not only conversed together during the performance and its intervals, but also from time to time refreshed themselves with alcoholic liquors. Mrs. Ormiston Chant and her friends made a number of allegations affecting both the sobriety and the morals of these merrymakers; and she endeavoured to procure the closing of the Promenade and above all of the bars which abutted on it. It seemed that the majority of the English public viewed these matters in a different light. Their cause was championed by the *Daily Telegraph*, in those days our leading popular newspaper. In a series of powerful articles headed 'Prudes on the Prowl' the *Daily Telegraph* inaugurated a wide and spirited correspondence to which persons were wont to contribute above such pseudonyms as 'Mother of Five,' 'Gentleman and Christian,' 'Live and Let Live,' 'John Bull' and so forth. The controversy aroused keen public interest; but nowhere was it more searchingly debated than among my Sandhurst friends. We were accustomed to visit this very promenade in the brief leave allowed to us twice a month from Saturday noon till Sunday midnight. We were scandalised by Mrs. Chant's charges and insinuations. We had never seen anything to complain of in the behaviour of either sex. Indeed the only point upon which criticism, as it seemed to us, might justly be directed was the strict and even rough manner in which the enormous uniformed commissionaires immediately removed, and even thrust forcibly into the street, anyone who had inadvertently overstepped the bounds of true temperance. We thought Mrs. Ormiston Chant's movement entirely uncalled-for and contrary to the best traditions of British freedom.

In this cause I was keenly anxious to strike a blow. I

noticed one day in the *Daily Telegraph* that a gentleman —whose name escapes me—proposed to found a League of Citizens to resist and counter the intolerance of Mrs. Chant and her backers. This was to be called 'The Entertainments Protection League.' The League proposed to form committees and an executive, to take offices and enrol members, to collect subscriptions, to hold public meetings and to issue literature in support of its views. I immediately volunteered my services. I wrote to the pious Founder at the address which he had given, expressing my cordial agreement with his aims and my readiness to co-operate in every lawful way. In due course I received an answer on impressively-headed notepaper informing me that my support was welcomed, and inviting my attendance at the first meeting of the Executive Committee, which was to be held on the following Wednesday at 6 o'clock in a London hotel.

Wednesday was a half-holiday, and well-conducted cadets could obtain leave to go to London simply by asking for it. I occupied the three days' interval in composing a speech which I thought I might be called upon to deliver to a crowded executive of stern-faced citizens, about to unfurl that flag of British freedom for which 'Hampden died on the battlefield and Sidney on the scaffold.' As I had never attempted to speak in public before, it was a serious undertaking. I wrote and rewrote my speech three or four times over, and committed it in all its perfection to my memory. It was a serious constitutional argument upon the inherent rights of British subjects; upon the dangers of State interference with the social habits of law-abiding persons; and upon the many evil consequences which inevitably follow upon repression not supported by healthy public opinion. It did not overstate the case, nor was it blind to facts. It sought to persuade by moderation and good-humour, and to convince by logic tempered with common sense. There was even in its closing phases an appeal for a patient mood towards our misguided opponents. Was there not always more error than malice in human affairs? This task completed I awaited eagerly and at the same time nervously the momentous occasion.

As soon as our morning tasks were done I gobbled a hasty luncheon, changed into plain clothes (we were taught to abhor the word 'mufti,' and such abominable expressions as 'civvies' were in those days unknown) and hastened to the railway station, where I caught a very slow train to London. I must mention that this was for me a time of straitened finance; in fact the cost of the return railway ticket left me with only a few shillings in my pocket, and it was more than a fortnight before my next monthly allowance of £10 was due. I whiled away the journey by rehearsing the points and passages on which I principally relied. I drove in a hansom cab from Waterloo to Leicester Square near which the hotel appointed for the meeting of the Executive was situated. I was surprised and a little disconcerted at the dingy and even squalid appearance of these back streets and still more at the hotel when my cab eventually drew up before it. However, I said to myself, they are probably quite right to avoid the fashionable quarters. If this movement is to prosper it must be based upon the people's will; it must respond to those simple instincts which all classes have in common. It must not be compromised by association with gilded youth or smart society. To the porter I said 'I have come to attend the meeting of the Entertainments Protection League announced to be held this day in your hotel.'

The porter looked rather puzzled, and then said 'I think there's a gentleman in the smoking-room about that.' Into the smoking-room, a small dark apartment, I was accordingly shown, and there I met face to face the Founder of the new body. He was alone. I was upset; but concealing my depression under the fast-vanishing rays of hope, I asked 'When do we go up to the meeting?' He too seemed embarrassed. 'I have written to several people, but they have none of them turned up, so there's only you and me. We can draw up the Constitution ourselves, if you like.' I said 'But you wrote to me on the headed paper of the League.' 'Well,' he said 'that only cost 5s. It's always a good thing to have a printed heading on your notepaper in starting these sort of things. It encourages people to come forward. You see it encouraged you!' He paused as if chilled by my reserve, then added, 'It's very difficult to get people to do anything in England now. They take everything lying down. I do not know what's happened to the country; they seem to have no spirit left.'

Nothing was to be gained by carrying the matter further and less than nothing by getting angry with the Founder of the League. So I bade him a restrained but decisive farewell, and walked out into the street with a magnificent oration surging within my bosom and only half a crown in my pocket. The pavements were thronged with people hurrying to and fro engrossed upon their petty personal interests, oblivious and indifferent to the larger issues of human government. I looked with pity not untinged with scorn upon these trivial-minded passers-by. Evidently it was not going to be so easy to guide public opinion in the right direction as I had supposed. If these weak products of democracy held their liberties so lightly, how would they defend the vast provinces and domains we had gained by centuries of aristocratic and oligarchic rule? For a moment I despaired of the Empire. Then I thought of dinner and was pallidly confronted with the half-a-crown! No, that would not do! A journey to London on a beautiful half-holiday, keyed up to the last point of expectation, with a speech that might have shaped the national destinies undelivered and undigested upon my stomach, and then to go back to Sandhurst upon a bun and a cup of tea! That was more than fortitude could endure. So I did what I have never done before or since. I had now reached the Strand. I saw the three golden balls hanging over Mr. Attenborough's well-known shop. I had a very fine gold watch which my father had given me on my latest birthday. After all, the Crown Jewels of great kingdoms had been pawned on hard occasions. 'How much do you want,' said the shopman after handling the watch respectfully. 'A fiver will do,' I said. Some particulars were filled up in a book. I received one of those tickets which hitherto I had only heard of in music-halls songs, and a five-pound note, and sallied forth again into the heart of London. I got home all right.

The next day my Sandhurst friends all wanted to know how the meeting had gone off. I had imparted to them beforehand some of the more cogent arguments I intended to use. They were curious to learn how they had gone down. What was the meeting like? They had rather admired me for having the cheek to go up to make a speech championing their views to an Executive Committee of grown-up people, politicians, aldermen and the like. They wanted to know all about it. I did not admit them to my confidence. Speaking generally I dwelt upon the difficulties of public agitation in a comfortable and upon the whole contented country. I pointed out the importance of proceeding step by step, and of making each step good before the next was taken. The first step was to form an Executive Committee —that had been done. The next was to draw up the constitution of the League and assign the various responsibilities and powers—this was proceeding. The third step would be a broad appeal to the public, and on the response to this everything depended. These statements were accepted rather dubiously; but what else could I do? Had I only possessed a newspaper of my own, I would have had my speech reported verbatim on its front page, punctuated by the loud cheers of the Committee, heralded by arresting headlines and soberly sustained by the weight of successive leading articles. Then indeed the Entertainments Protection League might have made real progress. It might, in those early nineties, when so many things were in the making, have marshalled a public opinion so vigilant throughout the English-speaking world, and pronounced a warning so impressive, that the mighty United States themselves might have been saved from Prohibition! Here again we see the footprints of Fate, but they turned off the pleasant lawns on to a dry and stony highway.

I was destined to strike another blow in this crusade. Mrs. Chant's campaign was not unsuccessful, indeed so menacing did it appear that our party thought it prudent to make a characteristically British compromise. It was settled that the offending bars were to be separated from the promenade by light canvas screens. Thus they would no longer be technically 'in' the promenade; they would be just as far removed from it in law as if they had been in the adjacent county; yet means of egress and ingress of sufficient width might be lawfully provided, together with any reduction of the canvas screens necessary for sufficient ventilation. Thus the temples of Venus and Bacchus, though adjacent, would be separated, and their attack upon human frailties could only be delivered in a successive or alternating and not in a concentrated form. Loud were the hosannas which arose from the steadfast ranks of the 'Prudes on the Prowl.' The music-hall proprietors for their part, after uttering howls of pain and protest, seemed to reconcile themselves quite readily to their lot. It was otherwise with the Sandhurst movement. We had not been consulted in this nefarious peace. I was myself filled with scorn at its hypocrisy. I had no idea in those days of the enormous and unquestionably helpful part that humbug plays in the social life of great peoples dwelling in a state of democratic freedom. I wanted a clear-cut definition of the duties of the state and of the rights of the individual, modified as might be necessary by public convenience and decorum.

On the first Saturday night after these canvas obstructions had been placed in the Empire Promenade it happened that quite a large number of us chanced to be there.

There were also a good many boys from the Universities about our own age, but of course mere bookworms, quite undisciplined and irresponsible. The new structures were examined with attention and soon became the subject of unfavourable comment. Then some young gentleman poked his walking-stick through the canvas. Others imitated his example. Naturally I could not hang back when colleagues were testifying after this fashion. Suddenly a most strange thing happened. The entire crowd numbering some two or three hundred people became excited and infuriated. They rushed upon these flimsy barricades and tore them to pieces. The authorities were powerless. Amid the cracking of timber and the tearing of canvas the barricades were demolished, and the bars were once more united with the promenade to which they had ministered so long.

In these somewhat unvirginal surroundings I now made my maiden speech. Mounting on the débris and indeed partially emerging from it, I addressed the tumultuous crowd. No very accurate report of my words has been preserved. They did not, however, fall unheeded, and I have heard about them several times since. I discarded the constitutional argument entirely and appealed directly to sentiment and even passion, finishing up by saying 'You have seen us tear down these barricades to-night; see that you pull down those who are responsible for them at the coming election.' These words were received with rapturous applause, and we all sallied out into the Square brandishing fragments of wood and canvas as trophies or symbols. It reminded me of the death of Julius Cæsar when the conspirators rushed forth into the street waving the bloody daggers with which they had slain the tyrant. I thought also of the taking of the Bastille, with the details of which I was equally familiar.

It seems even more difficult to carry forward a revolution than to start one. We had to catch the last train back to Sandhurst or be guilty of dereliction of duty. This train, which still starts from Waterloo shortly after midnight, conveys the daily toll of corpses to the London Necropolis. It ran only as far as Frimley near Aldershot which it reached at three o'clock in the morning, leaving us to drive eight or ten miles to the Royal Military College. On our arrival at this hamlet no conveyances were to be found. We therefore knocked up the local inn-keeper. It may well be that we knocked him up rather boisterously. After a considerable interval in which our impatience became more manifest, the upper half of the door was suddenly opened, and we found ourselves looking down the muzzle of a blunderbuss, behind which stood a pale and menacing face. Things are rarely pushed to extremes in England. We maintained a firm posture, explained our wants and offered money. The landlord, first reassured and finally placated, produced an old horse and a still more ancient fly, and in this seven or eight of us made a successful journey to Camberley, and without troubling the porter at the gates, reached our apartments by unofficial paths in good time for early morning parade.

This episode made a considerable stir, and even secured leading articles in most of the newspapers. I was for some time apprehensive lest undue attention should be focussed upon my share in the proceedings. Certainly there was grave risk, for my father's name was still electric. Although naturally proud of my part in resisting tyranny as is the duty of every citizen who wishes to live in a free country, I was not unaware that a contrary opinion was possible, and might even become predominant. Elderly people and those in authority cannot always be relied upon to take enlightened and comprehending views of what they call the indiscretions of youth. They sometimes have a nasty trick of singling out individuals and 'making examples.' Although always prepared for martyrdom, I preferred that it should be postponed. Happily by the time my name began to be connected with the event, public interest had entirely died down, and no one at the College or the War Office was so spiteful as to revive it. This was one of those pieces of good luck which ought always to be remembered to set against an equal amount of bad luck when it comes along, as come it must. It remains only for me to record that the County Council Elections went the wrong way. The Progressives, as they called themselves, triumphed. The barricades were rebuilt in brick and plaster, and all our efforts went for nothing. Still no one can say we did not do our best.

*   *   *   *   *

My course at Sandhurst soon came to an end. Instead of creeping in at the bottom, almost by charity, I passed out with honours eighth in my batch of a hundred and fifty. I mention this because it shows that I could learn quickly enough the things that mattered. It had been a hard but happy experience. There were only three terms, at the end of each of which one advanced almost automatically from junior to intermediate, and then to senior. The generations were so short that in a year one was a senior. One could feel oneself growing up almost every week.

In December, 1894, I returned home fully qualified to receive the Queen's commission. In contrast with my school days, I had made many friends, three or four of whom still survive. As for the rest they are gone. The South African War accounted for a large proportion not only of my friends but of my company; and the Great War killed almost all the others. The few that survived have been pierced through thigh or breast or face by the bullets of the enemy. I salute them all.

I passed out of Sandhurst into the world. It opened like Aladdin's Cave. From the beginning of 1895 down to the present time of writing I have never had time to turn round. I could count almost on my fingers the days when I have had nothing to do. An endless moving picture in which one was an actor. On the whole Great Fun! But the years 1895 to 1900 which are the staple of this story exceed in vividness, variety and exertion anything I have known—except of course the opening months of the Great War.

When I look back upon them I cannot but return my sincere thanks to the high gods for the gift of existence. All the days were good and each day better than the other. Ups and downs, risks and journeys, but always the sense of motion, and the illusion of hope. Come on now all you young men, all over the world. You are needed more than ever now to fill the gap of a generation shorn by the war. You have not an hour to lose. You must take your places in Life's fighting line. Twenty to twenty-five! These are the years! Don't be content with things as they are. 'The earth is yours and the fulness thereof.' Enter upon your inheritance, accept your responsibilities. Raise the glorious flags again, advance them upon the new enemies, who constantly gather upon the front of the human army, and have only to be assaulted to be overthrown. Don't take No for an answer. Never submit to failure. Do not be fobbed off with mere personal success or acceptance. You will make all kinds of mistakes; but as long as you are generous and true, and also fierce, you cannot hurt the world or even seriously distress her. She was made to be wooed and won by youth. She has lived and thrived only by repeated subjugations.

CHAPTER V

THE FOURTH HUSSARS

I MUST now introduce the reader to a man of striking character and presence who at this point began to play an important part in my life. Colonel Brabazon commanded the 4th Hussars. This regiment had arrived at Aldershot from Ireland in the preceding year and was now quartered in the East Cavalry Barracks. Colonel Brabazon had been a friend of my family for many years, and I had met him several times during my school days. I was complimented by receiving as a Sandhurst cadet an invitation to dine with him in the regimental Mess. This was a great treat. In those days the Mess of a cavalry regiment presented an impressive spectacle to a youthful eye. Twenty or thirty officers, all magnificently attired in blue and gold, assembled round a table upon which shone the plate and trophies gathered by the regiment in two hundred years of sport and campaigning. It was like a State banquet. In an all-pervading air of glitter, affluence, ceremony and veiled discipline, an excellent and lengthy dinner was served to the strains of the regimental string band. I received the gayest of welcomes, and having it would seem conducted myself with discretion and modesty, I was invited again on several occasions. After some months my mother told me that Colonel Brabazon was anxious that I should go into his regiment, but that my father had said 'No.' Indeed it appeared he still believed it would be possible by using his influence to secure me an infantry commission after all. The Duke of Cambridge had expressed displeasure at my diversion from the 60th Rifles and had declared that there were ways in which the difficulties might, when the time came, be surmounted. 'Meanwhile,' my father had written, 'Brabazon, who I know is one of the finest soldiers in the Army, had no business to go and turn that boy's head about going into the 4th Hussars.'

However, the head was decidedly turned. After my father's last sad home-coming he could take but little interest in my affairs. My mother explained to him how matters had arranged themselves, and he seemed quite willing, and even pleased, that I should become a Cavalry Officer. Indeed, one of the last remarks he made to me was, 'Have you got your horses?'

*   *   *   *   *

My father died on January 24 in the early morning. Summoned from a neighbouring house where I was sleeping, I ran in the darkness across Grosvenor Square, then lapped in snow. His end was quite painless. Indeed he had long been in stupor. All my dreams of comradeship with him, of entering Parliament at his side and in his support, were ended. There remained for me only to pursue his aims and vindicate his memory.

I was now in the main the master of my fortunes. My mother was always at hand to help and advise; but I was now in my 21st year and she never sought to exercise parental control. Indeed she soon became an ardent ally, furthering my plans and guarding my interests with all her influence and boundless energy. She was still at forty young, beautiful and fascinating. We worked together on even terms, more like brother and sister than mother and son. At least so it seemed to me. And so it continued to the end.

*   *   *   *   *

In March 1895 I was gazetted to the 4th Hussars. I joined the Regiment six weeks earlier in anticipation, and was immediately set with several other subalterns to the stiff and arduous training of a Recruit Officer. Every day long hours were passed in the Riding-School, at Stables or on the

Barrack Square. I was fairly well fitted for the riding-school by the two long courses through which I had already gone; but I must proclaim that the 4th Hussars exceeded in severity anything I had previously experienced in military equitation.

In those days the principle was that the newly-joined Officer was given a recruit's training for the first six months. He rode and drilled afoot with the troopers and received exactly the same instruction and training as they did. At the head of the file in the riding-school, or on the right of the squad on the Square, he had to try to set an example to the men. This was a task not always possible to discharge with conspicuous success. Mounting and dismounting from a bare-backed horse at the trot or canter; jumping a high bar without stirrups or even saddle, sometimes with hands clasped behind one's back; jogging at a fast trot with nothing but the horse's hide between your knees, brought their inevitable share of mishaps. Many a time did I pick myself up shaken and sore from the riding-school tan and don again my little gold braided pork-pie cap, fastened on the chin by a boot-lace strap, with what appearance of dignity I could command, while twenty recruits grinned furtively but delightedly to see their Officer suffering the same misfortunes which it was their lot so frequently to undergo. I had the ill-luck, at an early stage in these proceedings, to strain my tailor's muscle on which one's grip upon a horse depends. In consequence I suffered tortures. Galvanic treatment was then unknown; one simply had to go on tearing at a lacerated muscle with the awful penalty of being thought a booby, if one begged off even for a day.

The Regimental Riding Master, nicknamed 'Jocko,' who specialized in being a terrible tyrant, happened during these weeks to be in an exceedingly touchy temper. One of the senior Subalterns had inserted in the *Aldershot Times* as an advertisement: 'Major ——, Professor of Equitation, East Cavalry Barracks. Hunting taught in 12 lessons and steeplechasing in 18.' This had drawn upon him a flood of ridicule which perhaps led him to suppose that every smile that ever flitted across the face of one of his riding-school class was due to some inward satisfaction at his expense.

However, within measure, I am all for youth being made willingly to endure austerities; and for the rest it was a gay and lordly life that now opened upon me. Even before being released from the riding-school the young officers were often permitted to ride out with their troops at exercise or on route marches and even sometimes to ride serre-file[1] in actual drill. There is a thrill and charm of its own in the glittering jingle of a cavalry squadron manœuvring at the trot; and this deepens into joyous excitement when the same evolutions are performed at a gallop. The stir of the horses, the clank of their equipment, the thrill of motion, the tossing plumes, the sense of incorporation in a living machine, the suave dignity of the uniform—all combine to make cavalry drill a fine thing in itself.

I must explain for the benefit of the ignorant reader that cavalry manœuvre in column and fight in line, and that cavalry drill resolves itself into swift and flexible changes from one formation to the other. Thus by wheeling or moving in échelon a front can always be presented by a squadron almost at any moment in any direction. The same principles apply to the movements of larger bodies of horsemen; and regiments, brigades and even divisions of cavalry could be made to present a front in an incredibly short time as the preliminary to that greatest of all cavalry events—the Charge.

It is a shame that War should have flung all this aside in its greedy, base, opportunist march, and should turn instead to chemists in spectacles, and chauffeurs pulling the levers of aeroplanes or machine guns. But at Aldershot in 1895 none

[1]The third rank of a troop which being only partially filled by supernumeraries, interlocks with the front rank of the following troop whenever the squadron is in column.

of these horrors had broken upon mankind. The Dragoon, the Lancer and above all, as we believed, the Hussar still claimed their time-honoured place upon the battlefield. War, which used to be cruel and magnificent, has now become cruel and squalid. In fact it has been completely spoilt. It is all the fault of Democracy and Science. From the moment that either of these meddlers and muddlers was allowed to take part in actual fighting, the doom of War was sealed. Instead of a small number of well-trained professionals champion-ing their country's cause with ancient weapons and a beauti-ful intricacy of archaic manoeuvre, sustained at every mo-ment by the applause of their nation, we now have entire populations, including even women and children, pitted against one another in brutish mutual extermination, and only a set of blear-eyed clerks left to add up the butcher's bill. From the moment Democracy was admitted to, or rather forced itself upon the battlefield, War ceased to be a gentleman's game. To Hell with it! Hence the League of Nations.

All the same it was a very fine thing in the '90's to see General Luck—the Inspector-General—manoeuvre a cav-alry division of thirty or forty squadrons as if it were one single unit. When this massive and splendid array assumed a preparatory formation and was then ordered to change front through an angle of perhaps 15 degrees, the outside brigade had to gallop two miles in a cloud of dust so thick that you could not see even five yards before your face, and twenty falls and half a dozen accidents were the features of a morn-ing's drill. And when the line was finally formed and the regiment or brigade was committed to the charge, one could hardly help shouting in joyous wrath.

Afterwards when we were home in barracks, these enthusi-asms in my case were corrected by remembering that the Germans had twenty cavalry divisions each as imposing as this our only darling, of which I formed a part; and sec-ondly by wondering what would happen if half a dozen spoil-sports got themselves into a hole with a maxim gun and kept their heads.

Then there were splendid parades when Queen Victoria sat in her carriage at the saluting point and when the whole Aldershot garrison, perhaps 25,000 strong, blue and gold, scarlet and steel, passed before her, Horse, Foot and Artillery, not forgetting the Engineers and Army Service Corps, in a broad and scintillating flood. It seemed very wrong that all these European Powers,—France, Germany, Austria and Russia—could do this same thing in *their* countries on the same day in twenty different places. I wondered why our Statesmen did not arrange an International Convention whereby each country should be represented in case of war, just as they are at the Olympic Games, by equal teams, and we by a single complete army corps which should embody all that was best in the race, and so settle the sovereignty of the world. However, the Victorian Ministers were very unenterprising; they missed their chance; they simply let War pass out of the hands of the experts and properly-trained persons who knew all about it, and reduced it to a mere disgusting matter of Men, Money and Machinery.

Those of us who already began to understand the sort of demoralisation that was going to come over War were irresistibly drawn to the conclusion that the British Army would never again take part in a European conflict. How could we, when we only had about one army corps with one Cavalry Division together with the Militia—God help them—and the Volunteers—Hurrah!? Certainly no Jingo Lieutenant or Fire-eating Staff Officer in the Aldershot Command in 1895, even in his most sanguine moments, would have believed that our little army would again be sent to Europe. Yet there was to come a day when a Cavalry Captain—Haig by name —who drilled with us in the Long Valley this spring was to feel himself stinted because in a most important battle, he could marshal no more than forty British Divisions together with the First American Army Corps—in all a bare six hun-

66

dred thousand men—and could only support them by less than 400 brigades of Artillery.

I wonder often whether any other generation has seen such astounding revolutions of data and values as those through which we have lived. Scarcely anything material or established which I was brought up to believe was permanent and vital, has lasted. Everything I was sure or taught to be sure was impossible, has happened.

*   *   *   *   *

Colonel Brabazon was an impoverished Irish landlord whose whole life had been spent in the British Army. He personified the heroes of Ouida. From his entry into the Grenadier Guards in the early '60's he had been in the van of fashion. He was one of the brightest military stars in London society. A close lifelong friendship had subsisted between him and the Prince of Wales. At Court, in the Clubs, on the racecourse, in the hunting field, he was accepted as a most distinguished figure. Though he had always remained a bachelor, he was by no means a misogynist. As a young man he must have been exceptionally good-looking. He was exactly the right height for a man to be. He was not actually six feet, but he looked it. Now, in his prime, his appearance was magnificent. His clean-cut symmetrical features, his bright grey eyes and strong jaw, were shown to the best advantage by a moustache which the Kaiser might well have taken as his unattainable ideal. To all this he added the airs and manners of the dandies of the generation before his own, and an inability, real or affected, to pronounce the letter 'R.' Apt and experienced in conversation, his remarkable personality was never at a loss in any company, polite or otherwise.

His military career had been long and varied. He had had to leave the Grenadier Guards after six years through straitened finances, and passed through a period of serious difficulty. He served as a gentleman volunteer—a great privilege—in the Ashanti Campaign of 1874. Here he so distinguished himself that there was a strong movement in high circles to restore to him his commission. This almost unprecedented favour was in fact accorded him. The Prince of Wales was most anxious that he should be appointed to his own regiment—the 10th Hussars—in those days probably the most exclusive regiment in the Army. However, as no vacancy was immediately available he was in the interval posted to an infantry regiment of the Line. To the question, 'What do you belong to now, Brab?' he replied, 'I never can wemember, but they have gween facings and you get at 'em from Waterloo.'

Of the Stationmaster at Aldershot he inquired on one occasion in later years: 'Where is the London twain?' 'It has gone, Colonel.' 'Gone! Bwing another.'

Translated at length into the 10th Hussars he served with increasing reputation through the Afghan War in 1878 and 1879 and through the fierce fighting round Suakim in 1884. As he had gained two successive brevets upon active service he was in army rank actually senior to the Colonel of his own regiment. This produced at least one embarrassing situation conceivable only in the British Army of those days. The Colonel of the 10th had occasion to find fault with Brabazon's squadron and went so far in his displeasure as to order it home to barracks. Brabazon was deeply mortified. However, a few weeks later the 10th Hussars were brigaded for some manœuvres with another cavalry regiment. Regimental seniority no longer ruled, and Brabazon's army rank gave him automatically the command of the brigade. Face to face with his own commanding officer, now for the moment his subordinate, Brabazon had repeated the same remarks and cutting sentences so recently addressed to him, and finished by the harsh order, 'Take your wegiment home, Sir!' The fashionable part of the army had been agog with this episode. That Brabazon had the law on his side could not be gainsaid. In those days men were accustomed to assert their rights in a rigid manner which would now be thought unsuitable. There were, however, two opinions upon the matter.

As it was clear that his regimental seniority would never enable him to command the 10th, the War Office had offered him in 1893 the command of the 4th Hussars. This was in itself an inevitable reflection upon the senior officers of that regiment. No regiment relishes the arrival of a stranger with the idea of 'smartening them up'; and there must have been a great deal of tension when this terrific Colonel, blazing with medals and clasps, and clad in all his social and military prestige, first assumed command of a regiment which had even longer traditions than the 10th Hussars. Brabazon made little attempt to conciliate. On the contrary he displayed a masterful confidence which won not only unquestioning obedience from all, but intense admiration, at any rate from the Captains and subalterns. Some of the seniors, however, were made to feel their position. 'And what chemist do you get this champagne fwom?' he inquired one evening of an irascible Mess president.

To me, apart from service matters in which he was a strict disciplinarian, he was always charming. But I soon discovered that behind all his talk of war and sport, which together with questions of religion or irreligion and one or two other topics formed the staple of Mess conversation, there lay in the Colonel's mind a very wide reading. When, for instance, on one occasion I quoted, 'God tempers the wind to the shorn lamb,' and Brabazon asked, 'Where do you get that fwom?' I had replied with some complacency that, though it was attributed often to the Bible, it really occurred in Sterne's *Sentimental Journey*. 'Have you ever wead it?' he asked, in the most innocent manner. Luckily I was not only naturally truthful, but also on my guard. I admitted that I had not. It was it seemed one of the Colonel's special favourites.

The Colonel, however, had his own rebuffs. Shortly before I joined the regiment he came into sharp collision with no less a personage than Sir Evelyn Wood who then commanded at Aldershot. Brabazon had not only introduced a number of minor irregularities, mostly extremely sensible, into the working uniform of the regiment—as for instance chrome yellow stripes for drill instead of gold lace—but he had worn for more than thirty years a small 'Imperial' beard under his lower lip. This was of course contrary to the Queen's Regulations Section VII. 'The chin and underlip are to be shaved (except by pioneers, who will wear beards).' But in thirty years of war and peace no superior authority had ever challenged Brabazon's Imperial. He had established it as a recognized privilege and institution of which no doubt he was enormously proud. No sooner had he brought his regiment into the Aldershot command than Sir Evelyn Wood was eager to show himself no respecter of persons. Away went the chrome yellow stripes on the pantaloons, away went the comfortable serge jumpers in which the regiment was accustomed to drill; back came the gold lace stripes and the tight-fitting cloth stable-jackets of the old régime. Forced to obey, the Colonel carried his complaints unofficially to the War Office. There was no doubt he had reason on his side. In fact within a year these sensible and economical innovations were imposed compulsorily upon the whole army. But no one at the War Office or in London dared override Sir Evelyn Wood, armed as he was with the text of the Queen's Regulations. As soon as Sir Evelyn Wood learned that Brabazon had criticised his decisions, he resolved upon a bold stroke. He sent the Colonel a written order to appear upon his next parade 'shaved in accordance with the regulations.' This was of course a mortal insult. Brabazon had no choice but to obey. That very night he made the sacrifice, and the next morning appeared disfigured before his men, who were aghast at the spectacle, and shocked at the tale they heard. The Colonel felt this situation so deeply that he never referred to it on any occasion. Except when obliged by military duty, he never spoke of Sir Evelyn Wood again.

Such was the man under whom I now had the honour to serve and whose friendship I enjoyed, warm and unbroken, through the remaining twenty years of his life. The Colonel was a die-hard Tory of the strictest and most robust school. His three main and fundamental tenets were: Protection, Conscription, and the revival of the Contagious Diseases Acts. He judged Governments and politicians according as they conformed or seemed likely to conform to his programme. But nothing in politics, not even the Free Trade controversy, nor the Lloyd George budget, nor the Ulster quarrel, severed our relations.

*   *   *   *   *

We were all delighted in the summer of 1895 to read that the Radical Home Rule Government had been beaten in the House of Commons and that Lord Salisbury was again forming an Administration. Everybody liked Lord Rosebery because he was thought to be patriotic. But then he had such bad companions! These bad companions dragged him down, and he was so weak, so they said, that he had to give way to them against his true convictions. Then too he was kept in office by the Irish Nationalists, who everyone knew would never be satisfied till they had broken up the British Empire. I put in a word for John Morley, but they said he was one of the worst of the lot and mixed up with Fenians and traitors of every kind. Particular pleasure was expressed that the Government should have been defeated for having let down the supply of cordite. Supposing a war came, how would you fight without cordite? Someone said that really there was plenty of cordite, but that any stick was good enough to beat such dogs! Certainly the Liberals were very unpopular at this time in Aldershot. The General Election proved that the rest of the country took our view, for Lord Salisbury was returned with a majority of 150, and the

Conservatives ruled the country for ten years during which they fought a number of the wars which form a considerable part of this account. Indeed they were never turned out until they went in for Protection, and then the Liberals came in and made the greatest of wars. But all that is stopped now.

I was invited to the party at Devonshire House after the Ministerial banquets. There I found all the new Ministers looking very smart in their blue and gold uniforms. These uniforms were not so magnificent as ours, but they had a style about them which commended them to my eye. I talked especially with Mr. George Curzon, the new Under Secretary of State for Foreign Affairs. He looked very splendid and prosperous, and received my congratulations with much affability. He explained that although his post was a small one, yet it carried with it the representation in the House of Commons of the Foreign Office and all that that implied. So he hoped he would have a share in making the foreign policy instead of only defending and explaining it. There were also some of those poor young men who had been left out; but they had to smile more gaily than anyone else, and go round congratulating all the people who had got the jobs these poor ones wanted for themselves. As no one had even considered me for any of these posts, I felt free to give rein to jealousy.

*   *   *   *   *

At this time Mrs. Everest died. As soon as I heard she was seriously ill I travelled up to London to see her. She lived with her sister's family in North London. She knew she was in danger, but her only anxiety was for me. There had been a heavy shower of rain. My jacket was wet. When she felt it with her hands she was greatly alarmed for fear I should catch cold. The jacket had to be taken off and thoroughly dried before she was calm again. Her only desire was to see my brother Jack, and this unhappily could not be arranged. I set out for London to get a good specialist, and the two doctors consulted together upon the case, which was one of peritonitis. I had to return to Aldershot by the midnight train for a very early morning parade. As soon as it was over, I returned to her bedside. She still knew me, but she gradually became unconscious. Death came very easily to her. She had lived such an innocent and loving life of service to others and held such a simple faith, that she had no fears at all, and did not seem to mind very much. She had been my dearest and most intimate friend during the whole of the twenty years I had lived. I now telegraphed to the clergyman with whom she had served nearly a quarter of a century before. He lived in Cumberland. He had a long memory for faithful service. We met at the graveside. He had become an Archdeacon. He did not bring little Ella with him.

When I think of the fate of poor old women, so many of whom have no one to look after them and nothing to live on at the end of their lives, I am glad to have had a hand in all that structure of pensions and insurance which no other country can rival and which is especially a help to them.

CHAPTER VI

CUBA

In the closing decade of the Victorian era the Empire had enjoyed so long a spell of almost unbroken peace, that medals and all they represented in experience and adventure were becoming extremely scarce in the British Army. The veterans of the Crimea and the Indian Mutiny were gone from the active list. The Afghan and Egyptian warriors of the early eighties had reached the senior ranks. Scarcely a shot had been fired in anger since then, and when I joined the 4th Hussars in January, 1895, scarcely a captain, hardly ever a subaltern, could be found throughout Her Majesty's forces who had seen even the smallest kind of war. Rarity in a desirable commodity is usually the cause of enhanced value; and there has never been a time when war service was held in so much esteem by the military authorities or more ardently sought by officers of every rank. It was the swift road to promotion and advancement in every arm. It was the glittering gateway to distinction. It cast a glamour upon the fortunate possessor alike in the eyes of elderly gentlemen and young ladies. How we young officers envied the senior Major for his adventures at Abu Klea! How we admired the Colonel with his long row of decorations! We listened with almost insatiable interest to the accounts which they were good enough to give us on more than one occasion of stirring deeds and episodes already melting into the mist of time. How we longed to have a similar store of memories to unpack and display, if necessary repeatedly, to a sympathetic audience! How we wondered whether our chance would ever come—whether we too in our turn would have battles to fight over again and again in the agreeable atmosphere of the after-dinner mess table? Prowess at polo, in the hunting-field, or between the flags, might count for something. But the young soldier who had been 'on active service' and 'under fire' had an *aura* about him to which the Generals he served under, the troopers he led, and the girls he courted, accorded a unanimous, sincere, and spontaneous recognition.

The want of a sufficient supply of active service was therefore acutely felt by my contemporaries in the circles in which I was now called upon to live my life. This complaint was destined to be cured, and all our requirements were to be met to the fullest extent. The danger—as the subaltern regarded it—which in those days seemed so real of Liberal and democratic governments making war impossible was soon to be proved illusory. The age of Peace had ended. There was to be no lack of war. There was to be enough for all. Aye, enough and to spare. Few indeed of the keen, aspiring generations of Sandhurst cadets and youthful officers who entered the Royal Service so light-heartedly in these and later years were to survive the ghastly surfeit which fate had in store. The little tidbits of fighting which the Indian frontier and the Soudan were soon to offer, distributed by luck or favour, were fiercely scrambled for throughout the British Army. But the South African War was to attain dimensions which fully satisfied the needs of our small army. And after that the deluge was still to come!

The military year was divided into a seven months' summer season of training and a five months' winter season of leave, and each officer received a solid block of two and a half months' uninterrupted repose. All my money had been spent on polo ponies, and as I could not afford to hunt, I searched the world for some scene of adventure or excitement. The general peace in which mankind had for so many years languished was broken only in one quarter of the globe. The long-drawn guerrilla between the Spaniards and the Cuban rebels was said to be entering upon its most serious phase. The Captain-General of Spain, the famous Marshal Martinez Campos, renowned alike for victories over the Moors and *pronunciamientos* to the Spaniards, had been sent to the recalcitrant island; and 80,000 Spanish reinforcements were being rapidly shipped across the ocean in a supreme attempt to quell the revolt. Here then was fighting actually going on. From very early youth I had brooded about soldiers and war, and often I had imagined in dreams and day-dreams the sensations attendant upon being for the first time under fire. It seemed to my youthful mind that it must be a thrilling and immense experience to hear the whistle of bullets all around and to play at hazard from moment to moment with death and wounds. Moreover, now that I had assumed professional obligations in the matter, I thought that it might be as well to have a private rehearsal, a secluded trial trip, in order to make sure that the ordeal was one not unsuited to my temperament. Accordingly it was to Cuba that I turned my eyes.

I unfolded the project to a brother subaltern—Reginald Barnes—who afterwards long commanded Divisions in France, and found him keen. The Colonel and the Mess generally looked with favour upon a plan to seek professional experience at a seat of war. It was considered as good or almost as good as a season's serious hunting, without which no subaltern or captain was considered to be living a respectable life. Thus fortified, I wrote to my father's old friend and Fourth Party colleague, Sir Henry Wolff, then our Ambassador at Madrid, asking whether he could procure us the necessary permissions from the Spanish military authorities. The dear old gentleman, whose long-acquired influence at the Spanish Court was unrivalled in the Diplomatic Corps, of which he was the doyen, took the greatest trouble on my behalf. Excellent introductions, formal and personal, soon arrived in a packet, together with the Ambassador's assurance that we had only to reach Havana to be warmly welcomed by the Captain-General and shown all there was to see. Accordingly at the beginning of November, 1895, we sailed for New York, and journeyed thence to Havana.

The minds of this generation, exhausted, brutalised, mutilated and bored by War, may not understand the delicious yet tremulous sensations with which a young British Officer bred in the long peace approached for the first time an actual theatre of operations. When first in the dim light of early morning I saw the shores of Cuba rise and define themselves from dark-blue horizons, I felt as if I sailed with Captain Silver and first gazed on Treasure Island. Here was a place where real things were going on. Here was a scene of vital action. Here was a place where anything might happen. Here was a place where something would certainly happen. Here I might leave my bones. These musings were dispersed by the advance of breakfast, and lost in the hurry of disembarkation.

Cuba is a lovely island. Well have the Spaniards named it 'The Pearl of the Antilles.' The temperate yet ardent climate, the abundant rainfall, the luxurious vegetation, the unrivalled fertility of the soil, the beautiful scenery—all combined to make me accuse that absent-minded morning when our ancestors let so delectable a possession slip through their fingers. However, our modern Democracy has inherited enough—to keep or to cast away.

The City and Harbour of Havana thirty-five years ago presented a spectacle which, though no doubt surpassed by its present progress, was in every respect magnificent. We took up our quarters in a fairly good hotel, ate a great quantity of oranges, smoked a number of cigars, and presented our credentials to Authority. Everything worked perfectly. Our letters had no sooner been read than we were treated as an unofficial, but none the less important, mission sent at a time of stress by a mighty Power and old ally. The more we endeavoured to reduce the character of our visit, the more its underlying significance was appraised. The Captain-General was on tour inspecting various posts and garrisons; but all would be arranged exactly as we wished. We should find the Marshal at Santa Clara;[1] the journey was quite practicable; the trains were armoured; escorts travelled in special wagons at either end; the sides of the carriages were protected by strong plating; when firing broke out as was usual you had only to lie down on the floor of the carriage to arrive safely. We started next morning.

Marshal Martinez Campos received us affably and handed us over to one of his Staff Officers, a young Lieutenant, son of the Duke of Tetuan, by name Juan O'Donnell, who spoke English extremely well. I was surprised at the name, but was told it had become Spanish since the days of the Irish Brigade. O'Donnell explained that if we wished to see the fighting we ought to join a mobile column. Such a column it appeared had started from Santa Clara only that morning under General Valdez for Sancti Spiritūs, a town about 40 miles away beset by rebels. It was a pity we had missed it. We suggested that as it would only have made one march we could easily overtake it. Our young Spaniard shook his head: 'You would not get 5 miles.' 'Where, then, are the enemy?' we asked. 'They are everywhere and nowhere,' he replied. 'Fifty horsemen can go where they please—two cannot go anywhere.' However, it would be possible to intercept General Valdez. We must go by train to Cienfuegos, and then by sea to Tuna. The railway line from Tuna to Sancti Spiritūs was, he said, strongly guarded by blockhouses, and military trains had hitherto passed regularly. Thus by a journey of 150 miles we should reach Sancti Spiritūs in three days, and General Valdez would not arrive there with his troops until the evening of the fourth day. There we could join his column and follow his further operations. Horses and orderlies would be provided and the General would welcome us upon his staff as guests.

We accomplished our journey with some risk, but no accident. Sancti Spiritūs, its name notwithstanding, was a

[1]See map on page 87.

very second-rate place and in the most unhealthy state. Small-pox and yellow fever were rife. We spent the night in a filthy, noisy, crowded tavern, and the next evening General Valdez and his column marched in. It was a considerable force: four battalions comprising about 3,000 infantry, two squadrons of cavalry and a mule battery. The troops looked fit and sturdy and none the worse for their marches. They were dressed in cotton uniforms which may originally have been white, but now with dirt and dust had toned down to something very like khaki. They carried heavy packs and double bandoliers, and wore large straw Panama hats. They were warmly greeted by their comrades in the town and also, it seemed, by the inhabitants.

After a respectful interval we presented ourselves at the General's headquarters. He had already read the telegrams which commended us to him, and he welcomed us most cordially. Suarez Valdez was a General of Division. He was making a fortnight's march through the insurgent districts with the double purpose of visiting the townships and posts garrisoned by the Spaniards, and also of fighting the rebels wherever and whenever they could be found. He explained, through an interpreter, what an honour it was for him to have two distinguished representatives of a great and friendly Power attached to his column, and how highly he valued the moral support which this gesture of Great Britain implied. We said, back through the interpreter, that it was awfully kind of him, and that we were sure it would be awfully jolly. The interpreter worked this up into something quite good, and the General looked much pleased. He then announced that he would march at daybreak. The town was too full of disease for him to stay for one unnecessary hour. Our horses would be ready before daylight. In the meanwhile he invited us to dinner.

Behold next morning a distinct sensation in the life of a young officer! It is still dark, but the sky is paling. We are in what a brilliant though little-known writer has called 'The dim mysterious temple of the Dawn.'[1] We are on our horses, in uniform; our revolvers are loaded. In the dusk and half-light, long files of armed and laden men are shuffling off towards the enemy. He may be very near; perhaps he is waiting for us a mile away. We cannot tell; we know nothing of the qualities either of our friends or foes. We have nothing to do with their quarrels. Except in personal self-defence we can take no part in their combats. But we feel it is a great moment in our lives—in fact, one of the best we have ever experienced. We think that something is going to happen; we hope devoutly that something will happen; yet at the same time we do not want to be hurt or killed. What is it then that we do want? It is that lure of youth—adventure, and adventure for adventure's sake. You might call it tomfoolery. To travel thousands of miles with money one could ill afford, and get up at four o'clock in the morning in the hope of getting into a scrape in the company of perfect strangers, is certainly hardly a rational proceeding. Yet we knew there were very few subalterns in the British Army who would not have given a month's pay to sit in our saddles.

However, nothing happened. Daylight slowly broadened, and the long Spanish column insinuated itself like a snake into the endless forests and undulations of a vast, lustrous landscape dripping with moisture and sparkling with sunshine. We marched about 8 miles, and then, it being near nine o'clock and fairly open country having been reached, a halt was called for breakfast and the *siesta*. Breakfast was an important meal. The infantry lighted fires to cook their food; the horses were off-saddled and put to graze; and coffee and a stew were served at a table to the staff. It was a picnic. The general's aide-de-camp at length produced a long metal bottle in which he made a beverage which he described as 'runcotelle.' It is only in later years that the meaning of this expression, which I so well remember, has been revealed

[1]Mackay, *Twenty-one Days in India.*

to me. It was undoubtedly a 'Rum Cocktail.' Whatever its name, it was extremely good. By this time hammocks had been slung between the trees of a thicket. Into these hammocks we were now enjoined to retire. The soldiers and regimental officers extended themselves upon the ground after, I trust, taking the necessary military precautions, and every one slept in the shade for about four hours.

At two o'clock the *siesta* was over. Bustle arose in the silent midday bivouac. At three in the afternoon we were once more on the way, and marched four hours at a speed of certainly not less than 2¾ miles an hour. As dusk was falling we reached our camping ground for the night. The column had covered 18 or 19 miles, and the infantry did not seem in the least fatigued. These tough Spanish peasants, sons of the soil, could jog along with heavy loads over mere tracks with an admirable persistence. The prolonged midday halt was like a second night's rest to them.

I have no doubt that the Romans planned the time-table of their days far better than we do. They rose before the sun at all seasons. Except in war time we never see the dawn. Sometimes we see sunset. The message of the sunset is sadness; the message of the dawn is hope. The rest and the spell of sleep in the middle of the day refresh the human frame far more than a long night. We were not made by Nature to work, or even to play, from eight o'clock in the morning till midnight. We throw a strain upon our system which is unfair and improvident. For every purpose of business or pleasure, mental or physical, we ought to break our days and our marches into two. When I was at the Admiralty in the War, I found I could add nearly two hours to my working effort by going to bed for an hour after luncheon. The Latins are wiser and closer to Nature in their way of living than the Anglo-Saxons or Teutons. But they dwell in superior climates.

Following this routine, we marched for several days, through wonderful country, without a sign or sound or sight of war. Meanwhile we got quite friendly with our Spanish hosts; and speaking execrable French in common, though from different angles, we managed to acquire some understanding of their views. The Chief of the Staff, Lieut.-Col. Benzo, for instance, on one occasion referred to the war 'which we are fighting to preserve the integrity of our country.' I was struck by this. I had not, no doubt owing to my restricted education, quite realised that these other nations had the same sort of feeling about their possessions as we in England had always been brought up to have about ours. They felt about Cuba, it seemed, just as we felt about Ireland. This impressed me much. I thought it rather cheek that these foreigners should have just the same views and use the same sort of language about their country and their colonies as if they were British. However, I accepted the fact and put it in my mental larder. Hitherto I had (secretly) sympathised with the rebels, or at least with the rebellion; but now I began to see how unhappy the Spanish were at the idea of having their beautiful 'Pearl of the Antilles' torn away from them, and I began to feel sorry for them.

We did not see how they could win. Imagine the cost per hour of a column of nearly 4,000 men wandering round and round this endless humid jungle; and there were perhaps a dozen such columns, and many smaller, continuously on the move. Then there were 200,000 men in all the posts and garrisons, or in the block-houses on the railway lines. We knew that Spain was not a rich country as things went then. We knew by what immense efforts and sacrifices she maintained more than a quarter of a million men across 5,000 miles of saltwater—a dumb-bell held at arm's length. And what of the enemy? We had seen nothing of them, we had not heard even one rifle let off; but they evidently existed. All these elaborate precautions and powerful forces had been brought into being as the result of repeated disasters. In these forests and mountains were bands of ragged men not ill supplied with rifles and ammunition, and armed above all

with a formidable chopper-sword called a 'machete,' to
whom war cost nothing except poverty, risk and discomfort
—and no one was likely to run short of these. Here were the
Spaniards out-guerrillaed in their turn. They moved like
Napoleon's convoys in the Peninsula, league after league,
day after day, through a world of impalpable hostility,
slashed here and there by fierce onslaught.

We slept on the night of November 29 in the fortified
village of Arroyo Blanco. We had sent two battalions and
one squadron with the main part of the convoy to carry provisions to a series of garrisons. The rest of our force, numbering perhaps 1,700 men, were to seek the enemy and a
fight. The 30th November was my 21st birthday, and on
that day for the first time I heard shots fired in anger, and
heard bullets strike flesh or whistle through the air.

There was a low mist as we moved off in the early morning, and all of a sudden the rear of the column was involved
in firing. In those days when people got quite close together
in order to fight, and used—partly, at any rate—large-bore
rifles to fight with, loud bangs were heard and smoke-puffs
or even flashes could be seen. The firing seemed about a fur-
long away and sounded very noisy and startling. As however
no bullets seemed to come near me, I was easily reassured.
I felt like the optimist 'who did not mind what happened,
so long as it did not happen to him.' The mist hid everything from view. After a while it began to lift, and I found
we were marching through a clearing in the woods, nearly
100 yards wide. This was called a military road, and we
wended along it for several hours. The jungle had already
encroached avidly upon the track, and the officers drew their
machetes and cut down the branches or, in sport, cut in half
the great water-gourds which hung from them and discharged a quart of cold crystal liquid upon the unwary.

On this day when we halted for breakfast every man sat
by his horse and ate what he had in his pocket. I had been
provided with half a skinny chicken. I was engaged in gnaw-

ing the drumstick when suddenly, close at hand, almost in our faces it seemed, a ragged volley rang out from the edge of the forest. The horse immediately behind me,—not my horse—gave a bound. There was excitement and commotion. A party of soldiers rushed to the place whence the volley had been fired, and of course found nothing except a few empty cartridge cases. Meanwhile I had been meditating upon the wounded horse. It was a chestnut. The bullet had struck between his ribs, the blood dripped on the ground, and there was a circle of dark red on his bright chestnut coat about a foot wide. He hung his head, but did not fall. Evidently however he was going to die, for his saddle and bridle were soon taken off him. As I watched these proceedings I could not help reflecting that the bullet which had struck the chestnut had certainly passed within a foot of my head. So at any rate I had been 'under fire.' That was something. Nevertheless, I began to take a more thoughtful view of our enterprise than I had hitherto done.

All the next day we pursued the trail. The woods which before had borne a distant resemblance to an English covert, now gave place to forests of bottle-stemmed palm trees of all possible sizes and most peculiar shapes. Three or four hours of this sort of country led us again to more open ground, and after fording the river we halted for the night near a rude cabin which boasted a name on the map. It was hot, and my companion and I persuaded two of the younger staff officers to come with us and bathe in the river which encircled our bivouac on three sides. The water was delightful, being warm and clear, and the spot very beautiful. We were dressing on the bank when suddenly we heard a shot fired at no great distance. Another and another followed, and then came a volley. The bullets whizzed over our heads. It was evident that an attack of some sort was in progress. We pulled on our clothes anyhow, and retired along the river as gracefully as might be and returned to the General's headquarters. When we arrived, there was a regular skirmish going on half a mile away, and the bullets were falling all over the camp. The rebels were armed mainly with Remingtons, and the deep note of their pieces contrasted strangely with the shrill rattle of the magazine rifles of the Spaniards. After about half an hour the insurgents had had enough, and went off carrying away with them the wounded and dead with which it was hoped they were not unprovided.

We dined undisturbed in the verandah and retired to our hammocks in the little barn. I was soon awakened by firing. Not only shots but volleys resounded through the night. A bullet ripped through the thatch of our hut, another wounded an orderly just outside. I should have been glad to get out of my hammock and lie on the ground. However, as no one else made a move, I thought it more becoming to stay where I was. I fortified myself by dwelling on the fact that the Spanish officer whose hammock was slung between me and the enemy's fire was a man of substantial physique; indeed one might almost have called him fat. I have never been prejudiced against fat men. At any rate I did not grudge this one his meals. Gradually I dropped asleep.

After a disturbed night, the column started early in the morning. A mist gave cover to the rebel marksmen, who saluted us as soon as we got across the river with a well-directed fire. The enemy, falling back before us, took advantage of every position. Though not very many men were hit, the bullets traversed the entire length of the column, making the march very lively for everybody. At eight o'clock the head of the Spanish column debouched from the broken ground into open country. A broad grass ride with a wire fence on one side and a row of little stunted trees on the other ran from the beginning of the plain to the enemy's line. On each side of the ride were broad fields of rank grass, waist-high. Half-way up the ride, which was about a mile long, and on the right-hand side, was a grove of about a hundred palm trees. At the end of the ride and at right angles to it was a low, long hill, surmounted by a rail fence and backed by the dense forests. This was the enemy's position, which the General resolved immediately to attack.

The tactics were simple. As the leading Spanish battalion got clear of the broken ground, two companies were thrown forward on each flank and extended. The cavalry went to the right of the ride and the artillery proceeded up the centre. The General, his staff and his two British visitors, advanced solemnly up the ride about 50 yards in the rear of the firing line. The second battalion followed the guns in column of companies. For 300 yards there was no firing. Then from the distant crest line came a lot of little puffs of smoke, followed immediately by the report of the insurgent rifles. Twice this happened, and then the enemy's fire became continuous and spread right and left along his whole position. The Spanish infantry now began to reply and advanced continually. The firing on both sides became heavy. There were sounds about us sometimes like a sigh, sometimes like a whistle, and at others like the buzz of an offended hornet. The General and his staff rode forward until the smoke-crested crackling fence was only four or five hundred yards away. Here we halted, and sitting mounted, without the slightest cover or concealment, watched the assault of the infantry. During this period the air was full of whizzings, and the palm trees smitten by the bullets yielded resounding smacks and thuds. The Spaniards were on their mettle; and we had to do our best to keep up appearances. It really seemed very dangerous indeed, and I was astonished to see how few people were hit amid all this clatter. In our group of about twenty, only three or four horses and men were wounded, and not one killed. Presently, to my relief, the sound of the Mauser volleys began to predominate, and the rebel fire to slacken, till it finally ceased altogether. For a moment I could see figures scurrying to the shelter of the woods, and then came silence. The infantry advanced and occupied the enemy's position. Pursuit was impossible owing to the impenetrable jungle.

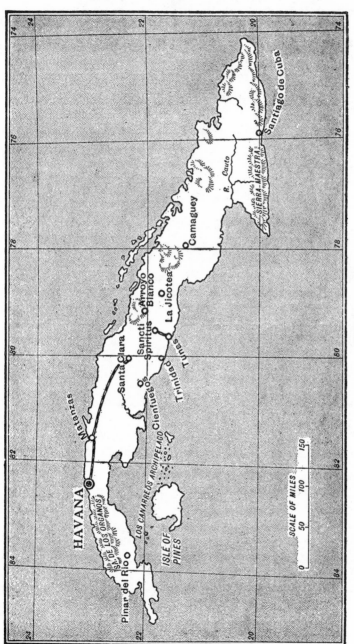

CUBA

As our column had now only one day's rations left, we withdrew across the plain to La Jicotea. Spanish honour and our own curiosity alike being satisfied, the column returned to the coast, and we to England. We did not think the Spaniards were likely to bring their war in Cuba to a speedy end.

CHAPTER VII

HOUNSLOW

IN the spring of 1896 the 4th Hussars marched to Hounslow and Hampton Court preparatory to sailing for India in the autumn. At Hounslow we yielded up our horses to some home-coming regiment, so that all cavalry training came to an end. The regiment would remain in the East for twelve or fourteen years, and officers were given the fullest leave and facilities for arranging their affairs. Before our horses departed we had a final parade on Hounslow Heath at which Colonel Brabazon, whose command was expiring, took leave of the regiment in a brief soldierly speech marked by distinction of phrasing.

I now passed a most agreeable six months; in fact they formed almost the only idle spell I have ever had. I was able to live at home with my mother and go down to Hounslow Barracks two or three times a week by the Underground Railway. We played polo at Hurlingham and Ranelagh. The Roehampton grounds had not then come into existence. I had now five quite good ponies, and was considered to show promise. I gave myself over to the amusements of the London Season. In those days English Society still existed in its old form. It was a brilliant and powerful body, with standards of conduct and methods of enforcing them now altogether forgotten. In a very large degree every one knew every one else and who they were. The few hundred great families who had governed England for so many generations and had seen her rise to the pinnacle of her glory, were inter-related to an enormous extent by marriage. Everywhere one met friends and kinsfolk. The leading figures of Society were in many cases the leading statesmen in Parliament, and also the leading sportsmen on the Turf.

Lord Salisbury was accustomed scrupulously to avoid calling a Cabinet when there was racing at Newmarket, and the House of Commons made a practice of adjourning for the Derby. In those days the glittering parties at Lansdowne House, Devonshire House or Stafford House comprised all the elements which made a gay and splendid social circle in close relation to the business of Parliament, the hierarchies of the Army and Navy, and the policy of the State. Now Lansdowne House and Devonshire House have been turned into hotels, flats and restaurants; and Stafford House has become the ugliest and stupidest museum in the world, in whose faded saloons Socialist Governments drearily dispense the public hospitality.

But none of these shadows had fallen across London in 1896. On the contrary, all minds were turning to the Diamond Jubilee in the coming year. I moved from one delightful company and scene to another, and passed the weekends in those beautiful places and palaces which were then linked by their actual owners with the long triumphant history of the United Kingdom. I am glad to have seen, if only for a few months, this vanished world. The picture which remains in my mind's eye is the Duchess of Devonshire's Fancy Dress Ball in 1897. It reproduced the scenes upon which Disraeli dilated in his novels. Indeed it revived one of his most celebrated descriptions; for outside in the Green Park large crowds of people had gathered in the summer night to watch the arriving and departing guests, to listen to the music, and perhaps to meditate upon the gulf which in those days separated the rulers and the ruled.

When in 1920 M. Paul Cambon brought to an end his long, memorable mission to the Court of St. James's, he was good enough to come to luncheon at my house. The talk turned upon the giant events through which we had passed and the distance the world had travelled since the beginning of the century. 'In the twenty years I have been here,' said the aged Ambassador, 'I have witnessed an English

Revolution more profound and searching than the French Revolution itself. The governing class have been almost entirely deprived of political power and to a very large extent of their property and estates; and this has been accomplished almost imperceptibly and without the loss of a single life.' I suppose this is true.

*　　*　　*　　*　　*

Lilian, widow of my uncle the 8th Duke of Marlborough, the daughter of a Commodore in the American navy, and very wealthy by an earlier marriage, had recently married in third wedlock Lord William Beresford. He was the youngest of Lord Waterford's three brothers, each of whom was a man of mark. The eldest, 'Charlie,' was the famous admiral. The second, Marcus, made a great place for himself in society and on the Turf; and the third 'Bill,' the soldier, had won the Victoria Cross in Zululand. All my life until they died I kept coming across these men.

Lord William and Lilian, Duchess, had married in riper years; but their union was happy, prosperous and even fruitful. They settled down at the beautiful Deepdene near Dorking, and bade me visit them continually. I took a strong liking to Bill Beresford. He seemed to have every quality which could fascinate a cavalry subaltern. He was a man of the world acquainted with every aspect of clubland and society. For long years he had been military secretary both to Lord Dufferin and Lord Lansdowne, successive Viceroys of India. He was a grand sportsman who had lived his whole life in companionship with horses. Polo, pig-sticking, pony-racing, horse-racing, together with shooting big game of every kind, had played a constant part in his affairs. As a young officer of the 12th Lancers he had won a large bet by walking after dinner from the Blues Mess at Knightsbridge to the cavalry barracks at Hounslow; there catching a badger kept by the 10th Hussars and carrying it back in a bag on his shoulders to the expectant Mess at Knightsbridge, in an exceedingly short time considering the distance. There was nothing in sport or in gambling about sport which he had not tasted. Lastly, he was an officer who had served in three or four wars, and who had in circumstances of forlorn hope rescued a comrade from Zulu assegais and bullets. His opinions about public affairs, though tinged with an official hue, were deeply practical, and on matters of conduct and etiquette they were held by many to be decisive.

Thus I paid frequent visits to Deepdene with its comfort and splendour, and I was never tired of listening to his wisdom or imparting my own. Always do I remember his declaration that there would never be another war between civilized peoples. 'Often,' he said, 'have I seen countries come up to the very verge, but something always happens to hold them back.' There was too much good sense in the world, he thought, to let such a hideous thing as that break out among polite nations. I did not accept this as conclusive; but it weighed with me, and three or four times when rumours of war filled the air, I rested myself upon it, and three or four times I saw it proved to be sure and true. It was the natural reflection of a life lived in the Victorian Age. However, there came a time when the world got into far deeper waters than Lord William Beresford or his contemporaries had ever plumbed.

It was at Deepdene in 1896 that I first met Sir Bindon Blood. This general was one of the most trusted and experienced commanders on the Indian frontier. He was my host's life-long friend. He had come home fresh from his successful storming of the Malakand Pass in the autumn of 1895. If future trouble broke out on the Indian frontier, he was sure to have a high command. He thus held the key to future delights. I made good friends with him. One Sunday morning on the sunny lawns of Deepdene I extracted from the general a promise that if ever he commanded another expedition on the Indian frontier, he would let me come with him.

I sustained one disturbing experience at Deepdene. I was invited, and it was a great honour for a 2nd lieutenant, to join a week-end party given to the Prince of Wales. Colonel Brabazon was also among the guests. I realized that I must be upon my best behaviour: punctual, subdued, reserved, in short display all the qualities with which I am least endowed. I ought to have caught a six o'clock train to Dorking; but I decided to travel by the 7.15 instead. This was running things very fine, but it was not until my journey was half completed that I realised that I should be almost certainly late for dinner. The train was due to arrive at 8.18, and then there would be ten minutes' drive from the station. So I proceeded, much to the concern of the gentleman who shared my carriage, to dress in the train between the stations. The train was horribly slow and seemed to lose a few minutes at each stop. Of course it stopped at every station. It was twenty to nine before I reached Dorking. I nipped out of the carriage to find a servant on the platform evidently disturbed. I jumped into the brougham and saw by the speed at which the two horses were being urged that a serious crisis awaited me at my destination. However, I thought, 'I will slip in and take my place almost unnoticed at the table, and make my apologies afterwards.'

When I arrived at Deepdene, I found the entire company assembled in the drawing-room. The party it seemed without me would be only thirteen. The prejudice of the Royal Family of those days against sitting down thirteen is well known. The Prince had refused point-blank to go in, and would not allow any rearrangement of two tables to be made. He had, as was his custom, been punctual to the minute at half-past eight. It was now twelve minutes to nine. There, in this large room, stood this select and distinguished company in the worst of tempers, and there on the other hand was I, a young boy asked as a special favour and compliment. Of course I had a perfectly good explanation. Oddly enough, it was one that I have had to use on more than one occasion since. I had not started soon enough! I put it aside. I stammered a few words of apology, and advanced to make my bow. 'Don't they teach you to be punctual in your regiment, Winston?' said the Prince in his most severe tone, and then looked acidly at Colonel Brabazon, who glowered. It was an awful moment! We went into dinner two by two and sat down an unexceptionable fourteen. After about a quarter of an hour the Prince, who was a naturally and genuinely kind-hearted man, put me at my ease again by some gracious chaffing remark.

I do think unpunctuality is a vile habit, and all my life I have tried to break myself of it. 'I have never been able,' said Dr. Welldon to me some years later, 'to understand the point of view of persons who make a practice of being ten minutes late for each of a series of appointments throughout the day.' I entirely agree with this dictum. The only straightforward course is to cut out one or two of the appointments altogether and so catch up. But very few men have the strength of mind to do this. It is better that one notability should be turned away expostulating from the doorstep, than that nine just deputations should each fume for ten minutes in a stuffy ante-room.

*   *   *   *   *

In December 1895 there had occurred in South Africa an event which seems to me when I look back over my map of life to be a fountain of ill. Lord Salisbury had been returned the summer before with a Conservative majority of 150. He looked forward to a reign limited only by the Septennial Act. He set before himself as his main task the wiping out of Mr. Gladstone's disgrace in the Soudan when General Gordon was murdered, and of his surrender in South Africa after our defeat at Majuba Hill. He proceeded upon both these courses with slow, sure steps and with the utmost cautiousness. He carefully fostered peace in Europe, and kept everything as quiet as possible at home. When Russian expansion in the Far East threatened the interests of Britain and the life of Japan, he was not above beating a retreat. He allowed the British China Fleet to be ordered out of Port Arthur by the Russians. He put up with the mockery which the Liberal Opposition of those days somewhat incongruously directed upon his pusillanimity. When the Olney Note about Venezuela—virtually an ultimatum—arrived from the United States, he sent the soft answer which turned away wrath. He confined his purposes to the British Empire. He kept the board clear for the Soudan and the Transvaal.

In this latter sphere Mr. Chamberlain was also active. The great 'Joe,' having kept Lord Salisbury in power from 1886 till 1892, had been the spear-point of the attacks which in 1895 had driven the Liberals from their brief spell of office. He had at last decided to join Lord Salisbury's new Administration; and the Colonial Office, which in Mid-Victorian times had been considered a minor appointment, became in his hands the main creative instrument of national policy. Lord Salisbury, moving ponderously forward towards the general squaring of accounts with the Khalifa at Khartoum and with President Kruger at Pretoria, found in the South African business a reinforcing and indeed overriding impulse from the Radical-Imperialist of Birmingham.

Apart from these personal and temperamental currents, the tide of events in South Africa carried everything steadily forward towards a crisis. The development of deep-level gold-mining in the Rand had in a few years made Johannesburg a recognizable factor not only in British, but in worldwide financial and economic affairs. The republic of Boer farmers, hitherto content to lead a pastoral life in the lonely regions into which their grandfathers had emigrated, now found themselves possessed of vast revenues from gold mines and responsible for a thriving modern city with a very large and rapidly growing polyglot population. A strong, capable and ambitious organism of government grew up at Pretoria. It became the magnet of Dutch aspirations throughout South Africa. It nourished itself by taxing the golden spoil which was drawn in ever-growing volume to the surface of the great Banket Reef. It reached out to Holland and Germany for European support and relationships. Behind all lay the unmeasured fighting strength of fifty or sixty thousand fierce, narrow, prejudiced, devout Boer farmers, constituting the finest mass of rifle-armed horsemen ever seen, and the most capable mounted warriors since the Mongols.

The new inhabitants of Johannesburg—the Outlanders, as they were called—in whom British elements predominated, were dissatisfied with the bad and often corrupt administration of the Boer Government; and still more so with its heavy and increasing taxes. They proclaimed the old watchword about 'No taxation without representation.' They demanded votes. But since their numbers would have swamped the Boer regime, and replaced the Transvaal sovereignty in those British hands from which it had been wrested in 1881, their rightful demand could by no means be conceded.

Mr. Chamberlain, with Lord Salisbury following steadily on behind, championed the cause of the Outlanders. On paper and for democratic purposes the case was overwhelming. But you can never persuade anyone by reasonable argument to give up his skin. The old inhabitants of the Transvaal were not going to yield their autonomy or any effective portion of it to the newcomers, however numerous or influential they might become. They intended by taxing them to procure the necessary means for keeping them in subjection. If the quarrel should come to actual fighting, President Kruger and his colleagues saw no reason why Europe should not intervene on their behalf or why they should not become masters of the whole of South Africa. They too had a good case. Had they not trekked into the wilderness to avoid British rule, with its perpetual interference between them and their native subjects and servants? If England could use the language of 'the Boston tea-party,' the Boers felt like the Southern planters on the eve of the War of Secession. They declared that the long arm of British Imperialism, clutching for gold, had pursued them even into their last refuges; and Mr. Chamberlain rejoined, in effect, that they were refusing to give civil rights to the modern productive elements who were making nine-tenths of the wealth of their country, because they were afraid they would no longer be allowed to larrup their own Kaffirs. Evil collision!

Mr. Cecil Rhodes was Chairman and creator of the Chartered Company. He was also with a considerable measure of Dutch support, Prime Minister of the Cape Colony. Dr. Jameson was an administrator of the Company serving under him. Jameson—a man of strong and impulsive personality —had gathered a force of 600 or 700 men at Mafeking so that if the Outlanders rose in rebellion to gain their civil and political liberties, as they frequently threatened to do, he could if necessary, if Mr. Rhodes were favourable and if the British Government approved, march rapidly across the 150 miles from Mafeking to Johannesburg and prevent needless bloodshed. Side by side with this there was an actual conspiracy in Johannesburg to demand by force the rights of citizenship for the Outlanders. No money was lacking, for the conspirators included the leading proprietors of the gold mines. In the main they were supported—though rather luke-warmly—by most of their employees and by the non-Dutch population of Johannesburg, which already in numbers exceeded the whole of the rest of the Transvaal. On an April morning a provisional government was formed in Johannesburg and Dr. Jameson with 700 horsemen and two guns started out across the veldt toward the city.

This event shook Europe and excited the whole world. The Kaiser sent his famous telegram to President Kruger and ordered German marines—who happened to be on the spot—to disembark at Delagoa Bay. Great Britain was censured in unmeasured terms in every country. The Boer com-

mandos, who had long been held in readiness, easily surrounded Dr. Jameson and his force, and after a sharp fight
forced them to surrender. At the same time other large
Transvaal forces quelled the rebellion in Johannesburg and
arrested all the leaders and millionaires concerned in it.
When the first news of Dr. Jameson's Raid reached England, his action was immediately disavowed by the British
Government. Cecil Rhodes at Cape Town laconically remarked, 'He has upset my applecart.' Lord Salisbury invoked all the resources of his patient and powerful diplomacy
to allay resentment. The Johannesburg ring-leaders having
been sentenced to death, were allowed to ransom themselves
for enormous sums. The Jameson raiders were delivered up
by the Boers to British justice, and their Chief and his lieutenants were tried and sentenced to two years' imprisonment.

A strict enquiry was made under the guidance of the Liberal Party to ascertain what degree of complicity (if any)
attached to Mr. Chamberlain, or to Mr. Rhodes. This enquiry took a long time, and in the end arrived at no definite
conclusion; and the affair gradually died down. It left behind it, however, a long succession of darkening consequences. British reputation throughout the world had received a grievous wound. The Dutch hurled Cecil Rhodes
from power in the Cape Colony. The British nation took the
German Emperor's telegram as a revelation of a hostile
mood, and they never forgot it. The Emperor for his part,
seeing himself completely powerless in the face of British
sea power, turned his mind to the construction of a German
fleet. The entire course of South African politics was turned
away from peaceful channels. The British colonists looked
to the Imperial Government for aid; and the Dutch race
throughout the sub-continent rallied around the standards of
the two Boer republics. The British Government gathered
themselves together after their disastrous set-back, while the
Transvaal taxed the Outlanders all the more and began to
arm heavily out of the proceeds. All the causes of the quarrel

were inflamed, and their trial was referred to a far more important court.

During this vivid summer my mother gathered constantly around her table politicians of both parties, and leading figures in literature and art, together with the most lovely beings on whom the eye could beam. On one occasion, however, she carried her catholicity too far. Sir John Willoughby, one of the Jameson raiders then on bail awaiting trial in London, was one of our oldest friends. In fact it was he who had first shown me how to arrange my toy cavalry soldiers in the proper formation of an advanced guard. Returning from Hounslow, I found him already arrived for luncheon. My mother was late. Suddenly the door opened and Mr. John Morley was announced. I scented trouble; but boldly presented them to each other. Indeed no other course was possible. John Morley drew himself up, and without extending his hand made a stiff little bow. Willoughby stared unconcernedly without acknowledging it. I squirmed inwardly, and endeavoured to make a pretence of conversation by asking commonplace questions of each alternately. Presently to my great relief my mother arrived. She was not unequal to the occasion, which was a serious one. Before the meal was far advanced no uninformed person would have noticed that two out of the four gathered round the table never addressed one another directly. Towards the end it seemed to me they would not have minded doing so at all. But having taken up their positions they had to stick to them. I suspected my mother of a design to mitigate the unusual asperities which gathered round this aspect of our affairs. She wanted to reduce the Raid to the level of ordinary politics. But blood had been shed; and that makes a different tale.

I need scarcely say that at 21 I was all for Dr. Jameson and his men. I understood fairly well the causes of the dispute on both sides. I longed for the day on which we should 'avenge Majuba.' I was shocked to see our Conservative

Government act so timidly in the crisis. I was ashamed to see them truckling to a misguided Liberal Opposition and even punishing these brave raiders, many of whom I knew so well. I was to learn more about South Africa in later years.

CHAPTER VIII

INDIA

THE time was now come for us to embark for the East. We sailed from Southampton in a trooper carrying about 1,200 men, and after a voyage of twenty-three days cast anchor in Bombay Harbour and pulled up the curtain on what might well have been a different planet.

It may be imagined how our whole shipful of officers and men were delighted after being cooped up for nearly a month to see the palms and palaces of Bombay lying about us in a wide crescent. We gazed at them over the bulwarks across the shining and surf-ribbed waters. Every one wanted to go on shore at once and see what India was like. The delays and formalities of disembarkation which oppress the ordinary traveller are multiplied for those who travel at the royal expense. However, at about three o'clock in the afternoon orders were issued that we were to land at eight o'clock when it would be cool; and in the meantime a proportion of officers might go ashore independently. A shoal of tiny boats had been lying around us all day long, rising and falling with the swell. We eagerly summoned some of these. It took about a quarter of an hour to reach the quays of the Sassoon Dock. Glad I was to be there; for the lively motion of the skiff to which I and two friends had committed ourselves was fast becoming our main preoccupation. We came alongside of a great stone wall with dripping steps and iron rings for hand-holds. The boat rose and fell four or five feet with the surges. I put out my hand and grasped at a ring; but before I could get my feet on the steps the boat swung away, giving my right shoulder a sharp and peculiar wrench. I scrambled up all right, made a few remarks of a general character, mostly beginning with the earlier letters of the alphabet, hugged my shoulder and soon thought no more about it.

Let me counsel my younger readers to beware of dislocated shoulders. In this, as in so many other things, it is the first step that counts. Quite an exceptional strain is required to tear the capsule which holds the shoulder joint together; but once the deed is done, a terrible liability remains. Although my shoulder did not actually go out, I had sustained an injury which was to last me my life; which was to cripple me at polo, to prevent me from ever playing tennis, and to be a grave embarrassment in moments of peril, violence and effort. Since then, at irregular intervals my shoulder has dislocated on the most unexpected pretexts: sleeping with my arm under the pillow, taking a book from the library shelves, slipping on a staircase, swimming, etc. Once it very nearly went out through a too expansive gesture in the House of Commons, and I thought how astonished the members would have been to see the speaker to whom they were listening, suddenly for no reason throw himself upon the floor in an instinctive effort to take the strain and leverage off the displaced arm bone.

This accident was a serious piece of bad luck. However, you never can tell whether bad luck may not after all turn out to be good luck. Perhaps if in the charge of Omdurman I had been able to use a sword, instead of having to adopt a modern weapon like a Mauser pistol, my story might not have got so far as the telling. One must never forget when misfortunes come that it is quite possible they are saving one from something much worse; or that when you make some great mistake, it may very easily serve you better than the best-advised decision. Life is a whole, and luck is a whole, and no part of them can be separated from the rest.

Let us resume our journey into what Colonel Brabazon in his farewell speech had called 'India, that famous appanage of the Bwitish Cwown.' We were sent into a rest camp at Poona, and arriving late in the evening passed our second night after landing in large double-fly tents upon a spacious plain. Daylight brought suave, ceremonious, turbanned applicants for the offices of butler, dressing boy, and head groom, which in those days formed the foundation of the cavalry subaltern's household. All bore trustworthy testimonials with them from the home-going regiment; and after brief formalities and salaams laid hold of one's worldly possessions and assumed absolute responsibility for one's whole domestic life. If you liked to be waited on and relieved of home worries, India thirty years ago was perfection. All you had to do was to hand over all your uniform and clothes to the dressing boy, your ponies to the syce, and your money to the butler, and you need never trouble any more. Your Cabinet was complete; each of these ministers entered upon his department with knowledge, experience and fidelity. They would devote their lives to their task. For a humble wage, justice, and a few kind words, there was nothing they would not do. Their world became bounded by the commonplace articles of your wardrobe and other small possessions. No toil was too hard, no hours were too long, no dangers too great for their unruffled calm or their unfailing care. Princes could live no better than we.

Among the group of suitors at our tent appeared two or three syces leading polo ponies and bearing notes from their masters; and then arrived with some commotion a splendid man in a red and gold frock-coat bearing an envelope with a puissant crest. He was a messenger from the Governor, Lord Sandhurst, inviting me and my companion, Hugo Baring, to dine that night at Government House. Thither, after a long day occupied mainly in scolding the troopers for forgetting to wear their pith-helmets and thus risking their lives, we repaired, and enjoyed a banquet of glitter, pomp and iced champagne. His Excellency, after the health of the Queen-Empress had been drunk and dinner was over, was good enough to ask my opinion upon several matters, and considering the magnificent character of his hospitality, I thought it would be unbecoming in me not to reply fully. I have forgotten the particular points of British and Indian affairs upon which he sought my counsel; all I can remember is that I responded generously. There were indeed moments when he seemed willing to impart his own views; but I thought it would be ungracious to put him to so much trouble; and he very readily subsided. He kindly sent his aide-de-camp with us to make sure we found our way back to camp all right. On the whole, after forty-eight hours of intensive study, I formed a highly favourable opinion about India. Sometimes, thought I, one sees these things more completely at first sight. As Kinglake says, 'a scrutiny so minute as to bring an object under an untrue angle of vision, is a poorer guide to a man's judgment than a sweeping glance which sees things in their true proportion.' We certainly felt as we dropped off to sleep the keenest realization of the great work which England was doing in India and of her high mission to rule these primitive but agreeable races for their welfare and our own. But almost immediately, it seemed, the trumpets sounded réveillé and we had to catch the 5.10 train for our thirty-six-hour journey to Bangalore.

The great triangular plateau of Southern India comprises the domains of the Nizam and the Maharajah of Mysore. The tranquility of these regions, together about the size of France, is assured in the ultimate resort by two British garrisons of two or three thousand troops apiece at Bangalore and Secunderabad. In each case there is added about double the number of Indian troops; so that sufficient forces of all arms are permanently available for every purpose of training and manœuvre. The British lines or cantonments[1] are in accordance with invariable practice placed five or six miles from the populous cities which they guard; and in the intervening space lie the lines of the Indian regiments. The British troops are housed in large, cool, colonnaded barracks. Here forethought and order have been denied neither time

[1] Pronounced 'cantoonments.'

nor space in the laying out of their plans. Splendid roads, endless double avenues of shady trees, abundant supplies of pure water; imposing offices, hospitals and institutions; ample parade-grounds and riding schools—characterize these centres of the collective life of considerable white communities.

The climate of Bangalore, at more than 3,000 feet above sea level, is excellent. Although the sun strikes with torrid power, the nights except in the hottest months are cool and fresh. The roses of Europe in innumerable large pots attain the highest perfection of fragrance and colour. Flowers, flowering shrubs and creepers blossom in glorious profusion. Snipe (and snakes) abound in the marshes, brilliant butterflies dance in the sunshine, and nautch-girls by the light of the moon.

No quarters are provided for the officers. They draw instead a lodging allowance which together with their pay and other incidentals fills each month with silver rupees a string net bag as big as a prize turnip. All around the cavalry mess lies a suburb of roomy one-storeyed bungalows standing in their own walled grounds and gardens. The subaltern receives his bag of silver at the end of each month of duty, canters home with it to his bungalow, throws it to his beaming butler, and then in theory has no further material cares. It was however better in a cavalry regiment in those days to supplement the generous rewards of the Queen-Empress by an allowance from home three or four times as great. Altogether we received for our services about fourteen shillings a day with about £3 a month on which to keep two horses. This, together with £500 a year paid quarterly, was my sole means of support: all the rest had to be borrowed at usurious rates of interest from the all-too-accommodating native bankers. Every officer was warned against these gentlemen. I always found them most agreeable; very fat, very urbane, quite honest and mercilessly rapacious. All you had to do was to sign little bits of paper, and produce a polo pony as if by magic. The smiling financier rose to his feet, covered his face with his hands, replaced his slippers, and trotted off contentedly till that day three months. They only charged *two per cent. a month* and made quite a good living out of it, considering they hardly ever had a bad debt.

We three, Reginald Barnes, Hugo Baring and I, pooling all our resources, took a palatial bungalow, all pink and white, with heavy tiled roof and deep verandahs sustained by white plaster columns, wreathed in purple bougainvillea. It stood in a compound or grounds of perhaps two acres. We took over from the late occupant about a hundred and fifty splendid standard roses: Maréchal Niel, La France, Gloire de Dijon, etc. We built a large tiled barn with mud walls, containing stabling for thirty horses and ponies. Our three butlers formed a triumvirate in which no internal dissensions ever appeared. We paid an equal contribution into the pot; and thus freed from mundane cares, devoted ourselves to the serious purpose of life.

This was expressed in one word—Polo. It was upon this, apart from duty, that all our interest was concentrated. But before you could play polo, you must have ponies. We had formed on the voyage a regimental polo club, which in return for moderate but regular subscriptions from all the officers (polo-players and non-polo-players alike) offered substantial credit facilities for the procuring of these indispensable allies. A regiment coming from home was never expected to count in the Indian polo world for a couple of years. It took that time to get a proper stud of ponies together. However, the president of our polo club and the Senior Officers, after prolonged and anxious discussions, determined upon a bold and novel stroke. The Bycullah stables at Bombay form the main emporium through which Arab horses and ponies are imported to India. The Poona Light Horse, a native regiment strongly officered by British, had in virtue of its permanent station an obvious advantage in the purchase of Arabian ponies. On our way through

Poona we had tried their ponies, and had entered into deeply important negotiations with them. Finally it was decided that the regimental polo club should purchase the entire polo stud of twenty-five ponies possessed by the Poona Light Horse; so that these ponies should form the nucleus around which we could gather the means of future victory in the Inter-Regimental Tournament. I can hardly describe the sustained intensity of purpose with which we threw ourselves into this audacious and colossal undertaking. Never in the history of Indian polo had a cavalry regiment from Southern India won the Inter-Regimental cup. We knew it would take two or three years of sacrifice, contrivance and effort. But if all other diversions were put aside, we did not believe that success was beyond our compass. To this task then we settled down with complete absorption.

I must not forget to say that there were of course also a great many military duties. Just before dawn, every morning, one was awakened by a dusky figure with a clammy hand adroitly lifting one's chin and applying a gleaming razor to a lathered and defenceless throat. By six o'clock the regiment was on parade, and we rode to a wide plain and there drilled and manœuvred for an hour and a half. We then returned to baths at the bungalow and breakfast in the mess. Then at nine stables and orderly room till about half-past ten; then home to the bungalow before the sun attained its fiercest ray. All the distances in the spread-out cantonment were so great that walking was impossible. We cantered on hacks from one place to another. But the noonday sun asserted his tyrannical authority, and long before eleven o'clock all white men were in shelter. We nipped across to luncheon at half-past one in blistering heat and then returned to sleep till five o'clock. Now the station begins to live again. It is the hour of Polo. It is the hour for which we have been living all day long. I was accustomed in those days to play every chukka I could get into. The whole system was elaborately organized for the garrison during the morning; and a smart little peon collected the names of all the officers together with the number of chukkas they wished to play. These were averaged out so as to secure 'the greatest good of the greatest number.' I very rarely played less than eight and more often ten or twelve.

As the shadows lengthened over the polo ground, we ambled back perspiring and exhausted to hot baths, rest, and at 8.30 dinner, to the strains of the regimental band and the clinking of ice in well-filled glasses. Thereafter those who were not so unlucky as to be caught by the Senior Officers to play a tiresome game then in vogue called 'Whist,' sat smoking in the moonlight, till half-past ten or eleven at the latest signalled the 'And so to bed.' Such was 'the long, long Indian day' as I knew it for three years; and not such a bad day either.

CHAPTER IX

EDUCATION AT BANGALORE

IT was not until this winter of 1896, when I had almost completed my twenty-second year, that the desire for learning came upon me. I began to feel myself wanting in even the vaguest knowledge about many large spheres of thought. I had picked up a wide vocabulary and had a liking for words and for the feel of words fitting and falling into their places like pennies in the slot. I caught myself using a good many words the meaning of which I could not define precisely. I admired these words, but was afraid to use them for fear of being absurd. One day, before I left England, a friend of mine had said: 'Christ's gospel was the last word in Ethics.' This sounded good; but what were Ethics? They had never been mentioned to me at Harrow or Sandhurst. Judging from the context I thought they must mean 'the public school spirit,' 'playing the game,' '*esprit de corps*,' 'honourable behaviour,' 'patriotism,' and the like. Then someone told me that Ethics were concerned not merely with the things you ought to do, but with why you ought to do them, and that there were whole books written on the subject. I would have paid some scholar £2 at least to give me a lecture of an hour or an hour and a half about Ethics. What was the scope of the subject; what were its main branches; what were the principal questions dealt with, and the chief controversies open; who were the high authorities and which were the standard books? But here in Bangalore there was no one to tell me about Ethics for love or money. Of tactics I had a grip: on politics I had a view: but a concise compendious outline of Ethics was a novelty not to be locally obtained.

This was only typical of a dozen similar mental needs that

now began to press insistently upon me. I knew of course that the youths at the universities were stuffed with all this patter at nineteen and twenty, and could pose you entrapping questions or give baffling answers. We never set much store by them or their affected superiority, remembering that they were only at their books, while we were commanding men and guarding the Empire. Nevertheless I had sometimes resented the apt and copious information which some of them seemed to possess, and I now wished I could find a competent teacher whom I could listen to and cross-examine for an hour or so every day.

Then someone had used the phrase 'the Socratic method.' What was that? It was apparently a way of giving your friend his head in an argument and progging him into a pit by cunning questions. Who was Socrates, anyhow? A very argumentative Greek who had a nagging wife and was finally compelled to commit suicide because he was a nuisance! Still, he was beyond doubt a considerable person. He counted for a lot in the minds of learned people. I wanted 'the Socrates story.' Why had his fame lasted through all the ages? What were the stresses which had led a government to put him to death merely because of the things he said? Dire stresses they must have been: the life of the Athenian Executive or the life of this talkative professor! Such antagonisms do not spring from petty issues. Evidently Socrates had called something into being long ago which was very explosive. Intellectual dynamite! A moral bomb! But there was nothing about in The Queen's Regulations.

Then there was history. I had always liked history at school. But there we were given only the dullest, driest pemmicanised forms like *The Student's Hume*. Once I had a hundred pages of *The Student's Hume* as a holiday task. Quite unexpectedly, before I went back to school, my father set out to examine me upon it. The period was Charles I. He asked me about the Grand Remonstrance; what did I know about that? I said that in the end the Parliament beat the

King and cut his head off. This seemed to me the grandest remonstrance imaginable. It was no good. 'Here,' said my father, 'is a grave parliamentary question affecting the whole structure of our constitutional history, lying near the centre of the task you have been set, and you do not in the slightest degree appreciate the issues involved.' I was puzzled by his concern; I could not see at the time why it should matter so much. Now I wanted to know more about it.

So I resolved to read history, philosophy, economics, and things like that; and I wrote to my mother asking for such books as I had heard of on these topics. She responded with alacrity, and every month the mail brought me a substantial package of what I thought were standard works. In history I decided to begin with Gibbon. Someone had told me that my father had read Gibbon with delight; that he knew whole pages of it by heart, and that it had greatly affected his style of speech and writing. So without more ado I set out upon the eight volumes of Dean Milman's edition of Gibbon's *Decline and Fall of the Roman Empire*. I was immediately dominated both by the story and the style. All through the long glistening middle hours of the Indian day, from when we quitted stables till the evening shadows proclaimed the hour of Polo, I devoured Gibbon. I rode triumphantly through it from end to end and enjoyed it all. I scribbled all my opinions on the margins of the pages, and very soon found myself a vehement partisan of the author against the disparagements of his pompous-pious editor. I was not even estranged by his naughty footnotes. On the other hand the Dean's apologies and disclaimers roused my ire. So pleased was I with *The Decline and Fall* that I began at once to read Gibbon's Autobiography, which luckily was bound up in the same edition. When I read his reference to his old nurse: 'If there be any, as I trust there are some, who rejoice that I live, to that dear and excellent woman their gratitude is due,' I thought of Mrs. Everest; and it shall be her epitaph.

From Gibbon I went to Macaulay. I had learnt *The Lays of Ancient Rome* by heart and loved them; and of course I knew he had written a history; but I had never read a page of it. I now embarked on that splendid romance, and I voyaged with full sail in a strong wind. I remembered then that Mrs. Everest's brother-in-law, the old prison warden, had possessed a copy of Macaulay's History, purchased in supplements and bound together, and that he used to speak of it with reverence. I accepted all Macaulay wrote as gospel, and I was grieved to read his harsh judgments upon the Great Duke of Marlborough. There was no one at hand to tell me that this historian with his captivating style and devastating self-confidence was the prince of literary rogues, who always preferred the tale to the truth, and smirched or glorified great men and garbled documents according as they affected his drama. I cannot forgive him for imposing on my confidence and on the simple faith of my old friend the warder. Still I must admit an immense debt upon the other side.

Not less than in his History, I revelled in his Essays: Chatham; Frederick the Great; Lord Nugent's Memorials of Hampden; Clive; Warren Hastings; Barère (the dirty dog); Southey's Colloquies on Society; and above all that masterpiece of literary ferocity, Mr. Robert Montgomery's Poems.

From November to May I read for four or five hours every day history and philosophy. Plato's Republic—it appeared he was for all practical purposes the same as Socrates; the Politics of Aristotle, edited by Dr. Welldon himself; Schopenhauer on Pessimism; Malthus on Population; Darwin's Origin of Species: all interspersed with other books of lesser standing. It was a curious education. First because I approached it with an empty, hungry mind, and with fairly strong jaws; and what I got I bit; secondly because I had no one to tell me: 'This is discredited.' 'You should read the answer to that by so and so; the two together will give you the gist of the argument.' 'There is a much better book on that subject,' and so forth. I now began for the first time to envy those young cubs at the university who had fine scholars to tell them what was what; professors who had devoted their lives to mastering and focussing ideas in every branch of learning; who were eager to distribute the treasures they had gathered before they were overtaken by the night. But now I pity undergraduates, when I see what frivolous lives many of them lead in the midst of precious fleeting opportunity. After all, a man's Life must be nailed to a cross either of Thought or Action. Without work there is no play.

When I am in the Socratic mood and planning *my* Republic, I make drastic changes in the education of the sons of well-to-do citizens. When they are sixteen or seventeen they begin to learn a craft and to do healthy manual labour, with plenty of poetry, songs, dancing, drill and gymnastics in their spare time. They can thus let off their steam on something useful. It is only when they are really thirsty for knowledge, longing to hear about things, that I would let them go to the university. It would be a favour, a coveted privilege, only to be given to those who had either proved their worth in factory or field or whose qualities and zeal were pre-eminent. However, this would upset a lot of things; it would cause commotion and bring me perhaps in the end a hemlock draught.

*   *   *   *   *

My various readings during the next two years led me to ask myself questions about religion. Hitherto I had dutifully accepted everything I had been told. Even in the holidays I always had to go once a week to Church, and at Harrow there were three services every Sunday, besides morning and evening prayers throughout the week. All this was very good. I accumulated in those years so fine a surplus in the Bank of Observance that I have been drawing confidently upon it ever since. Weddings, christenings, and funerals have brought in a steady annual income, and I have never made too close enquiries about the state of my account. It might well even be that I should find an overdraft. But now in these bright days of youth my attendances were well ahead of the Sundays. In the Army too there were regular church parades, and sometimes I marched the Roman Catholics to church, and sometimes the Protestants. Religious toleration in the British Army had spread till it overlapped the regions of indifference. No one was ever hampered or prejudiced on account of his religion. Everyone had the regulation facilities for its observance. In India the deities of a hundred creeds were placed by respectful routine in the Imperial Pantheon. In the regiment we sometimes used to argue questions like 'Whether we should live again in another world after this was over?' 'Whether we have ever lived before?' 'Whether we remember and meet each other after Death or merely start again like the Buddhists?' 'Whether some high intelligence is looking after the world or whether things are just drifting on anyhow?' There was general agreement that if you tried your best to live an honourable life and did your duty and were faithful to friends and not unkind to the weak and poor, it did not matter much what you believed or disbelieved. All would come out right. This is what would nowadays I suppose be called 'The Religion of Healthy-Mindedness.'

Some of the senior officers also dwelt upon the value of the Christian religion to women ('It helps to keep them straight'); and also generally to the lower orders ('Nothing can give them a good time here, but it makes them more contented to think they will get one hereafter'). Christianity, it appeared, had also a disciplinary value, especially when presented through the Church of England. It made people want to be respectable, to keep up appearances, and so saved lots of scandals. From this standpoint ceremonies and ritual ceased to be of importance. They were merely the same idea translated into different languages to suit different races and temperaments. Too much religion of any kind, however, was a bad thing. Among natives especially, fanaticism was highly dangerous and roused them to murder, mutiny or rebellion. Such is, I think, a fair gauging of the climate of opinion in which I dwelt.

I now began to read a number of books which challenged the whole religious education I had received at Harrow. The first of these books was *The Martyrdom of Man* by Winwood Reade. This was Colonel Brabazon's great book. He had read it many times over and regarded it as a sort of Bible. It is in fact a concise and well-written universal history of mankind, dealing in harsh terms with the mysteries of all religions and leading to the depressing conclusion that we simply go out like candles. I was much startled and indeed offended by what I read. But then I found that Gibbon evidently held the same view; and finally Mr. Lecky, in his *Rise and Influence of Rationalism* and *History of European Morals,* both of which I read this winter, established in my mind a predominantly secular view. For a time I was indignant at having been told so many untruths, as I then regarded them, by the schoolmasters and clergy who had guided my youth. Of course if I had been at a University my difficulties might have been resolved by the eminent professors and divines who are gathered there. At any rate, they would have shown me equally convincing books putting the opposite point of view. As it was I passed through a violent and aggressive anti-religious phase which, had it lasted, might easily have made me a nuisance. My poise was restored during the next few years by frequent contact with danger. I found that whatever I might think and argue, I did not hesitate to ask for special protection when about to come under the fire of the enemy: nor to feel sincerely grateful when I got home safe to tea. I even asked for lesser things than not to be killed too soon, and nearly always in these years, and indeed throughout my life, I got what I wanted. This practice seemed perfectly natural, and just as strong and real as the reasoning process which contradicted it so sharply. Moreover the practice was comforting and the reasoning led nowhere. I therefore acted in accordance with my feelings without troubling to square such conduct with the conclusions of thought.

It is a good thing for an uneducated man to read books of quotations. Bartlett's *Familiar Quotations* is an admirable work, and I studied it intently. The quotations when engraved upon the memory give you good thoughts. They also make you anxious to read the authors and look for more. In this or some other similar book I came across a French saying which seemed singularly opposite. 'Le cœur a ses raisons, que la raison ne connait pas.' It seemed to me that it would be very foolish to discard the reasons of the heart for those of the head. Indeed I could not see why I should not enjoy them both. I did not worry about the inconsistency of thinking one way and believing the other. It seemed good to let the mind explore so far as it could the paths of thought and logic, and also good to pray for help and succour, and be thankful when they came. I could not feel that the Supreme Creator who gave us our minds as well as our souls would be offended if they did not always run smoothly together in double harness. After all He must have foreseen this from the beginning and of course He would understand it all.

Accordingly I have always been surprised to see some of our Bishops and clergy making such heavy weather about reconciling the Bible story with modern scientific and historical knowledge. Why do they want to reconcile them? If you are the recipient of a message which cheers your heart and fortifies your soul, which promises you reunion with those you have loved in a world of larger opportunity and wider sympathies, why should you worry about the shape or colour of the travel-stained envelope; whether it is duly stamped, whether the date on the postmark is right or wrong? These matters may be puzzling, but they are certainly not important. What is important is the message and the benefits to you of receiving it. Close reasoning can conduct one to the precise conclusion that miracles are impossible: that 'it is much more likely that human testimony should err, than that the laws of nature should be violated'; and at the same time one may rejoice to read how Christ turned the water into wine in Cana of Galilee or walked on the lake or rose from the dead. The human brain cannot comprehend infinity, but the discovery of mathematics enables it to be handled quite easily. The idea that nothing is true except what we comprehend is silly, and that ideas which our minds cannot reconcile are mutually destructive, sillier still. Certainly nothing could be more repulsive both to our minds and feelings than the spectacle of thousands of millions of universes —for that is what they say it comes to now—all knocking about together for ever without any rational or good purpose behind them. I therefore adopted quite early in life a system of believing whatever I wanted to believe, while at the same time leaving reason to pursue unfettered whatever paths she was capable of treading.

Some of my cousins who had the great advantage of University education used to tease me with arguments to prove that nothing has any existence except what we think of it. The whole creation is but a dream; all phenomena are imaginary. You create your own universe as you go along. The stronger your imagination, the more variegated your universe. When you leave off dreaming, the universe ceases to exist. These amusing mental acrobatics are all right to play with. They are perfectly harmless and perfectly useless. I warn my younger readers only to treat them as a game. The metaphysicians will have the last word and defy you to disprove their absurd propositions.

I always rested upon the following argument which I devised for myself many years ago. We look up in the sky and see the sun. Our eyes are dazzled and our senses record the fact. So here is this great sun standing apparently on no better foundation than our physical senses. But happily there is a method, apart altogether from our physical senses, of testing the reality of the sun. It is by mathematics. By means of prolonged processes of mathematics, entirely separate from the senses, astronomers are able to calculate when an eclipse will occur. They predict by pure reason that a black spot will pass across the sun on a certain day. You go and look, and your sense of sight immediately tells you that their calculations are vindicated. So here you have the evidence of the senses reinforced by the entirely separate evidence of a vast independent process of mathematical reasoning. We have taken what is called in military map-making 'a cross bearing.' We have got independent testimony to the reality of the sun. When my metaphysical friends tell me that the data on which the astronomers made their calculations, were necessarily obtained originally through the evidence of the senses, I say 'No.' They might, in theory at any rate, be obtained by automatic calculating-machines set in motion by the light falling upon them without admixture of the human senses at any stage. When they persist that we should have to be told about the calculations and use our ears for that purpose, I reply that the mathematical process has a reality and virtue in itself, and that once discovered it constitutes a new and independent factor. I am also at this point accustomed to reaffirm with emphasis my conviction that the sun is real, and also that it is hot—in fact as hot as Hell, and that if the metaphysicians doubt it they should go there and see.

*　　　*　　　*　　　*　　　*

Our first incursion into the Indian polo world was dramatic. Within six weeks of our landing, the tournament for the Golconda Cup was played in Hyderabad. The capital of the Nizam's dominions and the neighbouring British garrison, five miles away in the cantonment of Secunderabad, maintained between them six or seven polo teams. Among these were the 19th Hussars, whom we had just relieved at Bangalore. There was ill-feeling between the men of the 4th and

19th Hussars, arising out of an unfavourable remark alleged
to have been made by some private soldier thirty years before
about the state of the 4th Hussars' barracks when the 19th
had taken over from them on some occasion. Although not
a single soul remained of those involved in the previous dispute, the sergeants and soldiers were found fully informed
about it, and as angry as if it had only taken place the month
before. These differences did not, however, extend to the
commissioned ranks, and we were most hospitably entertained by the Officers' Mess. I was accommodated in the
bungalow of a young Captain named Chetwode, now the
appointed Commander-in-Chief in India. Apart from other
garrison teams, there were two formidable Indian rivals: the
Vicar Al Umra, or Prime Minister's team, and the representatives of the famous Golconda Brigade, the bodyguard
of the Nizam himself. The Golcondas were considered in-
comparably the best team in Southern India. Many and close
were the contests which they had waged with Patiala and
Jodhpore, the leading native teams in Northern India. Immense wealth, manifested in ponies, was at their disposal,
and they had all the horsemanship and comprehension of
polo which were in those days the common ideal of young Indian and British officers.

Accompanied by the stud of ponies we had purchased complete from the Poona Light Horse, we set out anxious but
determined on the long journey across the Deccan. Our
hosts, the 19th, received us with open arms, and informed us
with all suitable condolences that we had had the great misfortune to draw the Golconda team in the first round. They
were sincere when they said what bad luck it was for us, after
being so little time in India, to be confronted in our first
match with the team that would certainly win the tournament.

In the morning we were spectators of a review of the entire garrison. The British troops, the regular Indian troops
and the Nizam's army paraded and defiled in martial pomp

before us, or perhaps it was before the official notabilities. At the end came a score of elephants drawing tandem-fashion gigantic cannon. It was then the custom for the elephants to salute as they marched past by raising their trunks, and this they all did with exemplary precision. Later on the custom was abolished because vulgar people tittered and the dignity of the elephants or their mahouts was wounded. Later on still, the elephants themselves were abolished, and we now have clattering tractors drawing far larger and more destructive guns. Thus civilisation advances. But I mourn the elephants and their salutations.

In the afternoon there was the polo match. Tournaments in Hyderabad were a striking spectacle. The whole ground was packed with enormous masses of Indian spectators of all classes watching the game with keen and instructed attention. The tents and canopied stands were thronged with the British community and the Indian rank and fashion of the Deccan. We were expected to be an easy prey, and when our lithe, darting, straight-hitting opponents scored 3 goals to nothing in the first few minutes, we almost shared the general opinion. However, without going into details which, though important, are effaced by the march of time and greater events, amid roars of excitement from the assembled multitudes we defeated the Golcondas by 9 goals to 3. On succeeding days we made short work of all other opponents, and established the record, never since broken, of winning a first-class tournament within fifty days of landing in India.

The reader may imagine with what reinforcement of resolve we applied ourselves to the supreme task that lay ahead. Several years were, however, to stand between us and its accomplishment.

With the approach of the hot weather season of 1897 it became known that a proportion of officers might have what was called 'three months' accumulated privilege leave,' to England. Having so newly arrived, hardly anybody wanted to go. I thought it was a pity that such good things should go a-begging, and I therefore volunteered to fill the gap. I sailed from Bombay towards the end of May in sweltering heat, rough weather and fearful seasickness. When I sat up again, we were two-thirds across the Indian Ocean, and I soon struck up an acquaintance with a tall thin Colonel, then in charge of Musketry Training in India, named Ian Hamilton. He pointed out to me what I had hitherto overlooked, that tension existed between Greece and Turkey. In fact those powers were on the point of war. Being romantic, he was for the Greeks, and hoped to serve with them in some capacity. Having been brought up a Tory, I was for the Turks; and I thought I might follow their armies as a newspaper correspondent. I also declared that they would certainly defeat the Greeks, as they were at least five to one and much better armed. He was genuinely pained; so I made it clear that I would take no part in the operations, but would merely see the fun and tell the tale. When we arrived at Port Said it was clear that the Greeks had already been defeated. They had run away from the unfair contest with equal prudence and rapidity, and the Great Powers were endeavouring to protect them by diplomacy from destruction. So instead of going to the battlefields of Thrace, I spent a fortnight in Italy, climbing Vesuvius, 'doing' Pompeii and, above all, seeing Rome. I read again the sentences in which Gibbon has described the emotions with which in his later years for the first time he approached the Eternal City, and though I had none of his credentials of learning, it was not without reverence that I followed in his footsteps.

This formed a well-conceived prelude to the gaieties of the London season.

CHAPTER X

THE MALAKAND FIELD FORCE

I was on the lawns of Goodwood in lovely weather and winning my money, when the revolt of the Pathan tribesmen of the Indian frontier began. I read in the newspapers that a Field Force of three brigades had been formed, and that at the head of it stood Sir Bindon Blood. Forthwith I telegraphed reminding him of his promise, and took the train for Brindisi to catch the Indian Mail. I impressed Lord William Beresford into my cause. He reinforced my appeals to the General. He entertained me at the Marlborough Club before my train left Victoria. These Beresfords had a great air. They made one feel that the world and everyone in it were of fine consequence. I remember the manner in which he announced my purpose to a circle of club friends many years my seniors. 'He goes to the East to-night—to the seat of war.' 'To the East'—the expression struck me. Most people would have said 'He is going out to India;' but to that generation the East meant the gateway to the adventures and conquests of England. 'To the Front?' they asked. Alas, I could only say I hoped so. However, they were all most friendly and even enthusiastic. I felt very important, but naturally observed a marked discretion upon Sir Bindon Blood's plan of campaign.

I only just caught the train; but I caught it in the best of spirits.

One voyage to India is enough; the others are merely repletion. It was the hottest season of the year, and the Red Sea was stifling. The hand-pulled punkahs, for in those days there were no electric fans, flapped vigorously to and fro in the crowded dining-saloon and agitated the hot food-smelling air. But these physical discomforts were nothing beside my mental anxieties. I was giving up a whole fortnight's leave. At Brindisi no answer had come from Sir Bindon Blood. It was sure to come at Aden. There I danced about from one foot to the other till the steward had distributed the last of the telegrams and left me forlorn. However, at Bombay was good news. The General's message was 'Very difficult; no vacancies; come up as a correspondent; will try to fit you in.   B. B.'

I had first of all to obtain leave from my regiment at Bangalore. This meant a two days' journey by railway in the opposite direction to that in which my hopes were directed. The regiment was surprised to see me back before my time, but an extra subaltern for duty was always welcome. Meanwhile I had been commissioned as war correspondent by the *Pioneer* newspaper, and my Mother had also arranged in England that my letters should be simultaneously published in the *Daily Telegraph*, for which that journal was willing to pay £5 a column. This was not much, considering that I had to pay all my own expenses. I carried these journalistic credentials when I presented in much anxiety Sir Bindon Blood's telegram to my commanding officer. But the Colonel was indulgent, and the fates were kind. Although the telegram was quite informal and unofficial, I was told that I could go and try my luck. That night therefore with my dressing-boy and campaigning kit I sped to the Bangalore railway station and bought a ticket for Nowshera. The Indian clerk, having collected from me a small sack of rupees, pushed an ordinary ticket through a pigeon hole. I had the curiosity to ask how far it was. The polite Indian consulted a railway time table and impassively answered 2,028 miles. Quite a big place, India! This meant a five days' journey in the worst of the heat. I was alone; but with plenty of books, the time passed not unpleasantly. Those large leather-lined Indian railway carriages, deeply-shuttered and blinded from the blistering sun and kept fairly cool by a circular wheel of wet straw which one turned from time to time, were well adapted to the local conditions. I spent five days in a dark padded moving cell, reading mostly by lamp-light or by some jealously admitted ray of glare.

I broke my journey for a night and day at Rawalpindi where I had a subaltern friend in the Fourth Dragoon Guards. There was a certain stir in Rawalpindi, although it was some hundreds of miles away from the front. The whole garrison was hoping to be sent north. All leave was stopped and the Dragoon Guards were expecting to be ordered any day to grind their swords. After dinner we repaired to the Sergeants' Mess, where a spirited sing-song was in progress. Nothing recalls the past so potently as a smell. In default of a smell the next best mnemonic is a tune. I have got tunes in my head for every war I have been to, and indeed for every critical or exciting phase in my life. Some day when my ship comes home, I am going to have them all collected in gramophone records, and then I will sit in a chair and smoke my cigar, while pictures and faces, moods and sensations long-vanished return; and pale but true there gleams the light of other days. I remember well the songs the soldiers sang on this occasion. There was a song called 'The New Photographee' about some shocking invention which had just been made enabling photographs to be taken through a screen or other opaque obstruction. This was the first I had heard of it. It appeared that there might soon be an end to all privacy. In the words of the song

'The | in | side | of | ev | er | y | thing | you | see, |
A ter | ri | ble | thing, | an | 'or | ri | ble | thing, | is | the | new |
    pho | tog | ra | phee.' |

Of course we treated it all as a joke, but afterwards I read in the newspaper that they might some day even be able to see the very bones in your body! Then there was the song, the chorus of which was—

'And England asks the question
When danger's nigh
Will the sons of India do or die?'

and naturally a reassuring answer was forthcoming. But the best of all was

> 'Great White Mother, far across the sea,
> Ruler of the Empire may she ever be.
> Long may she reign, glorious and free,
> In the Great White Motherland.'

I felt much uplifted by these noble sentiments especially after having been spaciously entertained at the regimental mess. I comported myself however with purposed discretion, because there was at this time some ill-feeling between this distinguished regiment and my own. An officer of the Fourth Dragoon Guards had telegraphed to one of our Captains in the ordinary routine of the service, saying 'Please state your lowest terms for an exchange into the Fourth Dragoon Guards.' To which our Captain had gaily replied '£10,000, a Peerage and a free kit.' The Dragoon Guards had taken umbrage at this and thought it was a reflection upon the standing of their regiment. This ruffling of plumes added zest to the competitions we were later on to have with this fine regiment in the polo championships of 1898 and 1899.

I must not allow the reader to forget that I am on my way post-haste to the front, and early on the sixth morning after I had left Bangalore I stood on the platform of Nowshera, the railhead of the Malakand Field Force. It was forty miles across the plains in really amazing heat, before the tonga—a kind of little cart drawn by relays of galloping ponies—began to climb the steep winding ascent to the Malakand Pass. This defile had been forced by Sir Bindon Blood three years before, and the headquarters for the new campaign, together with a brigade of all arms, were encamped upon its summit. Yellow with dust I presented myself at the Staff Office. The General was away. He had gone with a flying column to deal with the Bunerwals, a most formidable tribe with a valley of their own in which they had maintained themselves for centuries against all comers. In 1863 the Imperial Government had sent an expedition to Bunēr resulting in what is known in Anglo-Indian annals as the Umbeyla campaign. The Bunerwals had resisted with extraordinary spirit, and the skeletons of several hundred British soldiers and Sepoys mouldered round the once notorious Crag Picquet, stormed and retaken again and again. No one knew how long Sir Bindon Blood would be occupied in dealing with these famous and ferocious bandits. In the meanwhile I was made a member of the Staff Mess and told I might unroll my Wolseley valise in one of the tents. I decided in great docility to be always on my best behaviour for fear that anything should happen to get me a bad name in this new world into which I had climbed.

The General took only five days to coax and quell the Bunerwals, but it seemed a very long time to me. I endeavoured to turn it to the best advantage. I acquired an entirely new faculty. Until this time I had never been able to drink whisky. I disliked the flavour intensely. I could not understand how so many of my brother officers were so often calling for a whisky and soda. I liked wine, both red and white, and especially champagne; and on very special occasions I could even drink a small glass of brandy. But this smoky-tasting whisky I had never been able to face. I now found myself in heat which, though I stood it personally fairly well, was terrific, for five whole days and with absolutely nothing to drink, apart from tea, except either tepid water or tepid water with lime-juice or tepid water with whisky. Faced with these alternatives I 'grasped the larger hope.' I was sustained in these affairs by my high morale. Wishing to fit myself for active-service conditions I overcame the ordinary weaknesses of the flesh. By the end of these five days I had completely overcome my repugnance to the taste of whisky. Nor was this a momentary acquirement. On the contrary the ground I gained in those days I have firmly entrenched, and held throughout my whole life. Once one got the knack of it, the very repulsion from the flavour developed an attraction of its own; and to this day although I have always practised true temperance, I have never shrunk when occasion warranted it from the main basic standing refreshment of the white officer in the East.

Of course all this whisky business was quite a new departure in fashionable England. My father for instance could never have drunk whisky except when shooting on a moor or in some very dull chilly place. He lived in the age of the 'Brandy and Soda,' for which indeed there was much respectable warrant. However, surveying the proposition from an impartial standpoint after adequate experiment and reflection, I am clear that for ordinary daily use whisky in a diluted form is the more serviceable of these twin genii.

Now that I have been drawn into this subject while perched upon the Malakand Pass, let me say that I and other young officers had been brought up quite differently from the University boys of those times. The undergraduates of Oxford and Cambridge used to drink like fishes, and they even had clubs and formal dinners where it was an obligation for everyone to consume more liquor than he could carry. At Sandhurst, on the other hand, and in the Army, drunkenness was a disgraceful offence punishable not only by social reprobation often physically manifested, but if it ever got into the official sphere, by the sack. I had been brought up and trained to have the utmost contempt for people who got drunk—except on very exceptional occasions and a few anniversaries—and I would have liked to have the boozing scholars of the Universities wheeled into line and properly chastised for their squalid misuse of what I must ever regard as a good gift of the gods. In those days I was very much against drunkards, prohibitionists and other weaklings of excess: but now I can measure more charitably the frailties of nature from which their extravagances originate. Subalterns in those days were an intolerant tribe; they used to think that if a man got drunk or would not allow other people to have a drink, he ought to be kicked. Of course we all know much better now, having been civilised and ennobled by the Great War.

I had also in these five days to fit myself out in all respects for the approaching movement of our force. I had to buy two good horses, engage a military syce (groom), and complete my martial wardrobe in many particulars. Unluckily for them, but very conveniently for me, several officers had been killed in the preceding week, and their effects, including what they had stood up in, were, in accordance with Anglo-Indian campaigning custom, sold by auction as soon as the funeral (if any) was over. In this way I soon acquired a complete outfit. It struck me as rather grim to see the intimate belongings of one's comrade of the day before—his coat, his shirt, his boots, his water-bottle, his revolver, his blanket, his cooking-pot—thus unceremoniously distributed among strangers. But after all it was quite logical and in accordance with the highest principles of economics. Here was much the best market. All transport charges were already defrayed. The dead man disposed of his assets on what were virtually monopoly terms. The camp auctioneer realised far better prices than any widow or mother could have done for the worldly effects of Lieut. A.B. or Capt. X.Y. And as it was with the officers, so also was it much more frequently with the private soldier. Still I must admit that I felt a pang when a few weeks later I first slung round my shoulder the lanyard of a gallant friend I had seen killed the day before.

The time has come when I must put the reader into a more general comprehension of the campaign.[1] For three years the British had held the summit of the Malakand Pass and thus had maintained the road from the Swat Valley and across the Swat River by many other valleys to Chitral. Chitral was then supposed to be of great military importance. It has always seemed to get along quite happily since, but no doubt it was very important then. The tribesmen of the Swat Valley, irritated by the presence of the troops in what they

[1]See Map of Indian Frontier on page 133.

had for generations regarded as their own country, had suddenly burst out in a fury, attributed by the Government to religion, but easily explainable on quite ordinary grounds. They had attacked the garrisons holding the Malakand Pass and the little fort of Chakdara which, peeked up on a rock like a miniature Gibraltar, defended the long swinging bridge across the Swat River. The misguided tribesmen had killed quite a lot of people, including a number of women and children belonging to the friendly and pacified inhabitants. There had been a moment of crisis in the defence of the Malakand Pass from a sudden and surprise attack. However, the onslaught had been repulsed, and in the morning light the Guides Cavalry and the 11th Bengal Lancers had chased these turbulent and froward natives from one end of the Swat Valley to the other, claiming that they had speared and otherwise slain considerable numbers of them. The fort of Chakdara, the Lilliputian Gibraltar, had just survived its siege and saved its soul (and skin) alive. The swinging wire-rope bridge was intact, and by this bridge the punitive expedition of, say, 12,000 men and 4,000 animals was now about to march into the mountains, through the valleys of Dir and Bajaur, past the Mamund country, finally rejoining civilisation in the plains of India after subduing the Mohmands, another tribe who had also been extremely contumacious in the neighborhood of Peshawar.

Sir Bindon Blood returned in due course from the subjugation of the Bunerwals. He was a very experienced Anglo-Indian officer and he had reduced the Bunerwals to reason almost without killing anybody. He liked these wild tribesmen and understood the way to talk to them. The Pathans are strange people. They have all sorts of horrible customs and frightful revenges. They understand bargaining perfectly, and provided they are satisfied first of all that you are strong enough to talk to them on even terms, one can often come to an arrangement across the floor of the House, or rather 'behind the Chair.' Now, Sir Bindon Blood had cleared it all up quite happily with the Bunerwals. There had only been one fight and that a small one, in which his aide-de-camp Lord Fincastle and another officer had gained the V.C. by rescuing, in circumstances of peculiar valour, a wounded comrade, about to be finished off. Back then comes my old friend of Deepdene days, a General and Commander-in-Chief with his staff and escort around him and his young heroes in his train.

Sir Bindon Blood was a striking figure in these savage mountains and among these wild rifle-armed clansmen. He looked very much more formidable in his uniform, mounted, with his standard-bearer and cavalcade, than he had done when I had seen him in safe and comfortable England. He had seen a great deal of the British and Indian armies in war and peace, and he had no illusions on any point. He was very proud to be the direct descendant of the notorious Colonel Blood, who in the reign of King Charles II had attempted to steal by armed force the Crown Jewels from the Tower of London. The episode is in the history books. The Colonel was arrested as he quitted the Tower gates with important parts of the regalia in his hands. Brought to trial for high treason and several other capital offences, he was acquitted and immediately appointed to command the King's bodyguard. This strange sequence of events gave rise to scurrilous suggestions that his attempt to abstract the Crown Jewels from the Tower had the connivance of the Sovereign himself. It is certainly true that the King was very short of money in those hard times, and that the predecessors of Mr. Attenborough were already in existence in various parts of Europe. However this may be, Sir Bindon Blood regarded the attempted stealing of the Crown Jewels by his ancestor as the most glorious event in his family history, and in consequence he had warm sympathy with the Pathan tribes on the Indian frontier, all of whom would have completely understood the incident in all its bearings, and would have bestowed unstinted and discriminating applause upon all parties. If the General could have got them all together and told them the story at length by broadcast, it would never have been necessary for three brigades with endless tails of mule and camel transport to toil through the mountains and sparsely populated highlands in which my next few weeks were to be passed.

The General, then already a veteran, is alive and hale to-day. He had one personal ordeal in this campaign. A fanatic approaching in a deputation (called a *jirga*) whipped out a knife, and rushed upon him from about eight yards. Sir Bindon Blood, mounted upon his horse, drew his revolver, which most of us thought on a General of Division was merely a token weapon, and shot his assailant dead at two yards. It is easy to imagine how delighted everyone in the Field Force, down to the most untouchable sweeper, was at such an event.

It is not my purpose to relate the campaign. I have already written, as will presently appear, a standard history on the subject. Unhappily it is out of print. I will therefore summarise only in a few sentences its course. The three brigades of the Malakand Field Force moved in succession through all the valleys I have mentioned, trailing their coats before the tribesmen and causing them much inconvenience by driving off their cattle for rations and cutting their crops for forage. The Political Officers who accompanied the force, with white tabs on their collars, parleyed all the time with the chiefs, the priests and other local notables. These political officers were very unpopular with the army officers. They were regarded as marplots. It was alleged that they always patched things up and put many a slur upon the prestige of the Empire without ever letting anyone know about it. They were accused of the grievous crime of 'shilly-shallying,' which being interpreted means doing everything you possibly can before you shoot. We had with us a very brilliant political officer, a Major Deane, who was much disliked because he always stopped military operations. Just when we were looking forward to having a splendid fight and all the guns were loaded and everyone keyed up, this

Major Deane—and why was he a Major anyhow? so we said—being in truth nothing better than an ordinary politician—would come along and put a stop to it all. Apparently all these savage chiefs were his old friends and almost his blood relations. Nothing disturbed their friendship. In between the fights, they talked as man to man and as pal to pal, just as they talked to our General as robber to robber.

We knew nothing about the police *vs.* the crook gangs in Chicago, but this must have been in the same order of ideas. Undoubtedly they all understood each other very well and greatly despised things like democracy, commercialism, money-getting, business, honesty and vulgar people of all kinds. We on the other hand wanted to let off our guns. We had not come all this way and endured all these heats and discomforts—which really were trying—you could lift the heat with your hands, it sat on your shoulders like a knapsack, it rested on your head like a nightmare—in order to participate in an interminable interchange of confidences upon unmentionable matters between the political officers and these sulky and murderous tribesmen. And on the other side we had the very strong spirit of the 'die-hards' and the 'young bloods' of the enemy. They wanted to shoot at us and we wanted to shoot at them. But we were both baffled by what they called the elders, or as one might now put it 'the old gang,' and by what we could see quite plainly—the white tabs or white feathers on the lapels of the political officers. However, as has hitherto usually been the case, the carnivorous forces had their way. The tribes broke away from their 'old gang' and were not calmed by our political officers. So a lot of people were killed, and on our side their widows have had to be pensioned by the Imperial Government, and others were badly wounded and hopped around for the rest of their lives, and it was all very exciting and, for those who did not get killed or hurt, very jolly.

I hope to convey to the reader by these somewhat irreverent sentences some idea of the patience and knowledge of the Government of India. It is patient because among other things it knows that if the worst comes to the worst, it can shoot anybody down. Its problem is to avoid such hateful conclusions. It is a sedate Government tied up by laws, tangled about with parleys and many intimate relationships; tied up not only by the House of Commons, but by all sorts

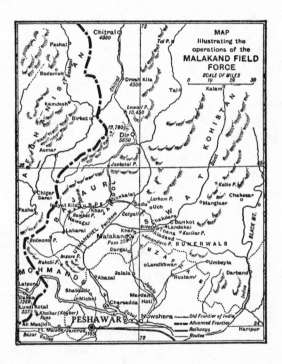

of purely Anglo-Indian restraints varying from the grandest conceptions of liberal magnanimity down to the most minute obstructions and inconveniences of red tape. So societies in quiet years should be constructed; overwhelming force on the side of the rulers, innumerable objections to the use of any part of it. Still from time to time things will happen and there are lapses, and what are called 'regrettable incidents' will occur, and it is with one of these that the next few pages of this account must deal.

CHAPTER XI

THE MAMUND VALLEY

CAMPAIGNING on the Indian frontier is an experience by itself. Neither the landscape nor the people find their counterparts in any other portion of the globe. Valley walls rise steeply five or six thousand feet on every side. The columns crawl through a maze of giant corridors down which fierce snow-fed torrents foam under skies of brass. Amid these scenes of savage brilliancy there dwells a race whose qualities seem to harmonise with their environment. Except at harvest-time, when self-preservation enjoins a temporary truce, the Pathan tribes are always engaged in private or public war. Every man is a warrior, a politician and a theologian. Every large house is a real feudal fortress made, it is true, only of sunbaked clay, but with battlements, turrets, loopholes, flanking towers, drawbridges, etc., complete. Every village has its defence. Every family cultivates its vendetta; every clan, its feud. The numerous tribes and combinations of tribes all have their accounts to settle with one another. Nothing is ever forgotten, and very few debts are left unpaid. For the purposes of social life, in addition to the convention about harvest-time, a most elaborate code of honour has been established and is on the whole faithfully observed. A man who knew it and observed it faultlessly might pass unarmed from one end of the frontier to another. The slightest technical slip would, however, be fatal. The life of the Pathan is thus full of interest; and his valleys, nourished alike by endless sunshine and abundant water, are fertile enough to yield with little labour the modest material requirements of a sparse population.

Into this happy world the nineteenth century brought two new facts; the breech-loading rifle and the British Government. The first was an enormous luxury and blessing; the second, an unmitigated nuisance. The convenience of the breech-loading, and still more of the magazine, rifle was nowhere more appreciated than in the Indian highlands. A weapon which would kill with accuracy at fifteen hundred yards opened a whole new vista of delights to every family or clan which could acquire it. One could actually remain in one's own house and fire at one's neighbour nearly a mile away. One could lie in wait on some high crag, and at hitherto unheard-of ranges hit a horseman far below. Even villages could fire at each other without the trouble of going far from home. Fabulous prices were therefore offered for these glorious products of science. Rifle-thieves scoured all India to reinforce the efforts of the honest smuggler. A steady flow of the coveted weapons spread its genial influence throughout the frontier, and the respect which the Pathan tribesmen entertained for Christian civilization was vastly enhanced.

The action of the British Government on the other hand was entirely unsatisfactory. The great organizing, advancing, absorbing power to the southward seemed to be little better than a monstrous spoil-sport. If the Pathans made forays into the plains, not only were they driven back (which after all was no more than fair), but a whole series of subsequent interferences took place, followed at intervals by expeditions which toiled laboriously through the valleys, scolding the tribesmen and exacting fines for any damage which they had done. No one would have minded these expeditions if they had simply come, had a fight and then gone away again. In many cases this was their practice under what was called the 'butcher and bolt policy' to which the Government of India long adhered. But towards the end of the nineteenth century these intruders began to make roads through many of the valleys, and in particular the great road to Chitral. They sought to insure the safety of these roads by threats, by forts and by subsidies. There was no objection to the last method so far as it went. But the whole of this tendency to road-making was regarded by the Pathans with profound distaste. All along the road people were expected to keep quiet, not to shoot one another, and, above all not to shoot at travellers along the road. It was too much to ask, and a whole series of quarrels took their origin from this source.

*   *   *   *   *

Our march to the Mohmand country led us past the mouth of the Mamund Valley. This valley is a pan-shaped plain nearly ten miles broad. No dispute existed between us and the Mamunds. Their reputation was pestilential, and the greatest care was taken to leave them alone. But the spectacle of the camp with its beautifully-ruled lines of shelters against the sun, with its cluster of hospital tents and multitudes of horses, camels, mules and donkeys, was too much for the Mamunds. Our fires twinkling in a wide quadrilateral through the night offered a target too tempting for human nature as developed on the Indian frontier to resist. Sniping by individuals was inevitable and began after dark upon the camp of our leading brigade. No great harm was done. A few men were wounded. Sir Bindon Blood continued his dinner impassively, although at one moment we had to put out the candles. In the morning, overlooking the Mamund impudence, we marched on to Nawagai. But the tribesmen were now excited, and when our second Brigade which was following at two days interval arrived, hundreds of men, armed with every kind of weapon from the oldest flintlock to the latest rifle, spent three exhilarating hours in firing continuously into the crowded array of men and animals. The great bulk of the troops had already dug themselves shallow pits, and the whole camp had been surrounded with a shelter trench. Nevertheless this night's sport cost them about forty officers and men, and many horses and pack animals besides. On this being reported, Sir Bindon Blood sent orders to retaliate. General Jeffreys commanding the second Brigade was told to enter the Mamund Valley on the following day and chastise the truculent assailants. The chastisement was to take the form of marching up their valley, which is a *cul de sac*, to its extreme point, destroying all the crops, breaking the reservoirs of water, blowing up as many castles as time permitted, and shooting anyone who obstructed the process. 'If you want to see a fight,' said Sir Bindon to me, 'you may ride back and join Jeffreys.' So availing myself of an escort of Bengal Lancers which was returning to the second Brigade, I picked my way gingerly through the 10 miles of broken ground which divided the two camps, and arrived at Jeffreys' Headquarters before nightfall.

All night long the bullets flew across the camp; but everyone now had good holes to lie in, and the horses and mules were protected to a large extent. At earliest dawn on September 16 our whole Brigade, preceded by a squadron of Bengal Lancers, marched in warlike formation into the Mamund Valley and was soon widely spread over its extensive area. There were three separate detachments, each of which had its own punitive mission to fulfil. As these diverged fanwise, and as our total number did not exceed twelve hundred fighting men, we were all soon reduced to quite small parties. I attached myself to the centre column whose mission it was to proceed to the farthest end of the valley. I began by riding with the cavalry.

We got to the head of the valley without a shot being fired. The villages and the plain were equally deserted. As we approached the mountain wall our field-glasses showed us clusters of tiny figures gathered on a conical hill. From these little blobs the sun threw back at intervals bright flashes of steel as the tribesmen waved their swords. This sight gave everyone the greatest pleasure, and our leading troop trotted and cantered forward to a small grove of trees which stood within rifle shot of the conical hill. Here we dismounted—perhaps fifteen carbines in all—and opened fire at seven hundred yards' range. Instantly the whole hill became spotted with white puffs of smoke, and bullets began to whistle through our little grove. This enjoyable skirmish crackled away for nearly an hour, and meanwhile the infantry toiled nearer and nearer to us across the plain. When they arrived, it was settled that the leading company of the 35th Sikhs should attack the conical hill and two more companies should proceed up a long spur to the left of it towards a village whose roofs could be seen amid the boulders and waving Indian corn of the mountain-side. The cavalry meanwhile would guard the plain and keep connection with the reserve of our force under the Brigadier, which now consisted mainly of the Buffs.[1]

I decided to go with the second party up the long spur towards the village. I gave my pony to a native and began to toil up the hillside with the Infantry. It was frightfully hot. The sun, nearing the meridian, beat upon one's shoulders. We plodded and stumbled upwards for nearly an hour—now through high patches of Indian corn, now over boulders, now along stony tracks or over bare slopes—but always mounting. A few shots were fired from higher up the mountain; but otherwise complete peace seemed to reign. As we ascended, the whole oval pan of the Mamund Valley spread out behind us, and pausing to mop my brow, I sat on a rock and surveyed it. It was already nearly eleven o'clock. The first thing that struck me was that there were no troops to be seen. About half a mile from the foot of the spur a few of the Lancers were dismounted. Far off against the distant mountain wall a thin column of smoke rose from a burning castle. Where was our Army? They had marched out twelve hundred strong only a few hours ago, and now the valley had swallowed them all up. I took out my glasses and searched the plain. Mud villages and castles here and there, the deep-cut water-courses, the gleam of reservoirs, occasional belts of cultivation, isolated groves of trees—all in a sparkling atmosphere backed by serrated cliffs—but of a British-Indian brigade, no sign.

[1] The East Kent Regiment.

It occurred to me for the first time that we were a very small party: five British officers including myself, and probably eighty-five Sikhs. That was absolutely all; and here we were at the very head of the redoubtable Mamund Valley, scrambling up to punish its farthest village. I was fresh enough from Sandhurst to remember the warnings about 'dispersion of forces,' and certainly it seemed that the contrast between the precautions which our strong force had taken moving out of camp in the morning, and the present position of our handful of men, was remarkable. However, like most young fools I was looking for trouble, and only hoped that something exciting would happen. It did!

At last we reached the few mud houses of the village. Like all the others, it was deserted. It stood at the head of the spur, and was linked to the mass of the mountains by a broad neck. I lay down with an officer and eight Sikhs on the side of the village towards the mountain, while the remainder of the company rummaged about the mud houses or sat down and rested behind them. A quarter of an hour passed and nothing happened. Then the Captain of the company arrived.

'We are going to withdraw,' he said to the subaltern. 'You stay here and cover our retirement till we take up a fresh position on that knoll below the village.' He added, 'The Buffs don't seem to be coming up, and the Colonel thinks we are rather in the air here.'

It struck me this was a sound observation. We waited another ten minutes. Meanwhile I presumed, for I could not see them, the main body of the company was retiring from the village towards the lower knoll. Suddenly the mountain-side sprang to life. Swords flashed from behind rocks, bright flags waved here and there. A dozen widely-scattered white smoke-puffs broke from the rugged face in front of us. Loud explosions resounded close at hand. From high up on the crag, one thousand, two thousand, three thousand feet above us, white or blue figures appeared, dropping down the mountainside from ledge to ledge like monkeys down the branches of a tall tree. A shrill crying arose from many points. Yi! Yi! Yi! Bang! Bang! Bang! The whole hillside began to be spotted with smoke, and tiny figures descended every moment nearer towards us. Our eight Sikhs opened an independent fire, which soon became more and more rapid. The hostile figures continued to flow down the mountain-side, and scores began to gather in rocks about a hundred yards away from us. The targets were too tempting to be resisted. I borrowed the Martini of the Sikh by whom I lay. He was quite content to hand me cartridges. I began to shoot carefully at the men gathering in the rocks. A lot of bullets whistled about us. But we lay very flat, and no harm was done. This lasted perhaps five minutes in continuous crescendo. We had certainly found the adventure for which we had been looking. Then an English voice close behind. It was the Battalion Adjutant.

'Come on back now. There is no time to lose. We can cover you from the knoll.'

The Sikh whose rifle I had borrowed had put eight or ten cartridges on the ground beside me. It was a standing rule to let no ammunition fall into the hands of the tribesmen. The Sikh seemed rather excited, so I handed him the cartridges one after the other to put in his pouch. This was a lucky inspiration. The rest of our party got up and turned to retreat. There was a ragged volley from the rocks; shouts, exclamations, and a scream. I thought for the moment that five or six of our men had lain down again. So they had: two killed and three wounded. One man was shot through the breast and pouring with blood; another lay on his back kicking and twisting. The British officer was spinning round just behind me, his face a mass of blood, his right eye cut out. Yes, it was certainly an adventure.

It is a point of honour on the Indian frontier not to leave wounded men behind. Death by inches and hideous mutilation are the invariable measure meted out to all who fall in battle into the hands of the Pathan tribesmen. Back came the Adjutant, with another British officer of subaltern rank, a

Sikh sergeant-major, and two or three soldiers. We all laid hands on the wounded and began to carry and drag them away down the hill. We got through the few houses, ten or twelve men carrying four, and emerged upon a bare strip of ground. Here stood the Captain commanding the company with half a dozen men. Beyond and below, one hundred and fifty yards away, was the knoll on which a supporting party should have been posted. No sign of them! Perhaps it was the knoll lower down. We hustled the wounded along, regardless of their protests. We had no rearguard of any kind. All were carrying the wounded. I was therefore sure that worse was close at our heels. We were not half-way across the open space when twenty or thirty furious figures appeared among the houses, firing frantically or waving their swords.

I could only follow by fragments what happened after that. One of the two Sikhs helping to carry my wounded man was shot through the calf. He shouted with pain; his turban fell off; and his long black hair streamed over his shoulders—a tragic golliwog. Two more men came from below and seized hold of our man. The new subaltern and I got the golliwog by the collar and dragged him along the ground. Luckily it was all down hill. Apparently we hurt him so much on the sharp rocks that he asked to be let go alone. He hopped and crawled and staggered and stumbled, but made a good pace. Thus he escaped. I looked round to my left. The Adjutant had been shot. Four of his soldiers were carrying him. He was a heavy man, and they all clutched at him. Out from the edge of the houses rushed half a dozen Pathan swordsmen. The bearers of the poor Adjutant let him fall and fled at their approach. The leading tribesman rushed upon the prostrate figure and slashed it three or four times with his sword. I forgot everything else at this moment except a desire to kill this man. I wore my long Cavalry sword well sharpened. After all, I had won the Public School fencing medal. I resolved on personal combat à *l'arme blanche*. The savage saw me coming. I was not more than twenty yards away. He picked up a big stone and hurled it at me with his left hand, and then awaited me, brandishing his sword. There were others waiting not far behind him. I changed my mind about the cold steel. I pulled out my revolver, took, as I thought, most careful aim, and fired. No result. I fired again. No result. I fired again. Whether I hit him or not I cannot tell. At any rate he ran back two or three yards and plumped down behind a rock. The fusillade was continuous. I looked around. I was all alone with the enemy. Not a friend was to be seen. I ran as fast as I could. There were bullets, everywhere. I got to the first knoll. Hurrah, there were the Sikhs holding the lower one! They made vehement gestures, and in a few moments I was among them.

There was still about three-quarters of a mile of the spur to traverse before the plain was reached, and on each side of us other spurs ran downwards. Along these rushed our pursuers, striving to cut us off and firing into both our flanks. I don't know how long we took to get to the bottom. But it was all done quite slowly and steadfastly. We carried two wounded officers and about six wounded Sikhs with us. That took about twenty men. We left one officer and a dozen men dead and wounded to be cut to pieces on the spur.

During this business I armed myself with the Martini and ammunition of a dead man, and fired as carefully as possible thirty or forty shots at tribesmen on the left-hand ridge at distances from eighty to a hundred and twenty yards. The difficulty about these occasions is that one is so out of breath and quivering with exertion, if not with excitement. However, I am sure I never fired without taking aim.

We fetched up at the bottom of the spur little better than a mob, but still with our wounded. There was the company reserve and the Lieutenant-Colonel commanding the battalion and a few orderlies. The wounded were set down, and all the survivors of the whole company were drawn up two deep, shoulder to shoulder, while the tribesmen, who must have now numbered two or three hundred, gathered in a wide and spreading half-moon around our flanks. I saw that the white officers were doing everything in their power to keep the Sikhs in close order. Although this formation presented a tremendous target, anything was better than being scattered. The tribesmen were all bunched together in clumps, and they too seemed frenzied with excitement.

The Colonel said to me, 'The Buffs are not more than half a mile away. Go and tell them to hurry or we shall all be wiped out.'

I had half turned to go on this errand, when a happy thought struck me. I saw in imagination the company overwhelmed and wiped out, and myself, an Orderly Officer to the Divisional General, arriving the sole survivor, breathless, at top speed, with tidings of disaster and appeals for help.

'I must have that order in writing, sir,' I said.

The Colonel looked surprised, fumbled in his tunic, produced his pocket-book and began to write.

But meanwhile the Captain had made his commands heard above the din and confusion. He had forced the company to cease their wild and ragged fusillade. I heard an order: 'Volley firing. Ready. Present.' Crash! At least a dozen tribesmen fell. Another volley, and they wavered. A third, and they began to withdraw up the hillside. The bugler began to sound the 'Charge.' Everyone shouted. The crisis was over, and here, Praise be to God, were the leading files of the Buffs.

Then we rejoiced and ate our lunch. But as it turned out, we had a long way to go before night.

*   *   *   *   *

The Buffs had now arrived, and it was obstinately decided to retake the spur down which we had been driven in order to recover prestige and the body of the Adjutant. This took us till five o'clock.

Meanwhile the other Company of the 35th Sikhs which had ascended the mountain on our right, had suffered even worse experiences. They eventually regained the plain, bearing along with them perhaps a dozen wounded, and leaving several officers and about fifteen soldiers to be devoured by the wolves. The shadows of evening had already fallen upon the valley, and all the detachments so improvidently dispersed in the morning, turned their steps towards the camp, gradually eneveloped by a thunderstorm and by the night, and closely followed by savage and exulting foes. I marched home with the Buffs and the much-mauled 35th Sikhs. It was dark when we entered the entrenchments which now surrounded the camp. All the other parties had already got home after unsatisfactory, though not serious, fighting. But where was the General? And where was his staff? And where was the mule battery?

The perimeter of the camp was strongly guarded, and we got ourselves some food amid the usual drizzle of sniping. Two hours passed. Where *was* the General? We now knew that he had with him besides the battery, a half-company of sappers and miners, and in all about ten white officers. Suddenly, from the valley there resounded the boom of a gun, calculated to be about three miles away. It was followed at short intervals by perhaps twenty more reports, then silence. What could be happening? Against what targets was the General firing his artillery in the blackness of night? Evidently he must be fighting at the very closest quarters. They must be all mixed up together; or were these guns firing signals for help? Ought we to set out to his relief? Volunteers were not lacking. The senior officers consulted together. As so often happens when things go wrong formalities were discarded, and I found myself taking part in the discussion. It was decided that no troops could leave the camp in the night. To send a rescue force to blunder on foot amid the innumerable pitfalls and obstacles of the valley in pitch darkness would be to cause a further disaster, and also to weaken the camp fatally if it were to be attacked, as well it might be. The General and the battery must fight it out wherever they were

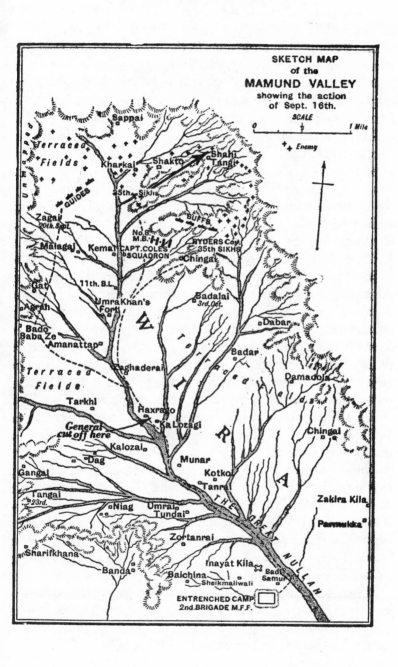

SKETCH MAP
of the
MAMUND VALLEY
showing the action
of Sept. 16th.

SCALE

0   1 Mile

+ + Enemy

Sappai

Terraced Fields

Kharkai   Shakto   Shahi Tangi

Unnamed

GUIDES   35th Sikhs

BUFFS

Zagai 20th Sept.   No.8. M.B.   RYDER'S Coy. 35th SIKHS

Malagai   Kemal CAPT. COLE'S SQUADRON   Chingai

Gat   11th. B.L.

Agrah   Umra Khan's Fort   Badalai 3rd. Oct.   Dabar

Bado Baba Ze   Amanattap   Badar   Damadola

Terraced Fields   Zaghaderai   d a

Tarkhi   Chingai

General cut off here   Haxrazo   Ka Lozagi

Kalozai   Munar

Dag   Kotko   Tanrai   Zakira Kila

Gangal   Parmukka

Tangai 23rd.   Niag   Umrai Tundai

Zortanrai

Sharifkhana   Inayat Kila   Bado Samur

Banda   Baichina   Sheikmaliwali

ENTRENCHED CAMP
2nd. BRIGADE M.F.F.

till daylight. Again the guns in the valley fired. So they had not been scuppered yet. I saw for the first time the anxieties, stresses and perplexities of war. It was not apparently all a gay adventure. We were already in jeopardy; and anything might happen. It was decided that the squadron of Bengal Lancers, supported by a column of infantry, should set out to relieve the General with the first light of dawn. It was now past midnight and I slept soundly, booted and spurred, for a few hours.

The open pan of the valley had no terrors for us in daylight. We found the General and his battery bunched up in a mud village. He had had a rough time. He was wounded in the head, but not seriously. Overtaken by the darkness, he had thrown his force into some of the houses and improvised a sort of fort. The Mamunds had arrived in the village at the same time, and all night long a fierce struggle had raged from house to house and in the alleys of this mud labyrinth. The assailants knew every inch of the ground perfectly. They were fighting in their own kitchens and parlours. The defenders simply hung on where they could, in almost total darkness, without the slightest knowledge of the ground or buildings. The tribesmen broke through the walls, or clambered on or through the roofs, firing and stabbing with their long knives. It was a fight in a rabbit warren. Men grappled with each other; shot each other in error; cannon were fired as you might fire a pistol at an enemy two or three yards away. Four of the ten British officers were wounded. A third of the sappers and gunners were casualties, and nearly all the mules were dead or streaming with blood. The haggard faces of the surviving officers added the final touch to this grim morning scene. However, it was all over now. So we proceeded to shoot the wounded mules and have breakfast.

When we all got back to camp, our General communicated by heliograph through a distant mountain top with Sir Bindon Blood at Nawagai. Sir Bindon and our leading brigade had themselves been heavily attacked the night before. They had lost hundreds of animals and twenty or thirty men, but otherwise were none the worse. Sir Bindon sent orders that we were to stay in the Mamund valley and lay it waste with fire and sword in vengeance. This accordingly we did, but with great precautions. We proceeded systematically, village by village, and we destroyed the houses, filled up the wells, blew down the towers, cut down the great shady trees, burned the crops and broke the reservoirs in punitive devastation. So long as the villages were in the plain, this was quite easy. The tribesmen sat on the mountains and sullenly watched the destruction of their homes and means of livelihood. When however we had to attack the villages on the sides of the mountains they resisted fiercely, and we lost for every village two or three British officers and fifteen or twenty native soldiers. Whether it was worth it, I cannot tell. At any rate, at the end of a fortnight the valley was a desert, and honour was satisfied.

CHAPTER XII

THE TIRAH EXPEDITION

IN the re-arrangements which were entailed by our losses on September 16 I was as an emergency measure posted to the 31st Punjaub Infantry, which had only three white officers besides the Colonel left. I have served officially as a regimental officer in peace or war altogether with the 4th Hussars, the 31st Punjaub Infantry, the 21st Lancers, the South African Light Horse, the Oxfordshire Yeomanry, the 2nd Grenadier Guards, the Royal Scots Fusiliers, and lastly, with the Oxfordshire Artillery. Very varied were the conditions in these different units in Asia, Africa and Europe; but this Punjaub Infantry business was the most peculiar of all. Although a cavalry officer, I had, of course, been trained in infantry drill at Sandhurst, and considered myself professionally competent in all minor operations, or major too, for the matter of that. The language difficulty was however more serious. I could hardly speak a word to the native soldiers who were perforce committed, in the scarcity of officers, to my direction. I had to proceed almost entirely by signals, gestures and dumb-crambo. To these I added three words, 'Maro' (kill), 'Chalo' (get on), and Tally ho! which speaks for itself. In these circumstances there could hardly be said to be that intimate connection between the Company Commander and his men which the drill books enjoin. However, in one way or another we got through without mishap three or four skirmishes, which I cannot dignify by the name of actions, but which were nevertheless both instructive and exciting to the handful of men who were engaged in them. I must have done it all by moral influence.

Although I could not enter very fully into their thoughts and feelings, I developed a regard for the Punjaubis. There was no doubt they liked to have a white officer among them when fighting, and they watched him carefully to see how things were going. If you grinned, they grinned. So I grinned industriously. Meanwhile I despatched accounts of the campaign both by telegram and letter to the *Pioneer* and also to the *Daily Telegraph*.

I now had good hopes of being permanently attached to the Malakand Field Force, and of roaming around these valleys for some time. However, the character of the operations changed. The tale of the 16th of September had been spread far and wide among the tribesmen, and of course the Mamunds probably made out they had had a great success. They exaggerated the number of our slain, and no doubt declared that their operations were proceeding according to plan. We said the same, but they did not read our newspapers. At any rate the whole frontier region was convulsed with excitement, and at the end of September the far more powerful Afridi tribes joined the revolt. The Afridis live in Tirah, a region of tremendous mountains lying to the north of Peshawar and the east of the Khyber Pass. The mountains of Tirah are higher and steeper than those on the Malakand side; and the valleys in Tirah are V-shaped instead of flat-bottomed. This greatly adds to the advantages of the tribesmen and to the difficulties of regular troops. In the middle of Tirah there is a flat plain like the Mamund Valley, but much larger, and accessible only by the V-shaped gorges through the mountain walls. This is called Tirah Maidān, and one may think of it as the centre of the maze at Hampton Court with mountains instead of hedges.

The Government of India in their wisdom now determined to send an expedition to Tirah Maidān. Here they would find all the granaries, herds and principal habitations of the Afridi tribes. These could all be destroyed, and the tribesmen together with their women and children driven up to the higher mountains in the depth of winter, where they would certainly be very uncomfortable. In order to inflict this chastisement, two whole divisions each of three brigades, say 35,000 men, together with large forces upon the communications and at the base, would be required. This army was accordingly mobilised, and concentrated about Peshawar and Kohat preparatory to invading Tirah. No white troops had ever yet reached the Maidān. The operations were considered to be the most serious undertaken on the frontier since the Afghan War, and the command was entrusted to an officer of the highest distinction and experience, Sir William Lockhart. Sir Bindon Blood, on the other hand, was to remain holding the tribes in check on the Malakand side. Our active operations thus came to an end, and about the same time reserve white officers of the Punjaubis came up to fill the vacancies in their regiment. I therefore turned my eyes to the Tirah Expeditionary Force and made strenuous efforts to be incorporated in it. However, I knew no one in high authority on that side. Colonel Ian Hamilton indeed commanded one of the brigades and would certainly have helped. Unluckily, he was thrown from his pony marching through the Kohat Pass, broke his leg, lost his brigade, missed the campaign, and nearly broke his heart. While I was in this weak position, detached from one force and not yet hooked on to the other, my Colonel far away in Southern India began to press for my return. In spite of Sir Bindon Blood's good-will, I fell between two stools and finished up at Bangalore.

My brother officers when I returned to them were extremely civil; but I found a very general opinion that I had had enough leave and should now do a steady spell of routine duty. The regiment was busy with the autumn training and about to proceed on manœuvres, and so less than a fortnight after hearing the bullets whistle in the Mamund valley, I found myself popping off blank cartridges in sham fights two thousand miles away. It seemed quite odd to hear the cracking of rifles on all sides, and nobody taking cover or bobbing their heads. Apart from this, the life was very much the same. It was just as hot, just as thirsty, and we marched and bivouacked day after day. Lovely country, Mysore, with splendid trees and innumerable sheets of stored water! We were manœuvring around a great mountain called Nundydroog, where the gold mines are, and where there are groves of trees whose leaves are brilliant scarlet.

There was certainly nothing to complain of, but as the weeks and months pased away, I watched with wistful eyes the newspaper accounts of the Tirah campaign. The two divisions had plunged into the mountains, and ultimately after much fighting and casualties in those days thought numerous, had reached the central plain or basin of Tirah. The next move was for them to come back before the worst of the winter had set in. This they did promptly, but none too soon. The indignant and now triumphant Afridis ran along the mountain ridges firing with deadly skill upon the long columns defiling painfully down the river bed, and forced to ford its freezing waters 10 to 12 times in every march. Hundreds of soldiers and thousands of animals were shot, and the retreat of the 2nd Division down the Bara valley was ragged in the extreme. Indeed at times, so we heard privately, it looked more like a rout than the victorious withdrawal of a punitive force. There was no doubt who had the punishment, nor who would have to pay the bill. Thirty-five thousand troops hunting, and being hunted by, Afridis around these gorges for a couple of months with 20,000 more guarding their communications make a nasty total when computed in rupees. Black were the brows of the wiseacres of Calcutta, and loud were the complaints of the Liberal Opposition at home.

I did not cry myself to sleep about the misadventures of the Tirah expedition. After all, they had been very selfish in not letting me come with them. I thought they would have to go in again in the spring, and I redoubled my efforts to join them. My mother co-operated energetically from her end. In my interest she left no wire unpulled, no stone unturned, no cutlet uncooked. Under my direction she had laid vigorous siege both to Lord Wolseley and Lord Roberts. These fortresses resisted obdurately. Lord Roberts wrote:

'I would, with the greatest pleasure, help your son, but it would be no use my communicating with General Lockhart as Sir George White is all powerful, and, as he refused to allow Winston to join General Blood's staff, after his having previously served with that officer in the Malakand Field Force, I feel sure he would not consent to his being sent with the Tirah Field Force.'

'I would telegraph to Sir George White, but I am certain that, under the circumstances, he would resent my doing so.'

Meanwhile, I was tethered in my garrison in Bangalore. At Christmas, however, it was easy to obtain ten days' leave. Ten days is not long. It was, in fact, long enough to reach the frontier and return. But I knew better than to present myself at the base headquarters of the field force without having prepared the ground beforehand. The military pussycat is a delightful animal, as long as you know how to keep clear of her claws, but once excited or irritated, she is capable of making herself extremely unpleasant. Moreover, if she falls into this mood, it is very difficult to get her out of it. I decided therefore to go not to the frontier, but to Calcutta, and to endeavour from the seat of the Indian Government to negotiate for a situation at the front. It took at that time three and a half days' continuous railway travelling to go from Bangalore to Calcutta, which, with an equal period for return, left about sixty hours to transact the all-important business. The Viceroy, Lord Elgin, under whom I was afterwards to serve as Under-Secretary of State in the Colonial Office, extended a large hospitality to young officers who had suitable introductions. I was royally entertained, and so well mounted that I won the fortnightly 'point to point' in which the garrison of Calcutta were wont at that time to engage. This was all very well, but my main business made no advance. I had, of course, used every resource at my disposal before I came on the spot, and I took the best advice of the highest authorities to whom I had access. They all agreed that the best chance was to beard the Adjutant-General, an extremely disagreeable person whose name I am glad to have forgotten. He could do it if he chose, and no one else could do it if he objected. Accordingly, I presented myself in his ante-room and applied for an interview. He declined point-blank to receive me, and I then began to realise that my quest was hopeless. There was an air of ironical amusement about the high military functionaries whom I met during these two days at lunch and dinner. They all knew what I had come about and what reception my suit would receive. From the Commander-in-Chief Sir George White downwards they were all extremely civil, but their friendliness seemed to carry with it a suggestion that there were some subjects better left unmentioned. And so at the end of my sixty hours I had again to clamber into the train and toil back discomfited to Bangalore.

During this winter I wrote my first book. I learned from England that my letters to the *Daily Telegraph* had been well received. Although written anonymously 'From a Young Officer,' they had attracted attention. The *Pioneer* too was complimentary. Taking these letters as the foundation, I resolved to build a small literary house. My friends told me that Lord Fincastle was also writing the story of the expedition. It was a race whose book would be finished first. I soon experienced a real pleasure in the task of writing, and the three or four hours in the middle of every day, often devoted to slumber or cards, saw me industriously at work. The manuscript was finished shortly after Christmas and sent home to my mother to sell. She arranged for its publication by Longmans.

Having contracted the habit of writing, I embarked on fiction. I thought I would try my hand at a novel. I found this much quicker work than the accurate chronicle of facts. Once started, the tale flowed on of itself. I chose as a theme a revolt in some imaginary Balkan or South American republic, and traced the fortunes of a liberal leader who overthrew an arbitrary Government only to be swallowed up by a socialist revolution. My brother officers were much amused by the story as it developed and made various suggestions for stimulating the love interest which I was not able to accept. But we had plenty of fighting and politics, interspersed with such philosophisings as I was capable of, all leading up to the grande finale of an ironclad fleet forcing a sort of Dardanelles to quell the rebellious capital. The novel was finished in about two months. It was eventually published in *Macmillan's Magazine* under the title of 'Savrola,' and being subsequently reprinted in various editions, yielded in all over several years about seven hundred pounds. I have consistently urged my friends to abstain from reading it.

Meanwhile my book on the Frontier War had been actually published.

In order not to lose two months by sending the proofs back to India, I had entrusted their correction to an uncle of mine, a very brilliant man and himself a ready writer. For some reason or other he missed many scores of shocking misprints and made no attempt to organise the punctuation. Nevertheless *The Malakand Field Force* had an immediate and wide success. The reviewers, though sarcastic about the misprints, etc., vied with each other in praise. When the first bundle of reviews reached me together with the volume as published, I was filled with pride and pleasure at the compliments, and consternated about the blunders. The reader must remember I had never been praised before. The only comments which had ever been made upon my work at school had been 'Indifferent,' 'Untidy,' 'Slovenly,'

'Bad,' 'Very bad,' etc. Now here was the great world with its leading literary newspapers and vigilant erudite critics, writing whole columns of praise! In fact I should blush even now to transcribe the glowing terms in which my 'style' was commended. The *Athenæum* said 'Pages of Napier punctuated by a mad printer's reader.' Others were less discriminating but even more complimentary. The *Pioneer* said something about 'a wisdom and comprehension far beyond his years.' That was the stuff! I was thrilled. I knew that if this would pass muster there was lots more where it came from, and I felt a new way of making a living and of asserting myself, opening splendidly out before me. I saw that even this little book had earned me in a few months two years' pay as a subaltern. I resolved that as soon as the wars which seemed to have begun again in several parts of the world should be ended, and we had won the Polo Cup, I would free myself from all discipline and authority, and set up in perfect independence in England with nobody to give me orders or arouse me by bell or trumpet.

One letter which I received gave me extreme pleasure, and I print it here as it shows the extraordinary kindness and consideration for young people which the Prince of Wales[1] always practised.

MARLBOROUGH HOUSE,
April 22/98.

MY DEAR WINSTON,

I cannot resist writing a few lines to congratulate you on the success of your book! I have read it with the greatest possible interest and I think the descriptions and the language generally excellent. Everybody is reading it, and I only hear it spoken of with praise. Having now seen active service you will wish to see more, and have as great a chance I am sure of winning the V.C. as Fincastle had; and I hope you will not follow the example of the latter, who I regret to say intends leaving the Army in order to go into Parliament.

[1]Afterwards King Edward VII.

You have plenty of time before you, and should certainly stick to the Army before adding M.P. to your name.

Hoping that you are flourishing,

I am,

Yours very sincerely,

A.E.

There was no more leave for me until the regimental polo team went north in the middle of March to play in the Annual Cavalry Tournament. I was fortunate enough to win a place, and in due course found myself at Meerut, the great cantonment where these contests usually take place. We were, I think, without doubt the second best team of all those who competed. We were defeated by the victors, the famous Durham Light Infantry. They were the only infantry regiment that ever won the Cavalry Cup. They were never beaten. All the crack regiments went down before them. The finest native teams shared a similar fate. All the wealth of Golconda and Rajputana, all the pride of their Maharajahs and the skill of their splendid players, were brushed firmly aside by these invincible foot soldiers. No record equals theirs in the annals of Indian polo. Their achievements were due to the brains and will-power of one man. Captain de Lisle, afterwards distinguished at Gallipoli and a Corps Commander on the western front, drilled, organised, and for four years led his team to certain and unbroken victory in all parts of India. We fell before his prowess in this the last year of his Indian polo career.

Meerut was 1,400 miles north of Bangalore, but it was still more than 600 miles from the front. Our leave expired three days after the final match of the tournament, and it took exactly three days in the train to return to Bangalore. A day and a half were required on the other hand to reach Peshawar and the front. I was by now so desperate that I felt the time had come to run a serious risk. Colonel Ian Hamilton was at length recovered from his accident, and had resumed the command of his brigade on their return from Tirah. He stood in high repute in the army, was a close personal friend and old brother officer of Sir George White, and on excellent terms with Sir William Lockhart. With Ian Hamilton I had long been in close correspondence, and he had made many efforts on my behalf. His reports were not very encouraging. There were many posts to be filled in the Expeditionary Force, but all appointments were made from Calcutta and *through the Adjutant General's department.* There was only one exception to this, namely appointments to the personal staff of Sir William Lockhart. I did not know Sir William Lockhart, nor so far as I could recollect had either my father or my mother made his acquaintance. How should I be able to obtain access to him, still more to persuade him to give me one of the two or three most coveted junior appointments on his staff? Besides, his staff was already complete. On the other hand, Colonel Ian Hamilton was in favour of my running the risk. 'I will do what I can,' he wrote. 'The Commander-in-Chief has an aide-de-camp of the name of Haldane, who was in the Gordon Highlanders with me. He has immense influence—in fact, they say throughout the Army, too much. If he were well disposed towards you, everything could be arranged. I have tried to prepare the ground. He is not friendly to you, but neither is he hostile. If you came up here, you might with your push and persuasiveness pull it off.'

Such was the gist of the letter which reached me on the morning after we had been defeated in the semi-final of the tournament. I looked out the trains north and south. There was obviously not time to take a day and a half's journey northwards to Peshawar, have a few hours there, and make the four and a half days' journey south within the limits of my expiring leave. I was bound, in short, if I took the northern train and failed to get an appointment at the front, to overstay my leave by at least forty-eight hours. I well knew that this was a military offence for which I should deservedly be punished. It would have been quite easy in ordinary circumstances to apply by telegraph for so short an extension; but once my plan of going to the front had been grasped by the regimental authorities, it was not an extension I should have received, but an order of immediate recall. In all the circumstances I decided to take the chance, and I started for Peshawar forthwith.

In the crisp air of the early morning I sought with a beating heart Sir William Lockhart at his headquarters, and sent my name in to his aide-de-camp. Out came the redoubtable Haldane, none too cordial but evidently interested and obviously in two minds. I don't remember what I said nor how I stated my case, but I must have hit the bull's eye more than once. For after about half an hour's walking up and down on the gravel-path Captain Haldane said, 'Well, I'll go and ask the Commander-in-Chief and see what he says.' Off he went, and I continued pacing the gravel alone. He was not gone long. 'Sir William has decided,' he said when he returned, 'to appoint you an extra orderly officer on his personal staff. You will take up your duties at once. We are communicating with the Government of India and your regiment.'

So forthwith my situation changed in a moment from disfavour and irregularity to commanding advantage. Red tabs sprouted on the lapels of my coat. The Adjutant-General published my appointment in the *Gazette*. Horses and servants were dispatched by the regiment from far-off Bangalore, and I became the close personal attendant of the Captain of the Host. To the interest and pleasure of hearing the daily conversation of this charming and distinguished man, who knew every inch of the frontier and had fought in every war upon it for forty years, was added the opportunity of visiting every part of his army, sure always of finding smiling faces.

For the first fortnight I behaved and was treated as befitted my youth and subordinate station. I sat silent at meals or only rarely asked a tactful question. But an incident presently occurred which gave me quite a different footing on Sir William Lockhart's staff. Captain Haldane used to take me with him on his daily walk, and we soon became intimate. He told me a good many things about the General and the staff, about the army and the operations as viewed from the inside, which showed me that much went on of which I and the general public were unconscious. One day he mentioned that a newspaper correspondent who had been sent home to England had written an article in the *Fortnightly Review* criticising severely, and as he said unfairly, the whole conduct of the Tirah expedition. The General and Headquarters Staff had been deeply wounded by this cruel attack. The Chief of the Staff, General Nicholson—who afterwards rose to the head of the British Army and was already well known as 'Old Nick'—had written a masterly, or at least a dusty, rejoinder. This had already been dispatched to England by the last mail.

Here at any rate I saw an opportunity of returning the kindness with which I had been treated by giving good and prompt advice. So I said that it would be considered most undignified and even improper for a high officer on the Staff of the Army in the Field to enter into newspaper controversy about the conduct of operations with a dismissed war-correspondent; that I was sure the Government would be surprised, and the War Office furious; that the Army Staff were expected to leave their defence to their superiors or to the politicians; and that no matter how good the arguments were, the mere fact of advancing them would be everywhere taken as a sign of weakness. Captain Haldane was much disturbed. We turned round and went home at once. All that night there were confabulations between the Commander-in-Chief and his staff officers. The next day I was asked how could the article already in the post be stopped. Ought the War Office to be told to put pressure upon the editor of the *Fortnightly Review*, and forbid him to print it when it was received? Would he be likely to obey such a request? I said he was presumably a gentleman, and that if he received a cable from the author asking him not to print the article, he would instantly comply, and bear his disappointment as he might. A cable was accordingly sent and received a reassuring reply. After this I began to be taken much more into the confidential circles of the staff and was treated as if I were quite a grown-up. Indeed I think that I was now very favourably situated for the opening of the Spring Campaign, and I began to have hopes of getting my teeth into serious affairs. The Commander-in-Chief seemed well pleased with me and I was altogether 'in the swim.' Unhappily for me at least my good fortune had come too late. The operations which were expected every day to recommence on an even larger scale gradually languished, then dissolved in prolonged negotiations with the tribesmen, and finally resulted in a lasting peace, the wisdom of which as a budding politician I was forced to approve, but which had nothing to do with the business that had brought me to Peshawar.

Thus the beaver builds his dam, and thus when his fishing is about to begin, comes the flood and sweeps his work and luck and fish away together. So he has to begin again.

CHAPTER XIII

A DIFFICULTY WITH KITCHENER

THE fighting on the Indian frontier had scarcely closed before the rumours of a new campaign in the Soudan began to ripen into certainty. The determination of Lord Salisbury's Government to advance to Khartoum, crush the Dervish power and liberate these immense regions from its withering tyranny, was openly avowed. Even while the Tirah Expeditionary Force was being demobilised, the first phase of the new operations began; and Sir Herbert Kitchener with a British and Egyptian force of about 20,000 men had already reached the confluence of the Nile and the Atbara, and had in a fierce action destroyed the Army of Mahmoud, the Khalifa's lieutenant, which had been sent to oppose him. There remained only the final phase of the long drama of the Soudan—the advance 200 miles southward to the Dervish capital and the decisive battle with the whole strength of the Dervish Empire.

I was deeply anxious to share in this.

But now I began to encounter resistances of a new and formidable character. When I had first gone into the Army, and wanted to go on active service, nearly everyone had been friendly and encouraging.

> . . . : all the world looked kind,
> (As it will look sometimes with the first stare
> Which Youth would not act ill to keep in mind).

The first stare was certainly over. I now perceived that there were many ill-informed and ill-disposed people who did not take a favourable view of my activities. On the contrary they began to develop an adverse and even a hostile attitude. They began to say things like this: 'Who the devil

is this fellow? How has he managed to get to these different campaigns? Why should he write for the papers and
serve as an officer at the same time? Why should a subaltern
praise or criticise his senior officers? Why should Generals
show him favour? How does he get so much leave from his
regiment? Look at all the hard-working men who have
never stirred an inch from the daily round and common task.
We have had quite enough of this—too much indeed. He is
very young, and later on he may be all right; but now a long
period of discipline and routine is what 2nd Lieutenant
Churchill requires.' Others proceeded to be actually abusive,
and the expressions 'Medal-hunter' and 'Self-advertiser'
were used from time to time in some high and some low
military circles in a manner which would, I am sure, surprise
and pain the readers of these notes. It is melancholy to be
forced to record these less amiable aspects of human nature,
which by a most curious and indeed unaccountable coincidence have always seemed to present themselves in the wake
of my innocent footsteps, and even sometimes across the
path on which I wished to proceed.

At any rate, quite early in the process of making my
arrangements to take part in the Soudan campaign, I became conscious of the unconcealed disapproval and hostility
of the Sirdar of the Egyptian Army, Sir Herbert Kitchener.
My application to join that army, although favoured by the
War Office, was refused, while several other officers of my
service and rank were accepted. The enquiries which I made
through various channels made it clear to me that the re-
fusal came from the highest quarter. I could not possibly
hope to overcome these ponderous obstacles from the cantonments of Bangalore in which I lay. As I was entitled
after the Tirah Expeditionary Force had been demobilised to
a period of leave, I decided to proceed without delay to the
centre of the Empire and argue the matter out in London.

On reaching London I mobilised whatever resources were
within my reach. My mother devoted the whole of her in-

fluence to furthering my wishes. Many were the pleasant luncheons and dinners attended by the powers of those days which occupied the two months of these strenuous negotiations. But all without avail! The obstacle to my going to Egypt was at once too powerful and too remote to be within her reach. She even went so far as to write personally to Sir Herbert Kitchener, whom she knew quite well, on my account. He replied with the utmost politeness that he had already more than enough officers for the campaign, that he was overwhelmed with applications from those who had what would appear to be far greater claims and qualifications, but that if at some future time opportunity occurred, he would be pleased, etc., etc.

We were already at the end of June. The general advance of the army must take place early in August. It was not a matter of weeks but of days.

But now at this moment a quite unexpected event occurred. Lord Salisbury, the Prime Minister, whose political relations with my father had not been without their tragic aspect, happened to read *The Malakand Field Force.* He appears to have been not only interested but attracted by it. Spontaneously and 'out of the blue,' he formed a wish to make the acquaintance of its author. One morning at the beginning of July, I received a letter from his Private Secretary, Sir Schomberg M'Donnell informing me that the Prime Minister had read my book with great pleasure and would very much like to discuss some parts of it with me. Could I make it convenient to pay him a visit one day at the Foreign Office? Four o'clock on the Tuesday following would be agreeable to him, if it fell in with my arrangements. I replied, as the reader will readily surmise, 'Will a duck swim?' or words to that effect.

The Great Man, Master of the British world, the unchallenged leader of the Conservative Party, a third time Prime Minister and Foreign Secretary at the height of his long career, received me at the appointed hour, and I entered for the first time that spacious room overlooking the Horse-guards Parade in which I was afterwards for many years from time to time to see much grave business done in Peace and War.

There was a tremendous air about this wise old States-man. Lord Salisbury, for all his resistance to modern ideas, and perhaps in some way because of it, played a greater part in gathering together the growing strength of the British Empire for a time of trial which few could foresee and none could measure, than any other historic figure that can be cited. I remember well the old-world courtesy with which he met me at the door and with a charming gesture of wel-come and salute conducted me to a seat on a small sofa in the midst of his vast room.

'I have been keenly interested in your book. I have read it with the greatest pleasure and, if I may say so, with ad-miration not only for its matter but for its style. The debates in both Houses of Parliament about the Indian frontier policy have been acrimonious, much misunderstanding has confused them. I myself have been able to form a truer pic-ture of the kind of fighting that has been going on in these frontier valleys from your writings than from any other documents which it has been my duty to read.'

I thought twenty minutes would be about the limit of my favour, which I had by no means the intention to outrun, and I accordingly made as if to depart after that period had expired. But he kept me for over half an hour, and when he finally conducted me again across the wide expanse of carpet to the door, he dismissed me in the following terms, 'I hope you will allow me to say how much you remind me of your father, with whom such important days of my politi-cal life were lived. If there is anything at any time that I can do which would be of assistance to you, pray do not fail to let me know.'

When I got back to my home I pondered long and anxi-ously over this parting invitation. I did not want to put the old Lord to trouble on my account. On the other hand, it seemed to me that the merest indication on his part would suffice to secure me what at that time I desired most of all in the world. A word from the Prime Minister, his great supporter, would surely induce Sir Herbert Kitchener to waive his quite disproportionate opposition to my modest desires. In after years when I myself disposed of these matters on an enormous scale, when young men begged to be allowed to take part in actual fighting and when the curmudgeons of red tape interposed their veto, I used to brush these objections aside saying, 'After all they are only asking to stop a bullet. Let them have their way.'

Accordingly, after several days' consideration I had recourse to Sir Schomberg M'Donnell whom I had seen and met in social circles since I was a child. By then it was the third week in July. There seemed absolutely no other way of reaching the Atbara Army before the advance to Khartoum began. I sought him out late one evening and found him dressing for dinner. Would the Prime Minister send a telegram to Sir Herbert Kitchener? The War Office had recommended me, my regiment had given me leave, the 21st Lancers were quite willing to accept me, there was no other obstacle of any sort or kind. Was it asking too much? Would he find out tentatively how Lord Salisbury felt about it?

'I am sure he will do his best,' he said. 'He is very pleased with you, but he won't go beyond a certain point. He may be willing to ask the question in such a way as to indicate what he would like the answer to be. You must not expect him to press it, if the answer is unfavourable.' I said I would be quite content with this.

'I'll do it at once,' said this gallant man, who was such an invaluable confidant and stand-by to Lord Salisbury during his long reign, and who in after years, at a very advanced age, insisted on proceeding to the trenches of the Great War, and was almost immediately killed by a shrapnel shell.

Off he went, discarding his dinner party, in search of his

Chief. Before darkness closed a telegram had gone to the Sirdar to the effect that while of course Lord Salisbury would not think of interfering with the Sirdar's wishes or discretion in the matter of subordinate appointments, he would be greatly pleased on personal grounds if my wish to take part in the impending operations could without disadvantage to the public service be acceded to. Swiftly, by return wire, came the answer: Sir Herbert Kitchener had already all the Officers he required, and if any vacancies occurred, there were others whom he would be bound to prefer before the young officer in question.

This sour intimation was in due course conveyed to me. If I had been found wanting at this moment in perseverance, I should certainly never have shared in the stirring episodes of the Battle of Omdurman. But in the interval a piece of information had come into my possession which opened up the prospect of one last effort.

Sir Francis Jeune, one of our most eminent Judges, had always been a friend of my family. His wife, now Lady St. Helier, moved much in military circles, and frequently met Sir Evelyn Wood, the Adjutant-General. Her subsequent work on the London County Council may be taken as the measure of the abilities which she employed and the influence which she exercised on men and affairs. She told me that Sir Evelyn Wood had expressed the opinion in her hearing at a dinner table that Sir Herbert Kitchener was going too far in picking and choosing between particular officers recommended by the War Office, and that he, for his part, was not at all disposed to see the War Office completely set aside by the Commander in the Field of what was after all a very small part of the British Army. The Egyptian Army no doubt was a sphere within which the Sirdar's wishes must be absolute, but the British contingent (of an Infantry Division, a Brigade of Artillery and a British Cavalry regiment, the 21st Lancers) was a part of the Expeditionary Force, the internal composition of which rested exclusively with the War Office. She told me indeed that Sir Evelyn Wood had evinced considerable feeling upon this subject. Then I said 'Have you told him that the Prime Minister has telegraphed personally on my behalf?' She said she had not. 'Do so,' I said, 'and let us see whether he will stand up for his prerogatives.'

Two days later I received the following laconic intimation from the War Office.

'You have been attached as a supernumerary Lieutenant to the 21st Lancers for the Soudan Campaign. You are to report at once at the Abassiyeh Barracks, Cairo, to the Regimental Headquarters. It is understood that you will proceed at your own expense and that in the event of your being killed or wounded in the impending operations, or for any other reason, no charge of any kind will fall on British Army funds.'

Oliver Borthwick, son of the proprietor of the *Morning Post* and most influential in the conduct of the paper, was a contemporary and a great friend of mine. Feeling the force of Napoleon's maxim that 'war should support **war**', I arranged that night with Oliver that I should write as opportunity served a series of letters to the *Morning Post* at £15 a column. The President of the Psychical Research Society extracted rather unseasonably a promise from me after dinner to 'communicate' with him, should anything unfortunate occur. I caught the 11 o'clock train for Marseilles the next morning. My mother waved me off in gallant style. Six days later I was in Cairo.

*   *   *   *   *

All was excitement and hustle at Abassiyeh Barracks. Two squadrons of the 21st Lancers had already started up the Nile. The other two were to leave the next morning. Altogether seven additional officers from other cavalry regiments had been attached to the 21st to bring them up to full war-strength. These officers were distributed in command of troops about the various squadrons. A troop had been reserved for me in one of the leading squadrons. But the delay and uncertainty about my coming had given this to another. Second-Lieutenant Robert Grenfell had succeeded in obtaining this vacancy. He had gone off in the highest spirits. At the base everyone believed that we should be too late for the battle. Perhaps the first two squadrons might get up in time, but no one could tell. 'Fancy how lucky I am,' wrote Grenfell to his family. 'Here I have got the troop that would have been Winston's, and we are to be the first to start.' Chance is unceasingly at work in our lives, but we cannot always see its workings sharply and clearly defined. As it turned out, this troop was practically cut to pieces in the charge which the regiment made in the battle of September 2, and its brave young leader was killed. He was the first of that noble line of Grenfells to give his life in the wars of the Empire. Two of his younger brothers were killed in the Great War, one after gaining the Victoria Cross; and his own ardent spirit was the equal of theirs.

The movement of the regiment 1,400 miles into the heart of Africa was effected with the swiftness, smoothness and punctuality which in those days characterised all Kitchener's arrangements. We were transported by train to Assiout; thence by stern-wheeled steamers to Assouan. We led our horses round the cataract at Philæ; re-embarked on other steamers at Shellal; voyaged four days to Wady Halfa; and from there proceeded 400 miles across the desert by the marvellous military railway whose completion had sealed the fate of the Dervish power. In exactly a fortnight from leaving Cairo we arrived in the camp and railway base of the army, where the waters of the Atbara flow into the mighty Nile.

The journey was delightful. The excellent arrangements made for our comfort and convenience, the cheery company, the novel and vivid scenery which streamed past, the excitement and thoughtless gaiety with which everyone looked

forward to the certainly-approaching battle and to the part
that would be played in it by the only British cavalry regiment with the army—all combined to make the experience
pleasant. But I was pursued and haunted by a profound,
unrelenting fear. I had not heard a word in Cairo of how
Sir Herbert Kitchener had received the over-riding by the
War Office of his wishes upon my appointment. I imagined
telegrams of protest on his part to the War Office which
would indeed put their resolution to the proof. Exaggerat-
ing, as one's anxious mind is prone to do, I pictured the
Adjutant-General seriously perturbed in Whitehall by the
stern remonstrance, or perhaps even obstinate resistance, of
the almost all-powerful Commander-in-Chief. I expected
every moment an order of recall. Besides, I was now under
the Sirdar's command. Nothing would be easier than for
him to utter the words, 'Send him back to the base; let him
come on with the remounts after the battle'; or a score of
equally detestable combinations. Every time the train drew
up at a station, every time the stern-wheeled steamers pad-
dled their way to a landing-stage, I scanned the crowd with
hunted eyes; and whenever the insignia of a Staff Officer
were visible, I concluded at once that the worst had overtaken me. I suppose a criminal flying from justice goes
through the same emotions at every stopping-point. Thank
God, there was no wireless in those days or I should never
have had a moment's peace. One could not, of course, escape
the ordinary telegraph. Its long coils wrapped one round
even then. But at least there were interludes of four or five
days when we plashed our way peacefully forward up the
great river out of all connection with the uncharitable world.

However, as the stages of the journey succeeded one
another without any catastrophe, Hope began to grow
stronger in my breast. By the time we reached Wady Halfa
I had begun to reason with myself in a more confident mood.
Surely on the eve of his most critical and decisive battle,
laden with all the immensely complicated business of a con-

centration and advance the smallest details of which, as is well known, he personally supervised, the Sirdar might find something else to occupy his mind and forget to put a spoke in the wheel of an unfortunate subaltern. Perhaps he might not have time or patience to wrangle with the War Office in cipher telegrams. He might forget. Best of all, he might not even have been told! And when on the evening of August 14 we ferried ourselves across from the Atbara camp to the left of the Nile, preparatory to beginning our 200 mile march to the Dervish capital, I felt entitled like Agag to believe that 'the bitterness of death was past.'

My efforts were not after all to miscarry. Sir Herbert Kitchener, as I afterwards learned, confronted with my appointment by the War Office, had simply shrugged his shoulders and passed on to what were after all matters of greater concern.

CHAPTER XIV

THE EVE OF OMDURMAN

NOTHING like the Battle of Omdurman will ever be seen again. It was the last link in the long chain of those spectacular conflicts whose vivid and majestic splendour has done so much to invest war with glamour. Everything was visible to the naked eye. The armies marched and manœuvred on the crisp surface of the desert plain through which the Nile wandered in broad reaches, now steel, now brass. Cavalry charged at full gallop in close order, and infantry or spearmen stood upright ranged in lines or masses to resist them. From the rocky hills which here and there flanked the great river the whole scene lay revealed in minute detail, curiously twisted, blurred and interspersed with phantom waters by the mirage. The finite and concrete presented itself in the most keenly-chiselled forms, and then dissolved in a shimmer of unreality and illusion. Long streaks of gleaming water, where we knew there was only desert, cut across the knees or the waists of marching troops. Batteries of artillery or long columns of cavalry emerged from a filmy world of uneven crystal on to the hard yellow-ochre sand, and took up their positions amid jagged red-black rocks with violet shadows. Over all the immense dome of the sky, dun to turquoise, turquoise to deepest blue, pierced by the flaming sun, weighed hard and heavy on marching necks and shoulders.

The 21st Lancers, having crossed to the left bank of the Nile at its confluence with the Atbara in the evening of August 15, journeyed forward by nine days' march to the advanced concentration camp just north of the Shabluka Cataract. This feature is peculiar. Across the 4,000-mile course of the Nile to the Mediterranean, Nature has here flung a high wall of rock. The river, instead of making a ten-mile detour round its western extremity, has preferred a frontal attack, and has pierced or discovered a way through the very centre of the obstructing mass. The Shabluka position was considered to be formidable. It was impossible to ascend the cataract in boats and steamers in any force that would be effective, unless the whole range of hills had first been turned from the desert flank. Such an operation would have presented a fine tactical opportunity to a Dervish army crouched behind the Shabluka hills ready to strike at the flank of any army making the indispensable turning movement. It was therefore no doubt with great relief that Sir Herbert Kitchener received from his cavalry, his scouts and his spies, the assurance that this strong position was left undefended by the enemy.

Nevertheless, all the precautions of war were observed in making the critical march through the desert round the end of the hills. All the mounted forces made a wide circling movement. For us, although we were only on the inner flank, the distance was perhaps 25 miles from our morning watering-place on the Nile bank north of the Shabluka to where we reached the river again at the evening bivouac on the southern and Omdurman side of the barrier. Those of us who, like my troop, composed the advance patrols, expected as we filtered through the thorn scrub to find enemies behind every bush, and we strained our ears and eyes and waited at every instant the first clatter of musketry. But except for a few fleeting horsemen, no hostile sight or sound disturbed or even diversified our march, and when the vast plain reddened in the sunset, we followed our lengthening shadows peacefully but thirstily again to the sweet waters of the river. Meanwhile the flat-bottomed gunboats and stern-wheel steamers, drawing endless tows of sailing boats carrying our supplies, had safely negotiated the cataract, and by the 27th all our forces, desert and river, were concentrated South of the Shabluka hills with only five clear marches over open plain to the city of our quest.

On the 28th the army set forth on its final advance. We moved in full order of battle and by stages of only eight or ten miles a day so as to save all our strength for the collision at any moment. We carried nothing with us but what we and our horses stood up in. We drew our water and food each night from the Nile and its armada. The heat in this part of Africa and at this time of the year was intense. In spite of thick clothes, spine-pads, broad-brimmed pitch helmets, one felt the sun leaning down upon one and piercing our bodies with his burning rays. The canvas water-bags which hung from our saddles, agreeably cool from their own evaporation, were drained long before the afternoons had worn away. How delicious it was in the evenings when, the infantry having reached and ordered their bivouac, the cavalry screen was withdrawn, and we filed down in gold and purple twilight to drink and drink and drink again from the swift abundant Nile.

Of course by this time everyone in the British cavalry had made up his mind that there was to be no battle. Was it not all humbug? Did the Dervishes exist, or were they just myths created by the Sirdar and his Anglo-Egyptian entourage? The better-informed held that, while there were no doubt a lot of Dervishes gathered at Omdurman, they had all decided to avoid battle and were already streaming off hundreds of miles along the roads to distant Kordofan. 'We shall be marching like this towards the Equator for months and months.' Well, never mind. It was a pleasant occupation, a jolly life; health was good, exercise exhilarating, food sufficient, and at dawn and dusk—at least—water unlimited. We were seeing a new land all the time, and perhaps after all some day we might see something else. But when I dined on the night of the 31st in the mess of the British officers of a Soudanese battalion, I found a different opinion. 'They are all there,' said these men, who had been fighting the Dervishes for ten years. They would certainly 'put up a battle' for the capital of their Empire. They weren't the sort to run. We should find them drawn up outside the city; and the city was now only 18 miles away.

Our march of September 1 began like all the others in perfect calm, but towards nine o'clock our patrols began to see things. Reports trickled back through troops to squadrons of white patches and gleams of light amid the mirage glitter which shrouded the southern horizon. The squadron to which I belonged was that day employed only in support of the advanced screen, and we rode slowly forward with suppressed and growing excitement. At about half-past ten we topped a broad swell of sand and saw before us, scarcely a mile away, all our advanced patrols and parties halted in a long line, observing something which lay apparently immediately across their path. Soon we also were ordered to halt, and presently a friendly subaltern who had been on patrol came along with what to us was momentous and decisive news. 'Enemy in sight,' he said, beaming. 'Where?' we asked. 'There, can't you see? Look at that long brown smear. That's them. They haven't bolted,' and he went on his way. We had all noticed this dark discoloration of the distant horizon, but had taken it to be a forest of thornbushes. The best field-glasses failed to disclose any other impression from the point where we were halted. Then came the regimental-sergeant-major, also coming back from the outpost line.

'How many are there?' we asked.

'A good army,' he replied. 'Quite a good army,' and he too went on his way.

Next came an order for the support to send a subaltern whose horse was not exhausted up to the Colonel in the outpost line.

'Mr. Churchill,' said my squadron leader, and off I trotted.

There was a shallow dip followed by another rise of

ground before I found Colonel Martin in the outpost line near some sandhills.[1]

'Good morning,' he said. 'The enemy has just begun to advance. They are coming on pretty fast. I want you to see the situation for yourself, and then go back as quickly as you can without knocking up your horse, and report personally to the Sirdar. You will find him marching with the infantry.'

So I was to meet Kitchener after all! Would he be surprised to see me? Would he be angry? Would he say 'What the devil are you doing here? I thought I told you not to come.' Would he be disdainfully indifferent? Or would he merely receive the report without troubling to inquire the name of the officer who brought it? Anyhow, one could not have a better reason of service for accosting the great man than the news that a hostile army was advancing against him. The prospect interested and excited me as much as the approaching battle, and the possibilities in the rear seemed in no way less interesting, and in some respects not less formidable, than the enemy on our front.

Having thoroughly observed the enemy and been told all that there was to tell in the outpost line, I started to trot and canter across the six miles of desert which separated the advanced cavalry from the main body of the army. The heat was scorching, and as I thought it almost certain we should be fighting on horseback all the afternoon, I took as much care of my horse as the urgency of my orders allowed. In consequence nearly forty minutes had passed before I began to approach the mass of the infantry. I paused for a moment to rest my horse and survey the scene from the spur of a black rocky hill which gave a general view. The sight was truly magnificent. The British and Egyptian army was advancing in battle array. Five solid brigades of three or four infantry battalions each, marching in open columns, echeloned back from the Nile. Behind these great blocks of men

[1]See map on page 195.

followed long rows of artillery, and beyond these there
trailed out interminable strings of camels carrying supplies.
On the river abreast of the leading brigade moved masses of
heavily-laden sailing-boats towed by a score of stern-wheel
steamers, and from this mass there emerged gleaming grimly
seven or eight large white gunboats ready for action. On the
desert flank and towards the enemy a dozen squadrons of
Egyptian cavalry at wide intervals could be seen supporting
the outpost line, and still further inland the grey and chocolate columns of the Camel Corps completed the spacious
panorama.

Having breathed my horse, for I did not wish to arrive in
a flurry, I rode towards the centre of the infantry masses.
Soon I saw at their head a considerable cavalcade following
a bright red banner. Drawing nearer I saw the Union Jack
by the side of the Egyptian flag. Kitchener was riding alone
two or three horses' lengths in front of his Headquarters
Staff. His two standard-bearers marched immediately behind
him, and the principal officers of the Anglo-Egyptian army
staff followed in his train exactly as one would expect from
the picture-books.

I approached at an angle, made a half circle, drew my
horse alongside and slightly in rear of him, and saluted. It
was the first time I had ever looked upon that remarkable
countenance, already well known, afterwards and probably
for generations to be familiar to the whole world. He turned
his grave face upon me. The heavy moustaches, the queer
rolling look of the eyes, the sunburnt and almost purple
cheeks and jowl made a vivid manifestation upon the senses.

'Sir,' I said, 'I have come from the 21st Lancers with a
report.' He made a slight nod as a signal for me to continue.
I described the situation in terms which I had studied on my
ride to make as compendious as possible. The enemy were in
sight, apparently in large numbers; their main body lay
about seven miles away and almost directly between our
present position and the city of Omdurman. Up to 11 o'clock

they had remained stationary, but at five minutes past eleven they were seen to be in motion, and when I left forty minutes before they were still advancing rapidly.

He listened in absolute silence to every word, our horses crunching the sand as we rode forward side by side. Then, after a considerable pause, he said, 'You say the Dervish Army is advancing. How long do you think I have got?' My answer came out in a flash: 'You have got at least an hour—probably an hour and a half, sir, even if they come on at their present rate.' He tossed his head in a way that left me in doubt whether he accepted or rejected this estimate, and then with a slight bow signified that my mission was discharged. I saluted, reined my horse in, and let his retinue flow past.

I began to calculate speeds and distances rather anxiously in order to see whether my precipitate answer conformed to reason. In the result I was pretty sure I was not far out. Taking four miles an hour as the maximum rate at which the Dervish jog-trot could cover what I judged to be seven miles, an hour and a half was a safe and sure margin.

These meditations were broken in upon by a friendly voice. 'Come along with us and have some lunch.' It was an officer on the Staff of Sir Reginald Wingate, the Director of the Intelligence of the army. He presented me to his Chief, who received me kindly. I need scarcely say that a square meal, a friend at court, and the prospect of getting the best information on coming events, were triply agreeable. Meanwhile I saw that the infantry everywhere were forming into lines making an arc against the Nile, and that in front of the leading brigade thorn-bushes were being busily cut down and fastened into a zeriba. Then right in our path appeared a low wall of biscuit boxes which was being rapidly constructed, and on the top of this wall I perceived a long stretch of white oil-cloth on which again were being placed many bottles of inviting appearance and large dishes of bully beef and mixed pickles. This grateful sight arising as if by enchantment in the wilderness on the verge of battle filled my heart with a degree of thankfulness far exceeding what one usually experiences when regular Grace is said.

Everybody dismounted, orderlies surged up to lead away the horses. As this repast came into view, I lost sight of Kitchener. He seemed to have withdrawn a little from the Staff. Whether he lunched on a separate pile of biscuit boxes all to himself or whether he had no luncheon at all, I neither knew nor cared. I attacked the bully beef and cool drink with concentrated attention. Everyone was in the highest spirits and the best of tempers. It was like a race luncheon before the Derby. I remember that I found myself next to the representative of the German General Staff—Baron von Tiedemann. 'This is the 1st of September,' he said. '*Our* great day and now *your* great day: Sedan and Soudan.' He was greatly pleased with this and repeated it several times to the company, some of whom thought they detected sarcasm. 'Is there really going to be a battle?' I asked General Wingate. 'Certainly, rather,' he replied. 'When?' I said, 'to-morrow?' 'No,' he said, 'here, now, in an hour or two.' It really was a good moment to live, and I, a poor subaltern who had thought himself under a ban, plied my knife and fork with determination amid the infectious gaiety of all these military magnates.

All the time one could see the lines of the Infantry being rapidly marshalled, and the thorn fences growing in front of them from minute to minute. Before us the bare sand plain swept gently up from the river to a crescent rise beyond which were our cavalry outposts and, presumably, the steadily advancing foe. In an hour that arena would swarm with charging Dervishes, and be heaped with dead, while the lines of infantry behind the thorn zeriba blazed their rifle-fire and all the cannon boomed. Of course we should win. Of course we should mow them down. Still, nevertheless, these same Dervishes, in spite of all the pre-

cision of modern weapons, had more than once as at Abu
Klea and Tamai broken British squares, and again and again
had pierced through or overwhelmed fronts held only by
Egyptian troops. I pictured on the plain, in my imagination, several possible variants of the battle that seemed so
imminent and so near; and then, as if to proclaim its opening—Bang, Bang, Bang, went the howitzer battery firing
from an island upon the Mahdi's tomb in Omdurman.

However, there was to be no battle on September 1. I
had scarcely rejoined my squadron in the outpost line when
the Dervish army came to a standstill, and after giving a
tremendous *feu de joie* seemed to settle down for the night.
We watched them all the afternoon and evening, and our
patrols skirmished and scampered about with theirs. It was
not until the light faded that we returned to the Nile
and were ordered to tuck away our men and horses within
the zeriba under the steep bank of the river.

In this sheltered but helpless posture we were informed
that trustworthy news had been received that the enemy
would attack by night. The most severe penalties were denounced against anyone who in any circumstances whatever
—even to save his life—fired a shot from pistol or carbine
inside the perimeter of the thorn fence. If the Dervishes
broke the line and penetrated the camp, we were to defend
ourselves by fighting on foot with our lances or swords.
We reassured ourselves by the fact that the 1st Battalion
of the Grenadiers and a battalion of the Rifle Brigade occupied the line of the zeriba 100 yards away and immediately above us. Confiding our safety to these fine troops, we
addressed ourselves to preparations for dinner.

In this domain a happy experience befell me. As I strolled
in company with a brother officer along the river bank we
were hailed from the gunboats which lay 20 or 30 feet
from the shore. The vessel was commanded by a junior
naval Lieutenant named Beatty who had long served in the
Nile flotillas, and was destined to fame on blue water. The

gunboat officers, spotlessly attired in white uniforms, were eager to learn what the cavalry had seen, and we were by no means unwilling to tell. We had a jolly talk across the stretch of water while the sun sank. They were particularly pleased to learn of the orders against the use of firearms inside the zeriba, and made many lugubrious jokes at our expense. This included offering us hospitality on the gunboat if the worst came to the worst. We put the suggestion aside with dignity and expressed our confidence in the plan of using cavalry swords and lances on foot amid the sand dunes against a Dervish mob in pitch darkness. After a good deal of chaff came the piece of good fortune.

'How are you off for drinks? We have got everything in the world on board here. Can you catch?' and almost immediately a large bottle of champagne was thrown from the gunboat to the shore. It fell in the waters of the Nile, but happily where a gracious Providence decreed them to be shallow and the bottom soft. I nipped into the water up to my knees, and reaching down seized the precious gift which we bore in triumph back to our mess.

This kind of war was full of fascinating thrills. It was not like the Great War. Nobody expected to be killed. Here and there in every regiment or battalion, half a dozen, a score, at the worst thirty or forty, would pay the forfeit; but to the great mass of those who took part in the little wars of Britain in those vanished light-hearted days, this was only a sporting element in a splendid game. Most of us were fated to see a war where the hazards were reversed, where death was the general expectation and severe wounds were counted as lucky escapes, where whole brigades were shorn away under the steel flail of artillery and machine-guns, where the survivors of one tornado knew that they would certainly be consumed in the next or the next after that.

Everything depends upon the scale of events. We young men who lay down to sleep that night within three miles of

60,000 well-armed fanatical Dervishes, expecting every moment their violent onset or inrush and sure of fighting at latest with the dawn—we may perhaps be pardoned if we thought we were at grips with real war.

CHAPTER XV

THE SENSATIONS OF A CAVALRY CHARGE

Long before the dawn we were astir, and by five o'clock the 21st Lancers were drawn up mounted outside the zeriba. My squadron-leader Major Finn, an Australian by birth, had promised me some days before that he would give me 'a show' when the time came. I was afraid that he would count my mission to Lord Kitchener the day before as quittance; but I was now called out from my troop to advance with a patrol and reconnoitre the ridge between the rocky peak of Jebel Surgham and the river. Other patrols from our squadron and from the Egyptian cavalry were also sent hurrying forward in the darkness. I took six men and a corporal. We trotted fast over the plain and soon began to breast the unknown slopes of the ridge. There is nothing like the dawn. The quarter of an hour before the curtain is lifted upon an unknowable situation is an intense experience of war. Was the ridge held by the enemy or not? Were we riding through the gloom into thousands of ferocious savages? Every step might be deadly; yet there was no time for **overmuch** precaution. The regiment was coming on behind us, and dawn was breaking. It was already half light as we climbed the slope. What should we find at the summit? For cool, tense excitement I commend such moments.

Now we are near the top of the ridge. I make one man follow a hundred yards behind, so that whatever happens, he may tell the tale. There is no sound but our own clatter. We have reached the crest line. We rein in our horses. Every minute the horizon extends; we can already see 200 yards. Now we can see perhaps a quarter of a mile. All is quiet; no life but our own breathes among the rocks and sand hummocks of the ridge. No ambuscade, no occupation in force! The farther plain is bare below us: we can now see more than half a mile.

So they have all decamped! Just what we said! All bolted off to Kordofan; no battle! But wait! The dawn is growing fast. Veil after veil is lifted from the landscape. What is this shimmering in the distant plain? Nay—it is lighter now—what are these dark markings beneath the shimmer? *They are there!* These enormous black smears are thousands of men; the shimmering is the glinting of their weapons. It is now daylight. I slip off my horse; I write in my field service notebook 'The Dervish army is still in position a mile and a half south-west of Jebel Surgham.' I send this message by the corporal direct as ordered to the Commander-in-Chief. I mark it XXX. In the words of the drill book 'with all despatch' or as one would say 'Hell for leather.'

A glorious sunrise is taking place behind us; but we are admiring something else. It is already light enough to use field-glasses. The dark masses are changing their values. They are already becoming lighter than the plain; they are fawn-coloured. Now they are a kind of white, while the plain is dun. In front of us is a vast array four or five miles long. It fills the horizon till it is blocked out on our right by the serrated silhouette of Surgham Peak. This is an hour to live. We mount again, and suddenly new impressions strike the eye and mind. These masses are not stationary. They are advancing, and they are advancing fast. A tide is coming in. But what is this sound which we hear: a deadened roar coming up to us in waves? They are cheering for God, his Prophet and his holy Khalifa. They think they are going to win. We shall see about that presently. Still I must admit that we check our horses and hang upon the crest of the ridge for a few moments before advancing down its slopes.

But now it is broad morning and the slanting sun adds brilliant colour to the scene. The masses have defined themselves into swarms of men, in ordered ranks bright with glittering weapons, and above them dance a multitude of gorgeous flags. We see for ourselves what the Crusaders saw. We must see more of it. I trot briskly forward to somewhere near the sandhills where the 21st Lancers had halted the day before. Here we are scarcely 400 yards away from the great masses. We halt again and I make four troopers fire upon them, while the other two hold their horses. The enemy come on like the sea. A crackle of musketry breaks out on our front and to our left. Dust spurts rise among the sandhills. This is no place for Christians. We scamper off; and luckily no man nor horse is hurt. We climb back on to the ridge, and almost at this moment there returns the corporal on a panting horse. He comes direct from Kitchener with an order signed by the Chief of Staff. 'Remain as long as possible, and report how the masses of attack are moving.' Talk of Fun! Where will you beat this! On horseback, at daybreak, within shot of an advancing army, seeing everything, and corresponding direct with Headquarters.

So we remained on the ridge for nearly half an hour and I watched close up a scene which few have witnessed. All the masses except one passed for a time out of our view beyond the peak of Surgham on our right. But one, a division of certainly 6,000 men moved directly over the shoulder of the ridge. Already they were climbing its forward slopes. From where we sat on our horses we could see both sides. There was our army ranked and massed by the river. There were the gunboats lying expectant in the stream. There were all the batteries ready to open. And meanwhile on the other side, this large oblong gay-coloured crowd in fairly good order climbed swiftly up to the crest of exposure. We were about 2,500 yards from our own batteries, but little more than 200 from their approaching target. I called these Dervishes 'The White Flags.' They reminded me of the armies in the Bayeux tapestries, because of their rows of white and yellow standards held upright. Meanwhile the Dervish centre far out in the plain had come within range, and one after another the British and Egyptian batteries opened upon it. My eyes were rivetted by a nearer scene. At the top of the hill 'The White Flags' paused to rearrange their ranks and drew out a broad and solid parade along the crest. Then the cannonade turned upon them. Two or three batteries and all the gunboats, at least thirty guns, opened an intense fire. Their shells shrieked towards us and burst in scores over the heads and among the masses of the White Flag-men. We were so close, as we sat spellbound on our horses, that we almost shared their perils. I saw the full blast of Death strike this human wall. Down went their standards by dozens and their men by hundreds. Wide gaps and shapeless heaps appeared in their array. One saw them jumping and tumbling under the shrapnel bursts; but none turned back. Line after line they all streamed over the shoulder and advanced towards our zeriba, opening a heavy rifle fire which wreathed them in smoke.

Hitherto no one had taken any notice of us; but I now saw Baggara horsemen in twos and threes riding across the plain on our left towards the ridge. One of these patrols of three men came within pistol range. They were dark, cowled figures, like monks on horseback—ugly, sinister brutes with long spears. I fired a few shots at them from the saddle, and they sheered off. I did not see why we should not stop out on this ridge during the assault. I thought we could edge back towards the Nile and so watch both sides while keeping out of harm's way. But now arrived a positive order from Major Finn, whom I had perforce left out of my correspondence with the Commander-in-Chief, saying 'Come back at once into the zeriba as the infantry are about to open fire.' We should in fact have been safer on the ridge, for we only just got into the infantry lines before the rifle-storm began.

*   *   *   *   *

It is not my purpose in this record of personal impressions to give a general account of the Battle of Omdurman. The story has been told so often and in such exact military detail that everyone who is interested in the subject is no doubt well acquainted with what took place. I shall only summarise the course of the battle so far as may be necessary to explain my own experiences.

The whole of the Khalifa's army, nearly 60,000 strong, advanced in battle order from their encampment of the night before, topped the swell of ground which hid the two armies from one another, and then rolled down the gently-sloping amphitheatre in the arena of which, backed upon the Nile, Kitchener's 20,000 troops were drawn up shoulder to shoulder to receive them. Ancient and modern confronted one another. The weapons, the methods and the fanaticism of the Middle Ages were brought by an extraordinary anachronism into dire collision with the organisation and inventions of the nineteenth century. The result was not surprising. As the successors of the Saracens descended the long smooth slopes which led to the river and their enemy, they encountered the rifle fire of two and a half divisions of trained infantry, drawn up two deep and in close order and supported by at least 70 guns on the river bank and in the gunboats, all firing with undisturbed efficiency. Under this fire the whole attack withered and came to a standstill, with a loss of perhaps six or seven thousand men, at least 700 yards away from the British-Egyptian line. The Dervish army, however, possessed nearly 20,000 rifles of various kinds, from the most antiquated to the most modern, and when the spearmen could get no farther, these riflemen lay down on the plain and began a ragged, unaimed but considerable fusillade at the dark line of the thorn-fence zeriba. Now for the first time they began to inflict losses on their antagonists, and in the short space that this lasted perhaps two hundred casualties occurred among the British and Egyptian troops.

Seeing that the attack had been repulsed with great slaughter and that he was nearer to the city of Omdurman than the Dervish army, Kitchener immediately wheeled his five brigades into his usual echelon formation, and with his left flank on the river proceeded to march south towards the city, intending thereby to cut off what he considered to be the remnants of the Dervish army from their capital, their base, their food, their water, their home, and to drive them out into the vast deserts which stared on every side. But the Dervishes were by no means defeated. The whole of their left, having overshot the mark, had not even been under fire. The Khalifa's reserve of perhaps 15,000 men was still intact. All these swarms now advanced with undaunted courage to attack the British and Egyptian forces, which were no longer drawn up in a prepared position, but marching freely over the desert. This second shock was far more critical than the first. The charging Dervishes succeeded everywhere in coming to within a hundred or two hundred yards of the troops, and the rear brigade of Soudanese, attacked from two directions, was only saved from destruction by the skill and firmness of its commander, General Hector Macdonald. However, discipline and machinery triumphed over the most desperate valour, and after an enormous carnage, certainly exceeding 20,000 men, who strewed the ground in heaps and swathes 'like snowdrifts,' the whole mass of the Dervishes dissolved into fragments and into particles and streamed away into the fantastic mirages of the desert.

The Egyptian cavalry and the camel corps had been protecting the right flank of the zeriba when it was attacked, and the 21st Lancers were the only horsemen on the left flank nearest to Omdurman. Immediately after the first attack had been repulsed we were ordered to leave the zeriba, ascertain what enemy forces, if any, stood between Kitchener and the city, and if possible drive these forces back and clear the way for the advancing army. Of course as a regimental officer one knows very little of what is taking

place over the whole field of battle. We waited by our horses
during the first attack close down by the river's edge, sheltered by the steep Nile bank from the bullets which whistled
overhead. As soon as the fire began to slacken and it was
said on all sides that the attack had been repulsed, a General arrived with his staff at a gallop with instant orders
to mount and advance. In two minutes the four squadrons
were mounted and trotting out of the zeriba in a southerly
direction. We ascended again the slopes of Jebel Surgham
which had played its part in the first stages of the action,
and from its ridges soon saw before us the whole plain of
Omdurman with the vast mud city, its minarets and domes,
spread before us six or seven miles away. After various halts
and reconnoitrings we found ourselves walking forward in
what is called 'column of troops.' There are four troops in
a squadron and four squadrons in a regiment. Each of these
troops now followed the other. I commanded the second
troop from the rear, comprising between twenty and twenty-
five Lancers.

Everyone expected that we were going to make a charge.
That was the one idea that had been in all minds since we
had started from Cairo. Of course there would be a charge.
In those days, before the Boer War, British cavalry had been
taught little else. Here was clearly the occasion for a charge.
But against what body of enemy, over what ground, in
which direction or with what purpose, were matters hidden
from the rank and file. We continued to pace forward over
the hard sand, peering into the mirage-twisted plain in a
high state of suppressed excitement. Presently I noticed, 300
yards away on our flank and parallel to the line on which we
were advancing, a long row of blue-black objects, two or
three yards apart. I thought there were about a hundred and
fifty. Then I became sure that these were men—enemy
men—squatting on the ground. Almost at the same moment
the trumpet sounded 'Trot,' and the whole long column of
cavalry began to jingle and clatter across the front of these

crouching figures. We were in the lull of the battle and there was perfect silence. Forthwith from every blue-black blob came a white puff of smoke, and a loud volley of musketry broke the odd stillness. Such a target at such a distance could scarcely be missed, and all along the column here and there horses bounded and a few men fell.

The intentions of our Colonel had no doubt been to move round the flank of the body of Dervishes he had now located, and who, concealed in a fold of the ground behind their riflemen, were invisible to us, and then to attack them from a more advantageous quarter; but once the fire was opened and losses began to grow, he must have judged it inexpedient to prolong his procession across the open plain. The trumpet sounded 'Right wheel into line,' and all the sixteen troops swung round towards the blue-black riflemen. Almost immediately the regiment broke into a gallop, and the 21st Lancers were committed to their first charge in war!

I propose to describe exactly what happened to me: what I saw and what I felt. I recalled it to my mind so frequently after the event that the impression is as clear and vivid as it was a quarter of a century ago. The troop I commanded was, when we wheeled into line, the second from the right of the regiment. I was riding a handy, sure-footed, grey Arab polo pony. Before we wheeled and began to gallop, the officers had been marching with drawn swords. On account of my shoulder I had always decided that if I were involved in hand-to-hand fighting, I must use a pistol and not a sword. I had purchased in London a Mauser automatic pistol, then the newest and the latest design. I had practised carefully with this during our march and journey up the river. This then was the weapon with which I determined to fight. I had first of all to return my sword into its scabbard, which is not the easiest thing to do at a gallop. I had then to draw my pistol from its wooden holster and bring it to full cock. This dual operation took an appreciable time, and until it was finished, apart from a few glances to my left to see what effect the fire was producing, I did not look up at the general scene.

Then I saw immediately before me, and now only half the length of a polo ground away, the row of crouching blue figures firing frantically, wreathed in white smoke. On my right and left my neighbouring troop leaders made a good line. Immediately behind was a long dancing row of lances couched for the charge. We were going at a fast but steady gallop. There was too much trampling and rifle fire to hear any bullets. After this glance to the right and left and at my troop, I looked again towards the enemy. The scene appeared to be suddenly transformed. The blue-black men were still firing, but behind them there now came into view a depression like a shallow sunken road. This was crowded and crammed with men rising up from the ground where they had hidden. Bright flags appeared as if by magic, and I saw arriving from nowhere Emirs on horseback among and around the mass of the enemy. The Dervishes appeared to be ten or twelve deep at the thickest, a great grey mass gleaming with steel, filling the dry watercourse. In the same twinkling of an eye I saw also that our right overlapped their left, that my troop would just strike the edge of their array, and that the troop on my right would charge into air. My subaltern comrade on the right, Wormald of the 7th Hussars, could see the situation too; and we both increased our speed to the very fastest gallop and curved inwards like the horns of the moon. One really had not time to be frightened or to think of anything else but these particular necessary actions which I have described. They completely occupied mind and senses.

The collision was now very near. I saw immediately before me, not ten yards away, the two blue men who lay in my path. They were perhaps a couple of yards apart. I rode at the interval between them. They both fired. I passed through the smoke conscious that I was unhurt. The trooper immediately behind me was killed at this place and at this moment, whether by these shots or not I do not know. I checked my pony as the ground began to fall away beneath his feet. The clever animal dropped like a cat four or five feet down on to the sandy bed of the watercourse, and in this sandy bed I found myself surrounded by what seemed to be dozens of men. They were not thickly packed enough at this point for me to experience any actual collision with them. Whereas Grenfell's troop, next but one on my left, was brought to a complete standstill and suffered very heavy losses, we seemed to push our way through as one has sometimes seen mounted policemen break up a crowd. In less time than it takes to relate, my pony had scrambled up the other side of the ditch. I looked round.

Once again I was on the hard, crisp desert, my horse at a trot. I had the impression of scattered Dervishes running to and fro in all directions. Straight before me a man threw himself on the ground. The reader must remember that I had been trained as a cavalry soldier to believe that if ever cavalry broke into a mass of infantry, the latter would be at their mercy. My first idea therefore was that the man was terrified. But simultaneously I saw the gleam of his curved sword as he drew it back for a ham-stringing cut. I had room and time enough to turn my pony out of his reach, and leaning over on the off side I fired two shots into him at about three yards. As I straightened myself in the saddle, I saw before me another figure with uplifted sword. I raised my pistol and fired. So close were we that the pistol itself actually struck him. Man and sword disappeared below and behind me. On my left, ten yards away, was an Arab horseman in a bright-coloured tunic and steel helmet, with chain-mail hangings. I fired at him. He turned aside. I pulled my horse into a walk and looked around again.

In one respect a cavalry charge is very like ordinary life. So long as you are all right, firmly in your saddle, your horse in hand, and well armed, lots of enemies will give you a wide berth. But as soon as you have lost a stirrup, have a rein cut, have dropped your weapon, are wounded, or your horse is wounded, then is the moment when from all quarters enemies rush upon you. Such was the fate of not a few of my comrades in the troops immediately on my left. Brought to an actual standstill in the enemy's mass, clutched at from every side, stabbed at and hacked at by spear and sword, they were dragged from their horses and cut to pieces by the infuriated foe. But this I did not at the time see or understand. My impressions continued to be sanguine. I thought we were masters of the situation, riding the enemy down, scattering them and killing them. I pulled my horse up and looked about me. There was a mass of Dervishes about forty or fifty yards away on my left. They were huddling and clumping themselves together, rallying for mutual protection. They seemed wild with excitement, dancing about on their feet, shaking their spears up and down. The whole scene seemed to flicker. I have an impression, but it is too fleeting to define, of brown-clad Lancers mixed up here and there with this surging mob. The scattered individuals in my immediate neighbourhood made no attempt to molest me. Where was my troop? Where were the other troops of the squadron? Within a hundred yards of me I could not see a single officer or man. I looked back at the Dervish mass. I saw two or three riflemen crouching and aiming their rifles at me from the fringe of it. Then for the first time that morning I experienced a sudden sensation of fear. I felt myself absolutely alone. I thought these riflemen would hit me and the rest devour me like wolves. What a fool I was to loiter like this in the midst of the enemy! I crouched over the saddle, spurred my horse into a gallop and drew clear of the *mêlée*. Two or three hundred yards away I found my troop already faced about and partly formed up.

The other three troops of the squadron were reforming

close by. Suddenly in the midst of the troop up sprang a Dervish. How he got there I do not know. He must have leaped out of some scrub or hole. All the troopers turned upon him thrusting with their lances: but he darted to and fro causing for the moment a frantic commotion. Wounded several times, he staggered towards me raising his spear. I shot him at less than a yard. He fell on the sand, and lay there dead. How easy to kill a man! But I did not worry about it. I found I had fired the whole magazine of my Mauser pistol, so I put in a new clip of ten cartridges before thinking of anything else.

I was still prepossessed with the idea that we had inflicted great slaughter on the enemy and had scarcely suffered at all ourselves. Three or four men were missing from my troop. Six men and nine or ten horses were bleeding from spear thrusts or sword cuts. We all expected to be ordered immediately to charge back again. The men were ready, though they all looked serious. Several asked to be allowed to throw away their lances and draw their swords. I asked my second sergeant if he had enjoyed himself. His answer was 'Well, I don't exactly say I enjoyed it, Sir; but I think I'll get more used to it next time.' At this the whole troop laughed.

But now from the direction of the enemy there came a succession of grisly apparitions; horses spouting blood, struggling on three legs, men staggering on foot, men bleeding from terrible wounds, fish-hook spears stuck right through them, arms and faces cut to pieces, bowels protruding, men gasping, crying, collapsing, expiring. Our first task was to succour these; and meanwhile the blood of our leaders cooled. They remembered for the first time that we had carbines. Everything was still in great confusion. But trumpets were sounded and orders shouted, and we all moved off at a trot towards the flank of the enemy. Arrived at a position from which we could enfilade and rake the watercourse, two squadrons were dismounted and in a few minutes with their fire at three hundred yards compelled the Dervishes to retreat. We therefore remained in possession of the field. Within twenty minutes of the time when we had first wheeled into line and began our charge, we were halted and breakfasting in the very watercourse that had so nearly proved our undoing. There one could see the futility of the much vaunted *Arme Blanche*. The Dervishes had carried off their wounded, and the corpses of thirty or forty enemy were all that could be counted on the ground. Among these lay the bodies of over twenty Lancers, so hacked and mutilated as to be mostly unrecognisable. In all out of 310 officers and men the regiment had lost in the space of about two or three minutes five officers and sixty-five men killed and wounded, and 120 horses—nearly a quarter of its strength.

Such were my fortunes in this celebrated episode. It is very rarely that cavalry and infantry, while still both unshaken, are intermingled as the result of an actual collision. Either the infantry keep their heads and shoot the cavalry down, or they break into confusion and are cut down or speared as they run. But the two or three thousand Dervishes who faced the 21st Lancers in the watercourse at Omdurman were not in the least shaken by the stress of battle or afraid of cavalry. Their fire was not good enough to stop the charge, but they had no doubt faced horsemen many a time in the wars with Abyssinia. They were familiar with the ordeal of the charge. It was the kind of fighting they thoroughly understood. Moreover, the fight was with equal weapons, for the British too fought with sword and lance as in the days of old.

*   *   *   *   *

A white gunboat seeing our first advance had hurried up the river in the hopes of being of assistance. From the crow's nest, its commander, Beatty, watched the whole event with breathless interest. Many years passed before I met

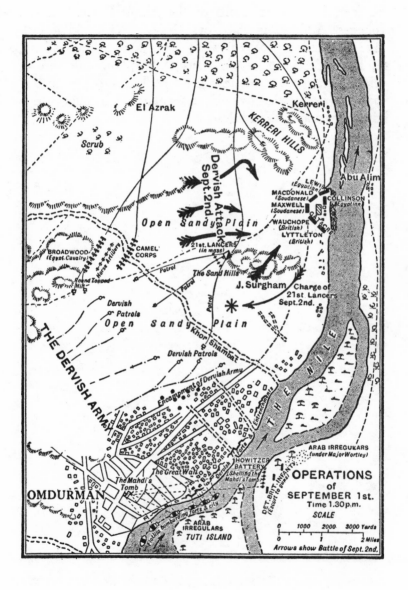

Scrub

El Azrak

KERRERI HILLS

Kerreri

Abu Alim

LEWIS (Egyptian)
MACDONALD (Soudanese)
COLLINSON (Egyptian)
MAXWELL (Soudanese)
WAUCHOPE (British)
LYTTLETON (British)

Dervish Attack Sept. 2nd

Open Sandy Plain

BROADWOOD (Egypt. Cavalry)
Horse Artillery
CAMEL CORPS
21st LANCERS (in mass)
Round Topped Hill
Dervish Patrols
The Sand Hills
J. Surgham Charge of 21st Lancers Sept. 2nd.

Patrol
Patrol
Patrol

Open Sandy Plain

THE DERVISH ARMY

Khor Shambat

Dervish Patrols

Encampment of Dervish Army

Dervish Entrenchments

THE NILE

The Mahdi's Tomb
The Great Wall
Dervish Entrenchment

OMDURMAN

Flotilla bombarding Forts & city

ARAB IRREGULARS
TUTI ISLAND

HOWITZER BATTERY (Shelling the Mahdi's Tomb)
DET. BRIT. INFANTRY (Escort to guns)

ARAB IRREGULARS (under Major Wortley)

OPERATIONS
of
SEPTEMBER 1st.
Time 1.30 p.m.
SCALE
0   1000   2000   3000 Yards
0   1   2 Miles

Arrows show Battle of Sept. 2nd.

this officer or knew that he had witnessed our gallop. When we met, I was First Lord of the Admiralty and he the youngest Admiral in the Royal Navy. 'What did it look like?' I asked him. 'What was your prevailing impression?' 'It looked,' said Admiral Beatty, 'like plum duff: brown currants scattered about in a great deal of suet.' With this striking, if somewhat homely, description my account of this adventure may fittingly close.

CHAPTER XVI

I LEAVE THE ARMY

THE defeat and destruction of the Dervish Army was so complete that the frugal Kitchener was able to dispense immediately with the costly services of a British cavalry regiment. Three days after the battle the 21st Lancers started northwards on their march home. I was allowed to float down the Nile in the big sailing-boats which contained the Grenadier Guards. In Cairo I found Dick Molyneux, a subaltern in the Blues, who like myself had been attached to the 21st. He had been seriously wounded by a sword-cut above his right wrist. This had severed all the muscles and forced him to drop his revolver. At the same time his horse had been shot at close quarters. Molyneux had been rescued from certain slaughter by the heroism of one of his troopers. He was now proceeding to England in charge of a hospital nurse. I decided to keep him company. While we were talking, the doctor came in to dress his wound. It was a horrible gash, and the doctor was anxious that it should be skinned over as soon as possible. He said something in a low tone to the nurse, who bared her arm. They retired into a corner, where he began to cut a piece of skin off her to transfer to Molyneux's wound. The poor nurse blanched, and the doctor turned upon me. He was a great raw-boned Irishman. 'Oi'll have to take it off you,' he said. There was no escape, and as I rolled up my sleeve he added genially 'Ye've heeard of a man being flayed aloive? Well, this is what it feels loike.' He then proceeded to cut a piece of skin and some flesh about the size of a shilling from the inside of my forearm. My sensations as he sawed the razor slowly to and fro fully justified his description of the ordeal. However, I managed to hold out until he had cut a beautiful

197

piece of skin with a thin layer of flesh attached to it. This precious fragment was then grafted on to my friend's wound. It remains there to this day and did him lasting good in many ways. I for my part keep the scar as a souvenir.

*   *   *   *   *

My father and mother had always been able to live near the centre and summit of the London world, and on a modest scale to have the best of everything. But they had never been at all rich, still less had they been able to save. On the contrary, debts and encumbrances had accumulated steadily during their intensely active public and private life. My father's expedition to South Africa in 1891 had however enabled him to obtain a share in very valuable gold-mining properties. He had acquired among other holdings 5,000 Rand Mines shares at their original par value. During the last year of his life these shares rose almost daily in the market, and at his death they were nearly twenty times the price he had paid for them. Soon afterwards they rose to fifty or sixty times this price; and had he lived another year he would have been possessed of a substantial fortune. In those days, when there was no taxation worth mentioning, and when the purchasing power of money was at least half as great again as it is now, even a quarter of a million sterling was real wealth. However, he died at the moment when his new fortune almost exactly equalled his debts. The shares, of course, were sold, and when everything was settled satisfactorily my mother was left with only the entailed property secured by her marriage settlements. This, however, was quite enough for comfort, ease and pleasure.

I was most anxious not to be a burden upon her in any way; and amid the movement and excitements of the campaigns and polo tournaments I reflected seriously upon the financial aspects of my military life. My allowance of £500 a year was not sufficient to meet the expenses of polo and the Hussars. I watched the remorseless piling up year by year of deficits which, although not large—as deficits go—were deficits none the less. I now saw that the only profession I had been taught would never yield me even enough money to avoid getting into debt, let alone to dispense with my allowance and become completely independent as I desired. To have given the most valuable years of one's education to reach a position of earning about 14*s.* a day out of which to keep up two horses and most costly uniforms seemed hardly in retrospect to have been a very judicious proceeding. To go on soldiering even for a few more years would plainly land me and all connected with me in increasing difficulties. On the other hand the two books I had already written and my war correspondence with the *Daily Telegraph* had already brought in about five times as much as the Queen had paid me for three years of assiduous and sometimes dangerous work. Her Majesty was so stinted by Parliament that she was not able to pay even a living wage. I therefore resolved with many regrets to quit her service betimes. The series of letters I had written for the *Morning Post* about the battle of Omdurman, although unsigned, had produced above £300. Living at home with my mother my expenses would be small, and I hoped to make from my new book about the Soudan Campaign, which I had decided to call *The River War,* enough to keep me in pocket money for at least two years. Besides this I had in contemplation a contract with the *Pioneer* to write them weekly letters from London at a payment of £3 apiece. I have improved upon this figure in later life; but at this time I reflected that it nearly equalled the pay I was receiving as a subaltern officer.

I therefore planned the sequence of the year 1899 as follows: To return to India and win the Polo Tournament: to send in my papers and leave the army: to relieve my mother from paying my allowance: to write my new book and the letters to the *Pioneer*: and to look out for a chance of entering Parliament. These plans as will be seen were in the main carried out. In fact from this year until the year 1919, when I inherited unexpectedly a valuable property under the will of my long dead great-grandmother Frances Anne, Marchioness of Londonderry, I was entirely dependent upon my own exertions. During all these twenty years I maintained myself, and later on my family, without ever lacking anything necessary to health or enjoyment. I am proud of this, and I commend my example to my son, indeed to all my children.

*　　*　　*　　*　　*

I decided to return to India at the end of November in order to prepare for the Polo Tournament in February. In the interval I found myself extremely well treated at home. My letters to the *Morning Post* had been read with wide attention. Everyone wanted to hear about the campaign and Omdurman and above all about the cavalry charge. I therefore often found myself at the dinner table, in the clubs or at Newmarket, which in those days I frequented, the centre of appreciative circles of listeners and inquirers much older than myself. There were also young ladies who took some interest in my prattle and affairs. The weeks therefore passed agreeably.

It was at this time that I met the group of new Conservative M.P.'s with whom I was afterwards to be much associated. Mr. Ian Malcolm invited me to a luncheon at which the other guests were Lord Hugh Cecil, Lord Percy (the elder brother of the late Duke of Northumberland) and Lord Balcarres (now Lord Crawford). These were the rising politicians of the Conservative Party; and many Parliaments have met without receiving such an accession to the strength and distinction of the assembly. They were all interested to see me, having heard of my activities, and also on account of my father's posthumous prestige. Naturally I was on my mettle, and not without envy in the presence of these young men only two or three years older than myself, all born with silver spoons in their mouths, all highly distinguished at Oxford or Cambridge, and all ensconced in safe Tory constituencies. I felt indeed I was the earthen pot among the brass.

Lord Hugh Cecil's intellectual gifts were never brighter than in the morning of life. Brought up for nearly twenty years in the house of a Prime Minister and Party Leader, he had heard from childhood the great questions of State discussed from the point of view of the responsible master of our affairs. The frankness and freedom with which the members of the Cecil family, male and female, talked and argued with each other were remarkable. Differences of opinion were encouraged; and repartee and rejoinder flashed to and fro between father and children, brother and sister, uncle and nephew, old and young, as if they were all on equal terms. Lord Hugh had already held the House of Commons rivetted in pin-drop silence for more than an hour while he discoursed on the government of an established church and the differences between Erastians and High Churchmen. He was an adept in every form of rhetoric or dialectic; and so quick, witty and unexpected in conversation that it was a delight to hear him.

Lord Percy, a thoughtful and romantic youth, an Irvingite by religion, of great personal charm and the highest academic achievement, had gained two years before the Newdigate Prize at Oxford for the best poem of the year. He had travelled widely in the highlands of Asia Minor and the Caucasus, feasting with princely barbarians and fasting with priestly fanatics. Over him the East exercised the spell it cast over Disraeli. He might, indeed, have stepped out of the pages of *Tancred* or *Coningsby*.

The conversation drifted to the issue of whether peoples have a right to *self* government or only to *good* government; what are the inherent rights of human beings and on what are they founded? From this we pushed on to Slavery as an institution. I was much surprised to find that

my companions had not the slightest hesitation in championing the unpopular side on all these issues; but what
surprised me still more, and even vexed me, was the difficulty I had in making plain my righteous and indeed obvious
point of view against their fallacious but most ingenious
arguments. They knew so much more about the controversy
and its possibilities than I did, that my bold broad generalities about liberty, equality and fraternity got seriously
knocked about. I entrenched myself around the slogan 'No
slavery under the Union Jack.' Slavery they suggested
might be right or wrong: the Union Jack was no doubt a
respectable piece of bunting: but what was the moral connection between the two? I had the same difficulty in discovering a foundation for the assertions I so confidently
made, as I have found in arguing with the people who contend that the sun is only a figment of our imagination. Indeed although I seemed to start with all the advantages, I
soon felt like going out into St. James's Street or Picadilly
and setting up without more ado a barricade and rousing a
mob to defend freedom, justice and democracy. However
at the end Lord Hugh said to me that I must not take such
discussions too seriously; that sentiments however worthy
required to be probed, and that he and his friends were not
really so much in favour of Slavery as an institution as I
might have thought. So it seemed that after all they were
only teasing me and making me gallop over ground which
they knew well was full of traps and pitfalls.

After this encounter I had the idea that I must go to
Oxford when I came back from India after the tournament.
I was I expect at this time capable of deriving both profit
and enjoyment from Oxford life and thought, and I began
to make inquiries about how to get there. It seemed that
there were, even for persons of riper years like myself,
Examinations, and that such formalities were indispensable.
I could not see why I should not have gone and paid my
fees and listened to the lectures and argued with the profes-

sors and read the books that they recommended. However, it appeared that this was impossible. I must pass examinations not only in Latin, but even in Greek. I could not contemplate toiling at Greek irregular verbs after having commanded British regular troops; so after much pondering I had to my keen regret to put the plan aside.

Early in November I paid a visit to the Central Offices of the Conservative Party at St. Stephen's Chambers, to inquire about finding a constituency. One of my more remote connections, Fitzroy-Stewart, had long worked there in an honorary capacity. He introduced me to the Party Manager, then Mr. Middleton, 'The Skipper' as he was called. Mr. Middleton was held in great repute because the Party had won the General Election of 1895. When parties lose elections through bad leadership or foolish policy or because of mere slackness and the swing of the pendulum, they always sack the party manager. So it is only fair that these functionaries should receive all the honours of success. 'The Skipper' was very cordial and complimentary. The Party would certainly find me a seat, and he hoped to see me in Parliament at an early date. He then touched delicately upon money matters. Could I pay my expenses, and how much a year could I afford to give to the constituency? I said I would gladly fight the battle, but I could not pay anything except my own personal expenses. He seemed rather damped by this, and observed that the best and safest constituencies always liked to have the largest contributions from their members. He instanced cases where as much as a thousand pounds a year or more was paid by the member in subscriptions and charities in return for the honour of holding the seat. Risky seats could not afford to be so particular, and 'Forlorn Hopes' were very cheap. However, he said he would do all he could, and that no doubt mine was an exceptional case on account of my father, and also he added on account of my experience at the wars, which would be popular with the Tory working-men.

On the way out I had another talk with Fitzroy-Stewart. My eye lighted upon a large book on his table on the cover of which was a white label bearing the inscription 'SPEAKERS WANTED.' I gazed upon this with wonder. Fancy that! Speakers were wanted and there was a bulky book of applications! Now I had always wanted to make a speech; but I had never on any occasion great or small been invited or indeed allowed to do so. There were no speeches in the 4th Hussars nor at Sandhurst either—if I might exclude one incident on which I was not concerned to dwell. So I said to Fitzroy-Stewart, 'Tell me about this. Do you mean to say there are a lot of meetings which *want* speakers?' 'Yes,' he replied; 'the Skipper told me I was not to let you go without getting something out of you. Can't I book you for one?' I was deeply agitated. On the one hand I felt immense eagerness; on the other the keenest apprehension. However, in life's steeplechase one must always jump the fences when they come. Regaining such composure as I could and assuming an indifference contrary to my feelings, I replied that perhaps if all the conditions were suitable and there was a real desire to hear me, I might be willing to accede to his request. He opened the book.

It appeared there were hundreds of indoor meetings and outdoor fêtes, of bazaars and rallies—all of which were clamant for speakers. I surveyed this prospect with the eye of an urchin looking through a pastrycook's window. Finally we selected Bath as the scene of my (official) maiden effort. It was settled that in ten days' time I should address a gathering of the Primrose League in a park, the property of a Mr. H. D. Skrine, situated on one of the hills overlooking that ancient city. I quitted the Central Office in suppressed excitement.

I was for some days in fear lest the plan should miscarry. Perhaps Mr. Skrine or the other local magnates would not want to have me, or had already found someone they liked better. However, all went well. I duly received a formal invitation and an announcement of the meeting appeared in the *Morning Post*. Oliver Borthwick now wrote that the *Morning Post* would send a special reporter to Bath to take down every word I said, and that the *Morning Post* would give it prominence. This heightened both my ardour and my nervousness. I spent many hours preparing my discourse and learning it so thoroughly by heart that I could almost have said it backwards in my sleep. I determined in defence of His Majesty's Government to adopt an aggressive and even a truculent mode. I was particularly pleased with one sentence which I coined, to the effect that 'England would gain far more from the rising tide of Tory Democracy than from the dried-up drainpipe of Radicalism.' I licked my chops over this and a good many others like it. These happy ideas, once they had begun to flow, seemed to come quite naturally. Indeed I very soon had enough to make several speeches. However, I had asked how long I ought to speak, and being told that about a quarter of an hour would do, I confined myself rigorously to 25 minutes. I found by repeated experiments with a stop-watch that I could certainly canter over the course in 20 minutes. This would leave time for interruptions. Above all one must not be hurried or flurried. One must not yield too easily to the weakness of audiences. There they were; what could they do? They had asked for it and they must have it.

The day arrived. I caught a train from Paddington. *There* was the reporter of the *Morning Post*, a companionable gentleman in a grey frock-coat. We travelled down together, and as we were alone in the carriage, I tried one or two tit-bits on him, as if they had arisen casually in conversation. We drove in a fly up the hills above Bath together. Mr. Skrine and his family received me hospitably. The fête was in progress throughout the grounds. There were cocoanut-shies and races and catchpenny shows of every kind. The weather was fine and everybody was enjoying themselves. Mindful of a former experience I inquired rather anxiously about the meeting. It was all right. At five o'clock they would ring a bell, and all these merrymakers would assemble at the mouth of a tent in which a platform had been erected. The Chairman of the Party in the district would introduce me. I was the only speaker apart from the votes of thanks.

Accordingly when the bell began to ring, we repaired to our tent and mounted the platform, which consisted of about four boards laid across some small barrels. There was neither table nor chair; but as soon as about a hundred persons had rather reluctantly, I thought, quitted their childish amusements in the park, the Chairman rose and in a brief speech introduced me to the audience. At Sandhurst and in the army compliments are few and far between, and flattery of subalterns does not exist. If you won the Victoria Cross or the Grand National Steeplechase or the Army Heavyweight Boxing Championship, you would only expect to receive from your friends warnings against having your head turned by your good luck. In politics it was apparently quite different. Here the butter was laid on with a trowel. I heard my father, who had been treated so scurvily, referred to in glowing terms as one of the greatest leaders the Conservatives had ever had. As for my adventures in Cuba, on the Indian frontier and up the Nile, I could only pray the regiment would never hear of what the Chairman said. When he descanted upon my 'bravery with the sword and brilliancy with the pen,' I feared that the audience would cry out 'Oh, rats!' or something similar. I was astonished and relieved to find that they lapped it all up as if it were gospel.

Then came my turn. Hardening my heart, summoning my resolution, I let off my speech. As I followed the well-worn grooves from stage to stage and point to point, I felt it was going quite well. The audience, which gradually increased in numbers, seemed delighted. They cheered a lot at all the right places when I paused on purpose to give them a chance, and even at others which I had not foreseen. At the end they clapped loudly and for quite a long time. So

I could do it after all! It seemed quite easy too. The reporter and I went home together. He had stood just in front
of me writing it down verbatim. He was warm in his congratulations, and the next day the *Morning Post* printed a
whole column, and even in addition, mark you, wrote an
appreciative leaderette upon the arrival of a new figure upon
the political scene. I began to be much pleased with myself
and with the world: and in this mood I sailed for India.

*   *   *   *   *

We have now to turn to other and more serious affairs.
All the officers of the regiment subscribed to send our polo
team to the tournament at Meerut. Thirty ponies under the
charge of a sergeant-major were embarked in a special train
for the 1,400-mile journey. Besides their *syces* they were
accompanied by a number of our most trustworthy non-commissioned officers including a farrier-sergeant, all under the
charge of a sergeant-major. The train covered about 200
miles a day, and every evening the ponies were taken out
rested and exercised. Thus they arrived at their destination
as fit as when they started. We travelled separately but arrived at the same time. We had arranged to play for a fortnight at Jodhpore before going to Meerut. Here we were
the guests of the famous Sir Pertab Singh. Sir Pertab was the
trusted regent of Jodhpore, as his nephew the Maharajah
was still a minor. He entertained us royally in his large,
cool, stone house. Every evening he and his young kinsmen,
two of whom, Hurji and Dokul Singh, were as fine polo-players as India has ever produced, with other Jodhpore nobles,
played us in carefully conducted instruction games. Old Pertab, who loved polo next to war more than anything in the
world, used to stop the game repeatedly and point out faults
or possible improvements in our play and combination. 'Faster,
faster, same like fly,' he would shout to increase the speed
of the game. The Jodhpore polo ground rises in great clouds
of red dust when a game is in progress. These clouds car-

ried to leeward on the strong breeze introduced a disturbing and somewhat dangerous complication. Turbanned figures emerged at full gallop from the dust-cloud, or the ball whistled out of it unexpectedly. It was difficult to follow the whole game, and one often had to play to avoid the dust-cloud. The Rajputs were quite used to it, and gradually it ceased to worry their guests.

The night before we were to leave Jodhpore for Meerut a grievous misfortune overtook me. Coming down to dinner, I slipped on the stone stairs and out went my shoulder. I got it put in again fairly easily, but the whole of the muscles were strained. By the next morning I had practically lost the use of my right arm. I knew from bitter experience that it would take three weeks or even more before I could hit a polo ball hard again, and even then it would only be under the precaution of having my elbow strapped to within a few inches of my side. The tournament was to begin in four days. The reader may well imagine my disappointment. My arm had been getting steadily stronger, and I had been playing No. 1 to the satisfaction of our team. Now I was a cripple. We luckily had a fifth man with us, so I told my friends when they picked me up, that they must take me out of the team. They considered this very gravely all the next day, and then our captain informed me that they had decided to play me in spite of everything. Even if I could not hit the ball at all and could only hold a stick in my hand, they thought that with my knowledge of the game and of our team-play I should give the best chance of success. After making sure that this decision had not been taken out of compassion but solely on its merits, I consented to do my best. In those days the off-side rule existed, and the No. 1 was engaged in a ceaseless duel with the opposing back who, turning and twisting his pony, always endeavoured to put his opponent off-side. If the No. 1 was able to occupy the back, ride him out of the game and hamper him at every turn, then he could serve his side far better than by overmuch hitting of the ball. We knew that Captain Hardress Lloyd, afterwards an international player against the United States, was the back and most formidable member of the 4th Dragoon Guards, the strongest team we should have to meet.

Accordingly with my elbow strapped tight to my side, holding a stick with many an ache and twinge, I played in the first two matches of the tournament. We were successful in both, and although I could only make a restricted contribution my friends seemed content. Our No. 2, Albert Savory, was a hard, brilliant hitter. I cleared the way for him. Polo is the prince of games because it combines all the pleasure of hitting the ball, which is the foundation of so many amusements, with all the pleasures of riding and horsemanship, and to both of these there is added that intricate, loyal team-work which is the essence of football or baseball, and which renders a true combination so vastly superior to the individuals of which it is composed.

The great day arrived. As we had foreseen we met the 4th Dragoon Guards in the Final. The match from the very first moment was severe and even. Up and down the hard, smooth Indian polo ground where the ball was very rarely missed and everyone knew where it should be hit to, we raced and tore. Quite soon we had scored one goal and our opponents two, and there the struggle hung in equipoise for some time. I never left the back, and being excellently mounted kept him very busy. Suddenly in the midst of a confused scrimmage close by the enemy goal, I saw the ball spin towards me. It was on my near side. I was able to lift the stick over and bending forward gave it a feeble forward tap. Through the goalposts it rolled. Two all! Apart from the crippled No. 1, we really had a very good team. Our captain, Reginald Hoare, who played No. 3, was not easily to be surpassed in India. Our back, Barnes, my companion in Cuba, was a rock, and almost unfailingly sent his strong back-handers to exactly the place where Savory was waiting for them with me to clear the way. For three years this contest had been the main preoccupation of our lives, and we had concentrated upon it every resource we possessed. Presently I had another chance. Again the ball came to me close to the hostile goal. This time it was travelling fast, and I had no more to do in one fleeting second than to stretch out my stick and send it rolling between the posts. Three to two! Then our opponents exerting themselves swept us down the ground and scored again. Three all!

I must explain that in Indian polo in those days, in order to avoid drawn matches, subsidiary goals could be scored. Half the width of the goalposts was laid off on either side by two small flags, and even if the goal were missed, a ball within these flags counted as a subsidiary. No number of subsidiaries equalled one goal, but when goals were equal, subsidiaries decided. Unfortunately our opponents had the best of us in subsidiaries. Unless we could score again we should lose. Once again fortune came to me, and I gave a little feeble hit at the ball among the ponies' hoofs, and for the third time saw it pass through the goal. This brought the 7th chukka to an end.

We lined up for the last period with 4 goals and 3 subsidiaries to our credit, our opponents having 3 goals and 4 subsidiaries. Thus if they got one more goal they would not merely tie, *but win the match outright*. Rarely have I seen such strained faces on both sides. You would not have thought it was a game at all, but a matter of life and death. Far graver crises cause less keen emotion. I do not remember anything of the last chukka except that as we galloped up and down the ground in desperate attack and counter-attack, I kept on thinking, 'Would God that night or Blücher would come.' They came in one of the most welcome sounds I have ever heard: the bell which ended the match, and enabled us to say as we sat streaming and exhausted on our ponies, 'We have won the Inter-Regimental Tournament of 1899.' Prolonged rejoicings, intense inward satisfaction, and nocturnal festivities from which the use of wine was not excluded, celebrated the victory. Do not grudge these young soldiers gathered from so many regiments their joy and sport. Few of that merry throng were destined to see old age. Our own team was never to play again. A year later Albert Savory was killed in the Transvaal, Barnes was grievously wounded in Natal, and I became a sedentary politician increasingly crippled by my wrenched shoulder. It was then or never for us; and never since has a cavalry regiment from Southern India gained the prize.

The regiment were very nice to me when eventually I departed for home, and paid me the rare compliment of drinking my health the last time I dined with them. What happy years I had had with them and what staunch friends one made! It was a grand school for anyone. Discipline and comradeship were the lessons it taught; and perhaps after all these are just as valuable as the lore of the universities. Still one would like to have both.

*　　*　　*　　*　　*

I had meanwhile been working continuously upon *The River War*. This work was extending in scope. From being a mere chronicle of the Omdurman campaign, it grew backwards into what was almost a history of the ruin and rescue of the Soudan. I read scores of books, indeed everything that had been published upon the subject; and I now planned a couple of fat volumes. I affected a combination of the styles of Macaulay and Gibbon, the staccato antitheses of the former and the rolling sentences and genitival endings of the latter; and I stuck in a bit of my own from time to time. I began to see that writing, especially narrative, was not only an affair of sentences, but of paragraphs. Indeed I thought the paragraph no less important than the sentence. Macaulay is a master of paragraphing. Just as the sentence contains one idea in all its fullness, so the paragraph should embrace a distinct episode; and as sentences should follow one another in harmonious sequence, so the paragraphs must fit on to one another like the automatic couplings of railway carriages. Chapterisation also began to dawn upon me. Each chapter must be self-contained. All the chapters should be of equal value and more or less of equal length. Some chapters define themselves naturally and obviously; but much more difficulty arises when a number of heterogeneous incidents none of which can be omitted have to be woven together into what looks like an integral theme. Finally the work must be surveyed as a whole and due proportion and strict order established from beginning to end. I already knew that chronology is the key to easy narrative. I already realised that 'good sense is the foundation of good writing.' I warned myself against the fault of beginning my story as some poor people do 'Four thousand years before the Deluge,' and I repeated earnestly one of my best French quotations, 'L'art d'être ennuyeux, c'est de tout dire.' I think I will repeat it again now.

It was great fun writing a book. One lived with it. It became a companion. It built an impalpable crystal sphere around one of interests and ideas. In a sense one felt like a goldfish in a bowl; but in this case the goldfish made his own bowl. This came along everywhere with me. It never got knocked about in travelling, and there was never a moment when agreeable occupation was lacking. Either the glass had to be polished, or the structure extended or contracted, or the walls required strengthening. I have noticed in my life deep resemblances between many different kinds of things. Writing a book is not unlike building a house or planning a battle or painting a picture. The technique is different, the materials are different, but the principle is the same. The foundations have to be laid, the data assembled, and the premises must bear the weight of their conclusions. Ornaments or refinements may then be added. The whole when finished is only the successful presentation of a theme. In battles however the other fellow interferes all the time and keeps upsetting things, and the best generals are those who arrive at the results of planning without being tied to plans.

On my homeward steamer I made friends with the most brilliant man in journalism I have ever met. Mr. G. W. Steevens was the 'star' writer of a certain Mr. Harmsworth's new paper called the *Daily Mail* which had just broken upon the world, and had forced the *Daily Telegraph* to move one step nearer Victorian respectability. Harmsworth relied enormously upon Steevens in these early critical days, and being well disposed to me, told him later on to write me up, which he did in his glowing fashion. 'Boom the Boomsters' was in those days the motto of the infant Harmsworth press, and on these grounds I was selected for their favours. But I anticipate.

I was working in the saloon of the Indiaman, and had reached an exciting point in my story. The Nile column had just by a forced night march reached Abu Hamed and was about to storm it. I was setting the scene in my most cere- monious style. 'The dawn was breaking and the mists, rising from the river and dispersing with the coming of the sun, revealed the outlines of the Dervish town and the half circle of rocky hills behind it. Within this stern amphitheatre one of the minor dramas of war was now to be enacted.' 'Ha! ha!' said Steevens, suddenly peering over my shoulder. 'Fin- ish it yourself then,' I said getting up; and I went on deck. I was curious to see how he would do it, and indeed I hoped for a valuable contribution. But when I came down again I found that all he had written on my nice sheet of paper was 'Pop-pop! pop-pop! Pop! Pop!' in his tiny handwrit- ing, and then at the bottom of the page printed in big letters 'BANG!!!' I was disgusted at this levity. But Steevens had many other styles besides that of the jaunty, breezy, slap- dash productions which he wrote for the *Daily Mail*. About this time there had appeared an anonymous article upon the future of the British Empire called 'The New Gibbon.' One would have thought it had been lifted bodily from the pages of the Roman historian. I was astounded when Steevens confessed himself the author.

Later on Steevens was kind enough to read my proofs and offer valuable advice which I transcribe. 'The parts of the book I have read,' he wrote, 'appear to me to be a valuable supplement to the works of G. W. Steevens, indeed, a valuable work altogether. I think it first rate, sound, well got up and put together, and full of most illuminating and descriptive pages. The only criticism I should make is that your philosophic reflections, while generally well expressed, often acute and sometimes true, are too devilish frequent. If I were you I should cut out the philosopher about January 1898, giving him perhaps a short innings at the very end. He will only bore people. Those who want such reflections can often supply them without assistance.' His gay, mocking spirit and rippling wit made him a delightful companion, and our acquaintance ripened into friendship during the summer months of 1899. This was the last summer he was to see. He died of typhoid fever in Ladysmith in the following February.

*　　　*　　　*　　　*　　　*

I paused in Cairo for a fortnight to collect materials for my book and enlist the co-operation of several important actors in the Soudan drama. In this way I met Girouard, the young Canadian Royal Engineer who had built the desert railway; Slatin Pasha, the little Austrian officer who had been ten years the Khalifa's prisoner and whose book *Fire and Sword in the Soudan* is a classic in its sphere; Sir Reginald Wingate, head of the Intelligence, to whom I was already indebted for an important meal; Garstin, head of the Egyptian Irrigation Service; together with a number of the leading Egyptian statesmen and personalities. All these able men had played their part in the measures of war and administration which in less than twenty years had raised Egypt from anarchy, bankruptcy and defeat to triumphant prosperity. I already knew their Chief, Lord Cromer. He invited me to visit him at the British Agency, and readily undertook to read my chapters on the liberation of the Soudan and Gordon's death, which I had already completed. Accordingly I sent him a bulky bundle of typescript, and was delighted and also startled to receive it back a few days later slashed about with blue pencil with a vigour which recalled the treatment my Latin exercises used to meet with at Harrow. I saw that Lord Cromer had taken an immense amount of trouble over my screed, and I therefore submitted dutifully to his comments and criticisms, which were often full and sometimes scathing. For instance I had written about General Gordon becoming private secretary to Lord Ripon at one period in his career 'the brilliant sun had become the satellite of a farthing dip.' On this Lord Cromer's comment was ' "brilliant sun" appears to be extravagant eulogy and "farthing dip" does less than justice to Lord Ripon's position as Viceroy. Lord Ripon would not mind, but his friends might be angry and most people would simply laugh at you.' I wrote back to say I was sacrificing this gem of which till then I had thought so highly, and I also accepted a great many other strictures in a spirit of becoming meekness. This disarmed and placated Lord Cromer, who continued to take a friendly interest in my work. He wrote 'My remarks were, I know, severe, and it is very sensible of you to take them in the spirit in which they were intended—which was distinctly friendly. I did for you what I have over and over again asked others to do for myself. I *always* invite criticism from friends before I write or do anything important. It is very much better to have one's weak points indicated by friendly critics before one acts, rather than by hostile critics when it is too late to alter. I hope your book will be a success and I think it will. One of the very few things which still interest me in life is to see young men get on.'

I saw Lord Cromer repeatedly during this fortnight and profited to the full by his knowledge and wisdom. He represented in an intense degree that phlegm and composure which used to be associated with high British administrators in the East. I was reminded of one of my best French quotations 'On ne règne sur les âmes que par le calme.' He was never in a hurry, never anxious to make an effect or sensation. He sat still and men came to him. He watched events until their combination enabled him to intervene smoothly and decisively. He could wait a year as easily as a week, and he had often waited four or five years before getting his way. He had now reigned in Egypt for nearly sixteen years. He rejected all high-sounding titles; he remained simply the British Agent. His status was indefinite; he might be nothing; he was in fact everything. His word was law. Working through a handful of brilliant lieutenants, who were mostly young and who, like their Chief, had trained themselves to keep in the background, Cromer controlled with minute and patient care every department of the Egyptian administration and every aspect of its policy. British and Egyptian Governments had come and gone; he had seen the Soudan lost and reconquered. He had maintained a tight hold upon the purse strings and a deft control of the whole movement of Egyptian politics. It was very pleasant to see him thus with his life's work shining around him, the embodiment of supreme power without pomp or apparent effort. I felt honoured by the consideration with which he treated me. We do not see his like nowadays, though our need is grave.

CHAPTER XVII

OLDHAM

IN the Spring of 1899 I became conscious of the fact that there was another Winston Churchill who also wrote books; apparently he wrote novels, and very good novels too, which achieved an enormous circulation in the United States. I received from many quarters congratulations on my skill as a writer of fiction. I thought at first these were due to a belated appreciation of the merits of *Savrola*. Gradually I realised that there was 'another Richmond in the field,' luckily on the other side of the Atlantic. I proceeded to indite my trans-Atlantic double a letter which with his answer is perhaps a literary curiosity.

LONDON,
June 7, 1899.

Mr. Winston Churchill presents his compliments to Mr. Winston Churchill, and begs to draw his attention to a matter which concerns them both. He has learnt from the Press notices that Mr. Winston Churchill proposes to bring out another novel, entitled *Richard Carvel*, which is certain to have a considerable sale both in England and America. Mr. Winston Churchill is also the author of a novel now being published in serial form in *Macmillan's Magazine*, and for which he anticipates some sale both in England and America. He also proposes to publish on the 1st of October another military chronicle on the Soudan War. He has no doubt that Mr. Winston Churchill will recognise from this letter—if indeed by no other means—that there is grave danger of his works being mistaken for those of Mr. Winston Churchill. He feels sure that Mr. Winston Churchill desires this as little as he does himself. In future to avoid mistakes as far as possible, Mr. Winston Churchill has decided to sign all published articles, stories, or other works, 'Winston Spencer Churchill,' and not 'Winston Churchill' as formerly. He trusts that this arrangement will commend itself to Mr. Winston Churchill, and he ventures to suggest, with a view to preventing further confusion which may arise out of this extraordinary coincidence, that both Mr. Winston Churchill and Mr. Winston Churchill should insert a short note in their respective publications explaining to the public which are the works of Mr. Winston Churchill and which those of Mr. Winston Churchill. The text of this note might form a subject for future discussion if Mr. Winston Churchill agrees with Mr. Winston Churchill's proposition. He takes this occasion of complimenting Mr. Winston Churchill upon the style and success of his works, which are always brought to his notice whether in magazine or book form, and he trusts that Mr. Winston Churchill has derived equal pleasure from any work of his that may have attracted his attention.

WINDSOR, VERMONT.
June 21, 1899.

Mr. Winston Churchill is extremely grateful to Mr. Winston Churchill for bringing forward a subject which has given Mr. Winston Churchill much anxiety. Mr. Winston Churchill appreciates the courtesy of Mr. Winston Churchill in adopting the name of 'Winston Spencer Churchill' in his books, articles, etc. Mr. Winston Churchill makes haste to add that, had he possessed any other names, he would certainly have adopted one of them. The writings of Mr. Winston Spencer Churchill (henceforth so called) have been brought to Mr. Winston Churchill's notice since the publication of his first story in the 'Century.' It did not seem then to Mr. Winston Churchill that the works of Mr. Winston Spencer Churchill would conflict in any way with his own attempts at fiction.

The proposal of Mr. Winston Spencer Churchill to affix

a note to the separate writings of Mr. Winston Spencer Churchill and Mr. Winston Churchill, the text of which is to be agreed on between them,—is quite acceptable to Mr. Winston Churchill. If Mr. Winston Spencer Churchill will do him the favour of drawing up this note, there is little doubt that Mr. Winston Churchill will acquiesce in its particulars.

Mr. Winston Churchill moreover, is about to ask the opinion of his friends and of his publishers as to the advisability of inserting the words 'The American,' after his name on the title-page of his books. Should this seem wise to them, he will request his publishers to make the change in future editions.

Mr. Winston Churchill will take the liberty of sending Mr. Winston Churchill copies of the two novels he has written. He has a high admiration for the works of Mr. Winston Spencer Churchill and is looking forward with pleasure to reading *Savrola.*

All was settled amicably, and by degrees the reading public accommodated themselves to the fact that there had arrived at the same moment two different persons of the same name who would from henceforward minister copiously to their literary, or if need be their political requirements. When a year later I visited Boston, Mr. Winston Churchill was the first to welcome me. He entertained me at a very gay banquet of young men, and we made each other complimentary speeches. Some confusion however persisted; all my mails were sent to his address and the bill for the dinner came in to me. I need not say that both these errors were speedily redressed.

* * * * *

One day I was asked to go to the House of Commons by a Mr. Robert Ascroft, Conservative member for Oldham. He took me down to the smoking-room and opened to me an important project. Oldham is a two-member constituency, and at this time the Conservatives held both seats. Ascroft the senior member had a strong position, as he was not only supported by the Conservative electors, but was also the tried and trusted solicitor for the Oldham Cotton Operatives Trade Unions. It appeared that his colleague had been for some time ailing, and Mr. Ascroft was on the look-out for some one to run in double harness with him. He evidently thought I should do. He made some sensible remarks. 'Young people' he said 'very often do not have as much money as older ones.' I knew nothing to enable me to contradict this painful fact. He seemed to think, however, that all obstacles could be surmounted, and I agreed to come down at an early date and address a meeting at Oldham under his auspices.

Some weeks passed—and the date of this meeting was already fixed, when to my regret the newspapers reported Mr. Ascroft's sudden death. It seemed strange that he, so strong and busy, seeming perfectly well, should flash away like this, while the colleague whose health had caused him so much anxiety, survived. Robert Ascroft was greatly respected by the Oldham working folk. They made a subscription of more than £2,000, the bulk collected in very small sums, to set up a statue to him as 'The Workers' Friend.' They stipulated—and I thought it characteristic of these Lancashire operatives—that the money was not to go to anything useful; no beds at a hospital, no extensions to a library, no fountain even, just a memorial. They did not want, they said, to give a present to themselves.

The vacancy now had to be filled, and they immediately pitched on me. I had been, it was said, virtually selected by the late honoured member. My name was already on the hoardings to address a meeting. Add to this my father's memory, and the case was complete. I received straight away without ever suing, or asking, or appearing before any committee, a formal invitation to contest the seat. At the

Conservative Central Office the 'Skipper' seemed quite content with the local decision, but he urged that advantage should be taken of the by-election to vacate both seats at the same time. In his view the Government was not at that moment in a good position to win Lancashire by-elections. They did not want to have a second vacancy at Oldham in a few months' time. Lord Salisbury could afford to be indifferent to the loss of a couple of seats. Better to lose them both now and have done with Oldham till the general election, when they could win them back. The significance of this attitude was not lost upon me. But in those days any political fight in any circumstances seemed to me better than no fight at all. I therefore unfurled my standard and advanced into the battle.

I now plunged into a by-election attended by the fullest publicity attaching to such episodes. I have fought up to the present fourteen contested elections, which take about a month of one's life apiece. It is melancholy, when one reflects upon our brief span, to think that no less than fourteen months of life have been passed in this wearing clatter. By-elections, of which I have had five, are even worse than ordinary elections because all the cranks and faddists of the country and all their associates and all the sponging, 'uplift' organisations fasten upon the wretched candidate. If he is a supporter of the administration, all the woes of the world, all the shortcomings of human society in addition are laid upon him, and he is vociferously urged to say what he is going to do about them.

In this case the Unionist administration was beginning to be unpopular. The Liberals had been out of office long enough for the electors to want a change. Democracy does not favour continuity. The Englishman will not, except on great occasions, be denied the indulgence of kicking out the Ministers of the Crown whoever they are and of reversing their policy whatever it is. I sailed out therefore upon an adverse tide. Moreover at that time the Conservatives were passing through the House of Commons a Tithes Bill making things a little easier for the poor clergy in the Church of England. The Nonconformists including the Wesleyans who were very influential in Lancashire could not be expected to feel much enthusiasm for this. The Radicals, quite shameless in their mockery, went so far as to describe this benevolent measure as 'The Clerical Doles Bill.' I need scarcely say that until I reached Oldham my heart had never bounded to any aspect of this controversy. Neither my education nor my military experiences had given me the slightest inkling of the passions which such a question could arouse. I therefore asked what it was all about. Most of my leading supporters seemed to agree with the Radicals in thinking the Clerical Doles Bill was a great mistake. As soon as they had explained the issues to me, I saw a solution. Of course the clergy ought to be kept up properly. How could they maintain their position, if they were not? But why not keep them all up equally, as we should do in the Army? Measure each religion according to its congregation, lump them together, and divide the extra money equally among them! This was fair, logical, reverent and conciliatory. I was surprised no one had thought of it before. But when I unfolded this plan to some of my committee, no one seemed to think it would meet the case. In fact they said it was no good at all. If everyone felt this, it was certainly true. So I dropped my eirenicon of concurrent endowment, and looked for other topics on which to woo what was then almost the largest constituency in the island.

At this point I was joined by my new colleague in the fight. His accession was deemed to be a master stroke of the Central Office. He was none other than Mr. James Mawdsley, a Socialist and the much respected secretary of the Operative Spinners' Association. Mr. Mawdsley was the most genuine specimen of the Tory working-man candidate I have ever come across. He boldly proclaimed admiration of Tory democracy and even of Tory Socialism. Both parties he declared were hypocritical, but the Liberals were the worse. He for his part was proud to stand upon the platform with a 'scion' of the ancient British aristocracy in the cause of the working people who knew him so well and had trusted him so long. I was much attracted by this development, and for some days it seemed successful. The partnership of 'The Scion and the Socialist' seemed a splendid new orientation of politics. Unhappily the offensive and disagreeable Radicals went about spoiling this excellent impression. They were aided by a lot of sulky fellows among the Trade Unionists. These accused poor Mr. Mawdsley of deserting his class. They were very rude about the Conservative party. They did not even stop short of being disrespectful about Lord Salisbury, going so far as to say he was not progressive, and out of harmony with modern democratic sentiment. We of course repudiated these calumnies. In the end however all the Liberal and Radical Trade Unionists went off and voted for their party, and we were left with our own strong supporters rather upset by the appearance of a wicked Socialist on their platforms.

Meanwhile our two opponents the Liberal champions proved themselves men of quality and mark. The senior, Mr. Emmott, came from a family which had driven many thousand spindles in Oldham for generations. Wealthy, experienced, in the prime of life, woven into the texture of the town, with abilities which afterwards raised him to high official rank, and at the head of the popular party in opposition to the Government, he was an antagonist not easily to be surpassed. The junior, Mr. Runciman, then a young and engaging figure, able, impeccable and very wealthy, was also a candidate of exceptional merit. My poor Trade Unionist friend and I would have had very great difficulty in finding £500 between us, yet we were accused of representing the vested interests of society, while our opponents, who were certainly good for a quarter of a million, claimed to champion in generous fashion the causes of the poor and needy. A strange inversion!

The fight was long and hard. I defended the virtues of the Government, the existing system of society, the Established Church and the unity of the Empire. 'Never before' I declared 'were there so many people in England, and never before had they had so much to eat.' I spoke of the vigour and the strength of Britain, of the liberation of the Soudan and of the need to keep out the foreign goods made by prison labour. Mr. Mawdsley followed suit. Our opponents deplored the misery of the working masses, the squalor of the slums, the glaring contrast between riches and poverty, and in particular, indeed above all, the iniquities of the Clerical Doles Bill. The contest would have been most uneven, but for the uncanny gift which the Lancashire working folk possess of balancing up the pros and cons of those who seek their votes. They apply all sorts of correctives to the obvious inequalities of the game. I delivered harangues from morning till night, and Mr. Mawdsley continued steadily to repeat his slogan that the Liberals were undoubtedly more hypocritical than the Tories.

Oldham is a purely working-class constituency, and was in those days an extremely prosperous community. Not only did they spin cotton goods for India, China and Japan, but in addition they made at the great works of Asa Lees the machinery which was ultimately to enable India, China and Japan to spin these cotton goods for themselves. There was no hotel in the town where one could hope to sleep, and few wealthy houses; but there were many thousands of contented working-class homes where for more than half a century things had been getting slowly and surely better. They were rising in the scale of prosperity, with woollen shawls over the girls' heads, wooden clogs on their feet, and barefoot children. I have lived to see them falling back in the world's affairs, but still at a level far superior to that which they then deemed prosperity. In those days the saying was 'clogs to clogs in four generations': the first makes the money, the second increases it, the third squanders it, and the fourth returns to the mill. I lived to see them disturbed because of a tax on silk stockings, with a style of life in my early days unknown, and yet gripped in the ever-narrowing funnel of declining trade and vanished ascendancy. No one can come in close contact with the working folk of Lancashire without wishing them well.

Half-way through the election all my principal supporters besought me to throw over the Clerical Doles Bill. As I was ignorant of the needs which had inspired it and detached from the passions which it aroused, the temptation to discard it was very great. I yielded to the temptation. Amid the enthusiastic cheers of my supporters I announced that, if returned, I would not vote for the measure. This was a frightful mistake. It is not the slightest use defending Governments or parties unless you defend the very worst thing about which they are attacked. At the moment I made my declaration the most vehement debates were taking place upon this Bill. At Westminster the Government were taunted with the fact that their own chosen candidate could not face a Lancashire electorate upon the issue, and at Oldham the other side, stimulated by my admission, redoubled their attacks upon the Bill. Live and learn! I think I may say without conceit that I was in those days a pretty good candidate. At any rate we had real enthusiasm on our side, and it rejoiced my heart to see these masses of working people who ardently, and for no material advantage, asserted their pride in our Empire and their love for the ancient traditions of the realm. However, when the votes were counted we were well beaten. In a poll of about 23,000 votes—then as big as was known in England—I was 1,300 behind and Mr. Mawdsley about 30 lower.

Then came the recriminations which always follow every kind of defeat. Everyone threw the blame on me. I have noticed that they nearly always do. I suppose it is because

they think I shall be able to bear it best. The high Tories
and the Carlton Club said 'Serve him right for standing
with a Socialist. No man of any principle would have done
such a thing!' Mr. Balfour, then leader of the House of
Commons, on hearing that I had declared against his Clerical Tithes Bill, said in the Lobby, quite justifiably I must
admit, 'I thought he was a young man of promise, but it
appears he is a young man of promises.' Party newspapers
wrote leading articles to say what a mistake it was to entrust
the fighting of great working-class constituencies to young
and inexperienced candidates, and everyone then made haste
to pass away from a dismal incident. I returned to London
with those feelings of deflation which a bottle of champagne
or even soda-water represents when it has been half emptied
and left uncorked for a night.

No one came to see me on my return to my mother's
house. However Mr. Balfour, always loyal and comprehending, wrote me a letter—every word in his own hand-
writing—which I have just unearthed from my most ancient
archives.

10.7.99.

I was very sorry to hear of your ill success at Oldham,
as I had greatly hoped to see you speedily in the House
where your father and I fought many a good battle side
by side in days gone by. I hope however you will not be
discouraged by what has taken place. For many reasons
this is a very unpropitious time to fight by-elections. At
by-elections the opposition can safely entrench themselves
behind criticism and are not driven to put a rival programme
in the field. This is at all times an advantage; it is doubly
an advantage when the rival programme would have to
include so unpromising an item as Home Rule. Moreover
opposition criticism falls just now upon willing ears. The
employers dislike the compensation bill; the doctors dislike
the vaccination bill; the general public dislike the clergy, so

the rating bill is unpopular: the clergy resented your repudiation of the bill: the Orangemen are sulky and refuse to be conciliated even by the promise to vote for the Liverpool proposals. Of course those benefited by our measures are not grateful, while those who suppose themselves to be injured resent them. Truly unpromising conditions under which to fight a Lancashire seat!

Never mind, it will all come right; and this small reverse will have no permanent ill effect upon your political fortunes.

At the end of this July I had a good long talk with Mr. Chamberlain. Although I had several times met him at my father's house, and he had greeted me on other occasions in a most kindly manner, this was the first time I really made his acquaintance. We were both the guests of my friend, Lady Jeune. She had a pleasant house upon the Thames: and in the afternoon we cruised along the river in a launch. Unlike Mr. Asquith, who never talked 'shop' out of business hours if he could help it, Mr. Chamberlain was always ready to discuss politics. He was most forthcoming and at the same time startlingly candid and direct. His conversation was a practical political education in itself. He knew every detail, every turn and twist of the game, and understood deeply the moving forces at work in both the great parties, of whose most aggressive aspirations he had in turn been the champion. In the main both in the launch and afterwards at dinner the conversation lay between us. South Africa had begun again to be a growing topic. The negotiations with President Kruger about the delicate, deadly question of suzerainty were gradually engaging national and indeed world attention. The reader may be sure I was keen that a strong line should be taken, and I remember Mr. Chamberlain saying, 'It is no use blowing the trumpet for the charge and then looking around to find nobody following.' Later we passed an old man seated upright in his chair on a lawn at the brink of the river. Lady Jeune said, 'Look, there is Labouchere.' 'A bundle of old rags!' was Mr. Chamberlain's comment as he turned his head away from his venomous political opponent. I was struck by the expression of disdain and dislike which passed swiftly but with intensity across his face. I realised as by a lightning flash, how stern were the hatreds my famous, agreeable, vivacious companion had contracted and repaid in his quarrel with the Liberal party and Mr. Gladstone.

For the rest I was plunged in *The River War*. All the hard work was done and I was now absorbed in the delightful occupation of playing with the proofs. Being now free from military discipline, I was able to write what I thought about Lord Kitchener without fear, favour or affection, and I certainly did so. I had been scandalised by his desecration of the Mahdi's Tomb and the barbarous manner in which he had carried off the Mahdi's head in a kerosene-can as a trophy. There had already been a heated debate in Parliament upon this incident, and I found myself sympathising in the gallery with the attacks which John Morley and Mr. C. P. Scott, the austere editor of the *Manchester Guardian*, had launched against the general. The Mahdi's head was just one of those trifles about which an immense body of rather gaseous feeling can be generated. All the Liberals were outraged by an act which seemed to them worthy of the Huns and Vandals. All the Tories thought it rather a lark. So here was I already out of step.

We planned to publish about the middle of October, and I was already counting the days till the two massive volumes, my *Magnum Opus* (up to date), upon which I had lavished a whole year of my life, should be launched upon an expectant public.

But when the middle of October came, we all had other things to think about.

CHAPTER XVIII

WITH BULLER TO THE CAPE

GREAT quarrels, it has been said, often arise from small occasions but never from small causes. The immediate preliminaries of the South African War were followed throughout England, and indeed the whole world, with minute attention. The long story of the relations of Briton and Boer since Majuba Hill, and the still longer tale of misunderstandings which had preceded that ill-omened episode, were familiar to wide publics. Every step in the negotiations and dispute of 1899 was watched with unceasing vigilance and debated in the sharpest challenge by the Opposition in the House of Commons. As the months of the summer and autumn passed, the dividing line in British politics was drawn between those who felt that war with the Boer Republics was necessary and inevitable and those who were resolved by every effort of argument, patience and prevision to prevent it.

The summer months were sultry. The atmosphere gradually but steadily became tense, charged with electricity, laden with the presage of storm. Ever since the Jameson raid three years before, the Transvaal had been arming heavily. A well-armed Police held the Outlanders in strict subjection, and German engineers were tracing the outlines of a fort overlooking Johannesburg to dominate the city with its artillery. Cannon, ammunition, rifles streamed in from Holland and Germany in quantities sufficient not only to equip the populations of the two Boer Republics, but to arm a still larger number of the Dutch race throughout the Cape Colony. Threatened by rebellion as well as war, the British Government slowly increased its garrisons in Natal and at the Cape. Meanwhile notes and dispatches of ever-deepening gravity, between Downing Street and Pretoria, succeeded one another in a sombre chain.

Suddenly in the early days of October the bold, daring men who directed the policy of the Transvaal resolved to bring the issue to a head. An ultimatum requiring the withdrawal of the British forces from the neighbourhood of the Republican frontiers, and the arrest of further reinforcements, was telegraphed from Pretoria on the 8th. The notice allowed before its expiry was limited to three days. And from that moment war was certain.

The Boer ultimatum had not ticked out on the tape machines for an hour before Oliver Borthwick came to offer me an appointment as principal War Correspondent of the *Morning Post.* £250 a month, all expenses paid, entire discretion as to movements and opinions, four months' minimum guarantee of employment—such were the terms; higher, I think, than any previously paid in British journalism to War Correspondents, and certainly attractive to a young man of twenty-four with no responsibilities but to earn his own living. The earliest steamer, the *Dunottar Castle,* sailed on the 11th, and I took my passage forthwith.

Preparations made in joyous expectation occupied my few remaining hours at home. London seethed with patriotic excitement and fierce Party controversy. In quick succession there arrived the news that the Boers themselves had taken the initiative and that their forces were advancing both towards the Cape Colony and Natal, that General Sir Redvers Buller had become the British Commander-in-Chief, that the Reserves were called out, and that our only Army Corps was to be sent at once to Table Bay.

I thought I would try to see Mr. Chamberlain before I sailed. Busy though the Minister was, he gave me rendezvous at the Colonial Office; and when I was unable to get there in time, he sent me a message to come to his house at Prince's Gardens early the next morning. There accordingly

I visited this extraordinary man at one of the most fateful moments in his public career. He was as usual smoking a cigar. He presented me with another. We talked for about ten minutes on the situation, and I explained what I was going to do. Then he said, 'I must go to the Colonial Office. You may drive with me, and we can talk on the way.'

In those days it took a quarter of an hour to drive in a hansom-cab from Prince's Gardens to Whitehall. I would not have had the journey shortened for anything. Mr. Chamberlain was most optimistic about the probable course of the war.

'Buller,' he said, 'may well be too late. He would have been wiser to have gone out earlier. Now, if the Boers invade Natal, Sir George White with his sixteen thousand men may easily settle the whole thing.'

'What about Mafeking?' I asked.

'Ah, Mafeking, that may be besieged. But if they cannot hold out for a few weeks, what is one to expect?'

Then he added prudently, 'Of course I have to base myself on the War Office opinion. They are all quite confident. I can only go by what they say.'

The British War Office of those days was the product of two generations of consistent House of Commons parsimony, unbroken by any serious call. So utterly unrelated to the actual facts were its ideas at this time that to an Australian request to be allowed to send a contingent of troops, the only reply was, 'Unmounted men preferred.' Nevertheless their own Intelligence Branch which lived in a separate building had prepared two volumes on the Boer Republics—afterwards presented to Parliament—which gave most full and accurate information. Sir John Ardagh, the head of this branch, told Lord Lansdowne, the Secretary of State for War, that 200,000 men would be required. His views were scouted; and the two volumes sent to Buller were returned within an hour with the message that he 'knew everything about South Africa.' Mr. George Wyndham, the Under Secretary of State, who dined with me one of these nights, alone seemed to appreciate the difficulties and magnitude of the task. The Boers, he said, were thoroughly prepared and acting on definite plans. They had large quantities of munitions, including a new form of heavy Maxim firing 1-inch shells. (This we afterwards learned to know quite well as the *Pompom*.) He thought that the opening of the campaign might be unpleasant, that the British forces might be attacked in detail, that they might be surrounded here and there by a far more mobile foe, and having been brought to a standstill, might be pounded to pieces with these same 1-inch Maxims. I must confess that in the ardour of youth I was much relieved to learn that the war would not be entirely one-sided or peter out in a mere parade of demonstration. I thought it very sporting of the Boers to take on the whole British Empire, and I felt quite glad they were not defenceless and had put themselves in the wrong by making preparations.

Let us learn our lessons. Never, never, never believe any war will be smooth and easy, or that anyone who embarks on the strange voyage can measure the tides and hurricanes he will encounter. The Statesman who yields to war fever must realise that once the signal is given, he is no longer the master of policy but the slave of unforeseeable and uncontrollable events. Antiquated War Offices, weak, incompetent or arrogant Commanders, untrustworthy allies, hostile neutrals, malignant Fortune, ugly surprises, awful miscalculations—all take their seats at the Council Board on the morrow of a declaration of war. Always remember, however sure you are that you can easily win, that there would not be a war if the other man did not think he also had a chance.

      *   *   *   *   *

One of my father's oldest friends, Billy Gerard, had some years before extracted a promise from Sir Redvers Buller (as I had done from Sir Bindon Blood) that, if ever that general received the command of an army in the field, he would take him on his staff. Lord Gerard was now an elderly man, of great wealth, extremely well known in society and one of the leading owners on the Turf. His approaching departure for the front was made the occasion of a dinner given by Sir Ernest Cassel in his honour at the Carlton Hotel. I was associated as a second string in this demonstration. The Prince of Wales and about forty men of the ruling generation formed a powerful and a merry company. Gerard's function was to look after the personal comfort of the Commander-in-Chief, and for this purpose he was presented at the dinner with I do not know how many cases of the very best champagne and the very oldest brandy which the cellars of London boasted. He was informed by the donors that he was to share these blessings freely with me whenever opportunity arose. Everyone was in that mood of gaiety and heartiness which so often salutes an outbreak of war. One of our company who was also starting for the front had from time to time in his past life shown less self-control in the use of alcohol than is to be desired. Indeed he had become a byword. As he rose to leave us, Lord Marcus Beresford said with great earnestness "Good-bye, old man, mind the V.C." To this our poor friend, deeply moved, replied "I'll do my best to win it." "Ah!" said Lord Marcus, "you are mistaken, I did not mean that, I meant the Vieux Cognac."

I may here add that these cases of champagne and brandy and my share in them fell among the many disappointments of war. In order to make sure that they reached the headquarters intact, Lord Gerard took the precaution of labelling them 'Castor Oil.' Two months later in Natal, when they had not yet arrived, he despatched an urgent telegram to the base at Durban asking for his castor oil. The reply came back that the packages of this drug addressed to His Lordship had by an error already been issued to the hospitals. There were now, however, ample stores of castor oil available at the base and the Commandant was forwarding a full supply forthwith!

Many of our South African experiences were to be upon a similar plane.

The *Dunottar Castle* sailed from Southampton on October 11, the day of the expiry of the Boer ultimatum. It did not only carry the Correspondent of the *Morning Post* and his fortunes; Sir Redvers Buller and the entire Headquarters Staff of our one (and only) organized army corps were also on its passenger list. Buller was a characteristic British personality. He looked stolid. He said little, and what he said was obscure. He was not the kind of man who could explain things, and he never tried to do so. He usually grunted, or nodded, or shook his head, in serious discussions; and shop of all kinds was sedulously excluded from his ordinary conversation. He had shown himself a brave and skilful officer in his youth, and for nearly twenty years he had filled important administrative posts of a sedentary character in Whitehall. As his political views were coloured with Liberalism, he was regarded as a very sensible soldier. His name had long been before the public; and with all these qualities it is no wonder that their belief in him was unbounded. 'My confidence,' said Lord Salisbury at the Guildhall, on November 9, 1899, 'in the British soldier is only equalled by my confidence in Sir Redvers Buller.' Certainly he was a man of a considerable scale. He plodded on from blunder to blunder and from one disaster to another, without losing either the regard of his country or the trust of his troops, to whose feeding as well as his own he paid serious attention. Independent, portentous, a man of the world, and a man of affairs—he gave the same sort of impression to the British at this juncture as we afterwards saw effected on the French nation through the personality of General Joffre.

While the issues of peace and war seemed to hang in their last flickering balance, and before a single irrevocable shot had been fired, we steamed off into grey storms. There was of course no wireless in those days, and therefore at this most exciting moment the Commander-in-Chief, the Headquarters Staff and the Correspondent of the *Morning Post* dropped completely out of the world. Still we expected news at Madeira, which was reached on the fourth day. There was no news at Madeira, except that negotiations were at an end and that troops on both sides were moving. In this suspense we glided off again, this time into the blue.

We had now to pass a fortnight completely cut off from all view of the drama which filled our thoughts. It was a fortnight of cloudless skies and calm seas, through which the Cape Liner cut her way with placid unconcern. She did not even increase her speed above the ordinary commercial rate. Such a measure would have been unprecedented. Nearly fifty years had passed since Great Britain had been at war with any white people, and the idea that time played any vital part in such a business seemed to be entirely absent from all her methods. Absolute tranquillity lapped the peaceful ship. The usual sports and games of a sea voyage occupied her passengers, civil and military alike. Buller trod the deck each day with sphinx-like calm. The general opinion among the Staff was that it would be all over before they got there. Some of our best officers were on board, and they simply could not conceive how 'irregular, amateur' forces like the Boers could make any impression against disciplined professional soldiers. If the Boers broke into Natal, they would immediately come up against General Penn Symonds who lay with a whole infantry brigade, a cavalry regiment and two batteries of artillery, at Dundee in the extreme north of Natal. The fear of the Staff was that such a shock would so discomfort them that they would never again try conclusions with regular forces. All this was very disheartening, and I did not wonder that Sir Redvers Buller often looked so glum.

Twelve days passed in silence, peace and speculation. I had constructed a dozen imaginary situations, ranging from the capture of Cape Town by Kruger to the capture of Pretoria by Sir George White or even by General Penn Symonds. None of them carried conviction to my mind. However, in two more days we should know all that had happened in this trance-like fortnight. The Interval would be over. The curtain would rise again on the world's scene. What should we see? I thought it must be very hard for General Buller to bear the suspense. What would he give to know what was taking place? How silly of the Government not to send out a torpedo boat to meet him five days from land and put him in possession of all the facts, so that he could adjust his mind to the problem and think over his first steps coolly and at leisure!

Suddenly there was a stir on deck. A ship was sighted right ahead, coming that is to say from the land of knowledge. We drew together rapidly. I think she would have passed us about a mile away but for the fact that some of the younger ones among us started a buzz of excitement. 'Surely we can get some news from her? Can't we stop her? She will have the Cape newspapers on board! Surely we are not going to let her go by without making an effort?'

These murmurs reached the ears of high seniority. Grave counsel was taken. It was decided that it would be unusual to stop a ship at sea. Possibly there might be a claim for damages against the Government, or some other penalty like that which happens if you pull the communication-cord without sufficient provocation. As a bold half-measure signals were made to the steamer, asking for news. On this she altered her course and steamed past us little more than a hundred yards' distance. She was a tramp steamer with perhaps twenty persons on board. They all gathered to look at us, and we—as the reader may well believe—returned the compliment. A blackboard was held up from the deck of the tramp, and on this we read the following legend:—

BOERS DEFEATED.
THREE BATTLES.
PENN SYMONDS KILLED.

Then she faded away behind us, and we were left to meditate upon this cryptic message.

The Staff were frankly consternated. There had evidently been fighting—actual battles! And a British General had been killed! It must therefore have been severe fighting. It was hardly possible the Boers would have any strength left. Was it likely, if they had been defeated in three battles, they would continue their hopeless struggle? Deep gloom settled down upon our party. Buller alone remained doggedly inscrutable, a tower of strength in times of trouble. He had read the message through his field-glasses, but had made no sign. It was not until some minutes had passed that a Staff Officer ventured to address him.

'It looks as if it will be over, sir.'

Thus pressed, the great man answered in the following words:

'I dare say there will be enough left to give us a fight outside Pretoria.'

His military instinct was sure and true. There was quite enough left!

This impressive utterance restored our morale. It was repeated from one to another, and it ran through the ship in a few moments. Every eye was brighter. Every heart felt lighter of its load. The Staff Officers congratulated one another, and the Aides-de-Camp skipped for joy. The optimism was so general that no one turned and rent me when I uplifted my voice and said 'that it would only have taken ten minutes to have stopped the ship and got proper information so that we should all know where we were.' On the contrary reasonable answer was made to me as follows:

'It is the weakness of youth to be impatient. We should know everything that had happened quite soon enough. Sir Redvers Buller had shown his characteristic phlegm in not seeking to anticipate the knowledge which would be at his disposal on landing at Cape Town. Moreover, as the remaining battle would, in the Commander-in-Chief's opinion, not take place until we reached Pretoria, and as Pretoria was upwards of seven hundred miles from Cape Town, there would be plenty of time to make all the arrangements necessary for disposing of what was left of the Boer resistance. Finally, the habit of questioning the decisions of superior officers in time of war, or in time of peace for that matter, was much to be regretted even in a War Correspondent, and more particularly in one who had quite recently worn the uniform of an officer.'

I, however, remained impenitent and unconvinced.

CHAPTER XIX

THE ARMOURED TRAIN

IT was dark when we anchored in Table Bay; but innumerable lights twinkled from the shore, and a stir of launches soon beset our vessel. High functionaries and naval and military officers arrived, bearing their reports. The Headquarters staff sat up all night to read them. I got hold of a bundle of newspapers and studied these with equal attention.[1]

The Boers had invaded Natal, had attacked our advanced forces at Dundee, and though defeated in the action of Talana Hill, had killed General Penn Symonds and very nearly rounded up the three or four thousand troops he had commanded as they made their hurried and hazardous retreat to Ladysmith. At Ladysmith Sir George White at the head of twelve or thirteen thousand men, with forty or fifty guns and a brigade of cavalry, attempted to bar their further advance. The intention of the British Government, though this I did not know at the time, was that he should retire southwards across the Tugela, delaying the Boer advance until he could be joined by the large reinforcements now hastening across the oceans from England and India. Above all, he was not to let himself be cut off and surrounded. The British war plan contemplated the temporary sacrifice of Northern Natal, the projecting triangle of which was obviously not defensible, and the advance of the main army under Buller from the Cape Colony through the Orange Free State to Pretoria. All this was soon deranged.

[1]For this and the following chapters, see map of the South African theatre, facing page 352.

I remember one night in after years that I said to Mr. Balfour at dinner how badly Sir George White had been treated. A look of implacable sternness suddenly replaced his easy, smiling, affable manner. A different man looked out upon me. 'We owe to him,' he said, 'the Ladysmith entanglement.'

On the very day of our arrival (October 31) grave events had taken place around Ladysmith. General White, who had gained a local success at Elandslaagte, attempted an ambitious offensive movement against the elusive, advancing, enveloping Boer commandos. A disaster had occurred. Nearly twelve hundred British infantry had been forced to surrender at Nicholson's Nek, and the rest of the widely-dispersed forces were thrown back upon Ladysmith. This they hastily converted into an entrenched camp of wide extent, and being speedily invested on all sides by the Boers, and their railway cut, settled down in a prolonged siege to await relief. The Boers, having encircled them on all sides, had left two-thirds of their forces to block them in, and were presumably about to pass on with the rest across the Tugela River into Southern Natal. Meanwhile in the west other Boer forces had similarly encircled Mafeking and Kimberley, and sat down stolidly to the process of starving them out. Finally, the Dutch areas of the Cape Colony itself were quivering upon the verge of rebellion. Throughout the vast sub-continent every man's hand was against his brother, and the British Government could, for the moment, be sure of nothing beyond the gunshot of the Navy.

Although I knew neither our plan nor the enemy's situation and all news of the day's disaster in Natal was still suppressed, it was clear as soon as we had landed that the first heavy fighting would come in Natal. Buller's Army Corps would take a month or six weeks to assemble in Cape Town and Port Elizabeth. There would be time to watch the Natal operations and come back to Cape Colony for the main advance. So I thought, and so, a few days later, to his subsequent sorrow, thought Sir Redvers Buller. All traffic through the Free State was of course interrupted, and to reach Natal involved a railway journey of 700 miles by De Aar Junction and Stormberg to Port Elizabeth, and thence by a small mailboat or tug to Durban—four days in all. The railroad from De Aar to Stormberg ran parallel to the hostile frontier. It was quite undefended and might be cut at any moment. However, the authorities thought there was a good chance of getting through, so in company with the correspondent of the *Manchester Guardian*, a charming young man, Mr. J. B. Atkins, later the Editor of the *Spectator*, I started forthwith. Our train was in fact the last that got round, and when we reached Stormberg the station staff were already packing up.

We sailed from East London upon a steamer of about 150 tons, in the teeth of a horrible Antarctic gale. Indeed I thought the little ship would be overwhelmed amid the enormous waves or else be cast away upon the rocks which showed their black teeth endlessly a bare mile away upon our port beam. But all these misgivings were quickly dispelled by the most appalling paroxysms of sea-sickness which it has ever been my lot to survive. I really do not think I could have lifted a finger to save my life. There was a stuffy cabin, or caboose, below decks in the stern of the vessel, in which six or seven members of the crew lived, slept and ate their meals. In a bunk of this I lay in an extreme of physical misery while our tiny ship bounded and reeled, and kicked and pitched, and fell and turned almost over and righted itself again, or, for all I know, turned right round, hour after hour through an endless afternoon, a still longer evening and an eternal night. I remembered that Titus Oates lived in good health for many years after his prodigious floggings, and upon this reflection, combined with a firm trust that Providence would do whatever was best, were founded such hopes as I could still retain.

There is an end to everything, and happily nothing fades

so quickly as the memory of physical pain. Still my voyage
to Durban is a recollection which, in the jingle of the 'Bab
Ballads'

> 'I shall carry to the catacombs of age,
> Photographically lined
> On the tablets of my mind,
> When a yesterday has faded from its page.'

*   *   *   *   *

We landed at Durban and travelled a night's journey to
Pietermaritzburg. The hospital was already full of wounded.
Here I found Reggie Barnes shot through the thigh. He had
been hit at close range in our brilliant little victory at
Elandslaagte Station in which my friend Ian Hamilton, now
a General, had commanded. He told me all about the fighting and how skilful the Boers were with horse and rifle.
He also showed me his leg. No bone was broken, but it was
absolutely coal black from hip to toe. The surgeon reassured
me afterwards that it was only bruising, and not mortifica-
tion as I feared. That night I travelled on to Estcourt, a
tiny tin township of a few hundred inhabitants, beyond
which the trains no longer ran.

It had been my intention to get into Ladysmith, where
I knew Ian Hamilton would look after me and give me a
good show. I was too late, the door was shut. The Boers
had occupied Colenso Station on the Tugela River and
held the iron railway bridge. General French and his staff,
which included both Haig and Herbert Lawrence,[1] had
just slipped through under artillery fire in the last train
out of Ladysmith on his way to the Cape Colony, where
the main cavalry forces were to be assembled. There was
nothing to do but to wait at Estcourt with such handfuls
of troops as were being hurriedly collected to protect the
southern part of Natal from the impending Boer invasion.
A single battalion of Dublin Fusiliers, two or three guns
and a few squadrons of Natal Caribineers, two companies of

[1]Commander-in-Chief, and Chief of the Staff respectively in 1917–18.

Durban Light Infantry and an armoured train, were the only forces which remained for the defence of the Colony. All the rest of the Natal Army was blockaded in Ladysmith. Reinforcements were hurrying to the spot from all parts of the British Empire; but during the week I was at Estcourt our weakness was such that we expected to be ourselves surrounded almost every day, and could do little but fortify our post and wear a confident air.

At Estcourt I found old friends. Leo Amery, the monitor I had unluckily pushed into the bathing pool at Harrow ten years before, afterwards long my colleague in Parliament and Government, was now one of the war correspondents of the *Times*. We were able for the first time to meet on terms of equality and fraternity, and together with my friend of the *Manchester Guardian* we took up our abode in an empty bell tent that stood in the shunting triangle of the railway station. That evening, walking in the single street of the town, whom should I meet but Captain Haldane, who had been so helpful in procuring me my appointment to Sir William Lockhart's staff during the Tirah Expedition. Haldane had been wounded at Elandslaagte, and had hoped to rejoin his battalion of Gordon Highlanders in Ladysmith, and being like me held up by the enemy, had been given the temporary command of a company of the Dublin Fusiliers. The days passed slowly and anxiously. The position of our small force was most precarious. At any moment ten or twelve thousand mounted Boers might sweep forward to attack us or cut off our retreat. Yet it was necessary to hold Estcourt as long and in as firm a posture as possible. Cavalry reconnaissances were pushed out every morning for ten or fifteen miles towards the enemy to give us timely notice of their expected advance; and in an unlucky moment it occurred to the General in command on the spot to send his armoured train along the sixteen miles of intact railway line to supplement the efforts of the cavalry.

Nothing looks more formidable and impressive than an

armoured train; but nothing is in fact more vulnerable and helpless. It was only necessary to blow up a bridge or culvert to leave the monster stranded far from home and help, at the mercy of the enemy. This situation did not seem to have occurred to our commander. He decided to put a company of the Dublin Fusiliers and a company of the Durban Light Infantry into an armoured train of six trucks, and add a small six-pounder naval gun with some sailors landed from H.M.S. *Terrible*, together with a break-down gang, and to send this considerable portion of his force out to reconnoitre towards Colenso. Captain Haldane was the officer he selected for the duty of commanding this operation. Haldane told me on the night of November 14 of the task which had been set him for the next day and on which he was to start at dawn. He did not conceal his misgivings on the imprudence of the enterprise, but he was of course, like everyone else at the beginning of a war, very keen upon adventure and a brush with the enemy. 'Would I come with him?' He would like it if I did! Out of comradeship, and because I thought it was my duty to gather as much information as I could for the *Morning Post*, also because I was eager for trouble, I accepted the invitation without demur.

The military events which followed are well known and have often been discussed. The armoured train proceeded about fourteen miles towards the enemy and got as far as Chieveley station without a sign of opposition or indeed of life or movement on the broad undulations of the Natal landscape. We stopped for a few moments at Chieveley to report our arrival at this point by telegraph to the General. No sooner had we done this than we saw, on a hill between us and home which overlooked the line at about 600 yards distance, a number of small figures moving about and hurrying forward. Certainly they were Boers. Certainly they were behind us. What would they be doing with the railway line? There was not an instant to lose. We started immediately on our return journey. As we approached the hill, I was stand-

ing on a box with my head and shoulders above the steel
plating of the rear armoured truck. I saw a cluster of Boers
on the crest. Suddenly three wheeled things appeared among
them, and instantly bright flashes of light opened and shut
ten or twelve times. A huge white ball of smoke sprang into
being and tore out into a cone, only as it seemed a few feet
above my head. It was shrapnel—the first I had ever seen
in war, and very nearly the last! The steel sides of the truck
tanged with a patter of bullets. There was a crash from the
front of the train, and a series of sharp explosions. The railway line curved round the base of the hill on a steep down
gradient, and under the stimulus of the enemy's fire, as well
as of the slope, our pace increased enormously. The Boer
artillery (two guns and a pom-pom) had only time for one
discharge before we were round the corner out of their sight.
It had flashed across my mind that there must be some trap
farther on. I was just turning to Haldane to suggest that
someone should scramble along the train and make the engine-driver reduce speed, when suddenly there was a tremendous shock, and he and I and all the soldiers in the
truck were pitched head over heels on to its floor. The armoured train travelling at not less than forty miles an hour
had been thrown off the metals by some obstruction, or by
some injury to the line.

In our truck no one was seriously hurt, and it took but a
few seconds for me to scramble to my feet and look over the
top of the armour. The train lay in a valley about 1,200
yards on the homeward side of the enemy's hill. On the
top of this hill were scores of figures running forward and
throwing themselves down in the grass, from which there
came almost immediately an accurate and heavy rifle fire.
The bullets whistled overhead and rang and splattered on
the steel plates like a hailstorm. I got down from my perch,
and Haldane and I debated what to do. It was agreed that
he with the little naval gun and his Dublin Fusiliers in the
rear truck should endeavour to keep down the enemy's fir-

ing, and that I should go and see what had happened to the train, what was the damage to the line, and whether there was any chance of repairing it or clearing the wreckage out of the way.

I nipped out of the truck accordingly and ran along the line to the head of the train.[1] The engine was still on the rails. The first truck, an ordinary bogey, had turned completely head over heels, killing and terribly injuring some of the plate-layers who were upon it; but it lay quite clear of the track. The next two armoured trucks, which contained the Durban Light Infantry, were both derailed, one still upright and the other on its side. They lay jammed against each other in disorder, blocking the homeward path of the rest. Behind the overturned trucks the Durban Light Infantry men, bruised, shaken and some severely injured, had found a temporary shelter. The enemy's fire was continuous, and soon there mingled with the rifles the bang of the field guns and the near explosion of their shells. We were in the toils of the enemy.

As I passed the engine another shrapnel burst immediately as it seemed overhead, hurling its contents with a rasping rush through the air. The driver at once sprang out of the cab and ran to the shelter of the overturned trucks. His face cut open by a splinter streamed with blood, and he complained in bitter, futile indignation. 'He was a civilian. What did they think he was paid for? To be killed by a bombshell—not he! He would not stay another minute.' It looked as if his excitement and misery—he was dazed by the blow on his head—would prevent him from working the engine further, and as only he understood the machinery, the hope of escape would thus be cut off. So I told him that no man was hit twice on the same day: that a wounded man who continued to do his duty was always rewarded for distinguished gallantry, and that he might never have this chance

[1]See diagram on page 251.

again. On this he pulled himself together, wiped the blood off his face, climbed back into the cab of his engine, and thereafter obeyed every order which I gave him.[1]

I formed the opinion that it would be possible, using the engine as a ram, to pull and push the two wrecked trucks clear of the line, and consequently that escape for the whole force was possible. The line appeared to be uninjured, no rail had been removed. I returned along the line to Captain Haldane's truck and told him through a loophole what was the position and what I proposed we should do. He agreed to all I said and undertook to keep the enemy hotly engaged meanwhile.

I was very lucky in the hour that followed not to be hit. It was necessary for me to be almost continuously moving up and down the train or standing in the open, telling the engine-driver what to do. The first thing was to detach the truck which was half off the rails from the one completely so. To do this the engine had to be removed so as to tug the partly-derailed truck backwards along the line until it was clear of the other wreckage, and then to throw it completely off the rails. The dead weight of the iron truck half on the sleepers was enormous, and the engine wheels skidded vainly several times before any hauling power was obtained. At last the truck was drawn sufficiently far back, and I called for volunteers to overturn it from the side, while the engine pushed it from the end. It was very evident that these men would be exposed to considerable danger. Twenty were called for and there was an immediate response, but only nine men, including the Major of the Durban Light Infantry and four or five of the Dublin Fusiliers, actually stepped out into the

[1]It was more than ten years before I was able to make good my promise. Nothing was done for this man by the military authorities; but when in 1910 I was Home Secretary, it was my duty to advise the King upon the awards of the Albert Medal. I therefore revived the old records, communicated with the Governor of Natal and the railway company, and ultimately both the driver and his fireman received the highest reward for gallantry open to civilians.

open. The attempt was nevertheless successful. The truck heeled over further under their pressure, and the engine giving a shove at the right moment, it fell off the line, and the track seemed clear. Safety and success appeared in sight together, but one of the bitterest disappointments of my life overtook them.

The footplate of the engine was about 6 in. wider than the tender and jammed against the corner of the newly overturned truck. It did not seem safe to push very hard, lest the engine itself should be derailed. We uncoupled the engine from the rear trucks, and time after time moved it back a yard or two and butted forward at the obstruction. Each time it moved a little, but soon it was evident that complications had set in. The newly-derailed truck had become jammed in a **T**-shaped position with the one originally off the line, and the more the engine pushed, the greater became the block.

It occurred to me that if the trucks only jammed tighter after the forward pushing, they might be loosened by again pulling backwards. Now however a new difficulty arose. The coupling chains of the engine would not reach by five or six inches those of the overturned truck. Search was made for a spare coupling. By a solitary gleam of good luck, one was found. The engine hauled at the wreckage and before the chain parted pulled it about a yard backwards and off the track. Now surely the line was clear at last. But again the corner of the engine footplate jammed with the corner of the truck, and again we came to a jarring halt. The heat and excitement of the work were such as to absorb me completely. I remember thinking that it was like working in front of an iron target at a rifle range at which men were continually firing. We struggled for seventy minutes among these clanging, rending iron boxes, amid the repeated explosions of shells and the ceaseless hammering of bullets, and with only five or six inches of twisted ironwork to make the difference between danger, captivity and shame on the one hand, and safety, freedom and triumph on the other.

Above all things we had to be careful not to throw the
engine off the line. But at last, as the artillery firing steadily
increased and the second gun came into action from the opposite flank, I decided to run a great risk. The engine was
backed to its fullest extent and driven full tilt at the obstruction. There was a harsh crunching tear, the engine
reeled on the rails, and as the obstructing truck reared upwards ground its way past and gained the homeward side,
free and, as it turned out, safe. But our three remaining
trucks were fifty yards away, still the wrong side of the obstruction, which had fallen back into its original place after
the engine had passed. What were we to do? Certainly we
could not take the engine back. Could we then drag the
trucks by hand up to the engine? They were narrower than
the engine and there would be just room for them to slip
past.

I went back again to Captain Haldane. He accepted the
plan. He ordered his men to climb out of their steel pen and
try to push it towards the engine. The plan was sound
enough, but it broke down under the force of circumstances.
The truck was so heavy that it required all hands to move
it; the fire was so hot and the confusion so great and increasing that the men drifted away from the exposed side. The
enemy, relieved of our counter-fire, were now plainly visible
in large numbers on the face of the hill, firing furiously. We
then agreed that the engine should go slowly back along the
line with all the wounded, who were now numerous, and
that the Dublins and the Durban men should retreat on foot,
sheltering themselves behind the engine which would go at
a foot's pace. Upwards of forty persons, of whom the greater
part were streaming with blood, were crowded on the engine and its tender, and we began to move slowly forward.
I was in the cab of the engine directing the engine-driver. It
was crammed so full of wounded men that one could scarcely
move. The shells burst all around, some striking the engine,

others dashing the gravel of the track upon it and its unhappy human freight. The pace increased, the infantry outside began to lag and then to be left behind. At last I forced
the engine-driver to stop altogether, but before I could get
the engine stopped we were already 300 yards away from
our infantry. Close at hand was the bridge across the Blue
Krantz River, a considerable span. I told the engine-driver
to cross the bridge and wait on the other side, and forcing
my way out of the cab I got down on to the line and went
back along it to find Captain Haldane, and to bring him and
his Dublin Fusiliers along.

But while these events had been taking place everything
else had been in movement. I had not retraced my steps 200
yards when, instead of Haldane and his company, two figures in plain clothes appeared upon the line. 'Plate-layers!'
I said to myself, and then with a surge of realization,
'Boers!' My mind retains its impression of these tall figures,
full of energy, clad in dark, flapping clothes, with slouch,
storm-driven hats, poising on their levelled rifles hardly a
hundred yards away. I turned again and ran back towards
the engine, the two Boers firing as I ran between the metals.
Their bullets, sucking to right and left, seemed to miss only
by inches. We were in a small cutting with banks about six
feet high on either side. I flung myself against the bank of
the cutting. It gave no cover. Another glance at the two figures; one was now kneeling to aim. Movement seemed the
only chance. Again I darted forward: again two soft kisses
sucked in the air; but nothing struck me. This could not endure. I must get out of the cutting—that damnable corridor!
I jigged to the left, and scrambled up the bank. The earth
sprang up beside me. I got through the wire fence unhurt.
Outside the cutting was a tiny depression. I crouched in this,
struggling to get my breath again.

Fifty yards away was a small plate-layer's cabin of masonry; there was cover there. About 200 yards away was the
rocky gorge of the Blue Krantz River; there was plenty of

THE ARMOURED TRAIN
Nov. 15th. 1899.

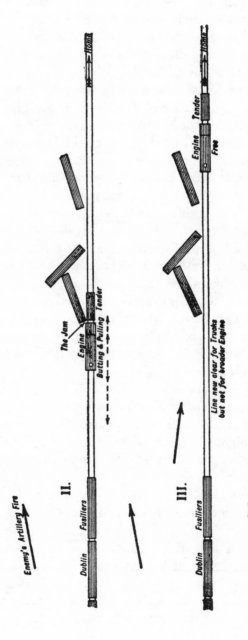

Durham Light Infantry

Break down men's truck overturned

On its side

Derailed

Naval Gun Dublin Fusiliers Engine Tender

I.

Enemy's Artillery Fire →

The Jam

Engine

Butting & Pulling Tender

Dublin Fusiliers

II.

Engine Tender

Free

Line new clear for Trucks but not for broader Engine

Dublin Fusiliers

III.

cover there. I determined to make a dash for the river. I rose to my feet. Suddenly on the other side of the railway, separated from me by the rails and two uncut wire fences, I saw a horseman galloping furiously, a tall, dark figure, holding his rifle in his right hand. He pulled up his horse almost in its own length and shaking the rifle at me shouted a loud command. We were forty yards apart. That morning I had taken with me, Correspondent-status notwithstanding, my Mauser pistol. I thought I could kill this man, and after the treatment I had received I earnestly desired to do so. I put my hand to my belt, the pistol was not there. When engaged in clearing the line, getting in and out of the engine, etc., I had taken it off. It came safely home on the engine. I have it now! But at this moment I was quite unarmed. Meanwhile, I suppose in about the time this takes to tell, the Boer horseman, still seated on his horse, had covered me with his rifle. The animal stood stock still, so did he, and so did I. I looked towards the river, I looked towards the plate-layer's hut. The Boer continued to look along his sights. I thought there was absolutely no chance of escape, if he fired he would surely hit me, so I held up my hands and surrendered myself a prisoner of war.

'When one is alone and unarmed,' said the great Napoleon, in words which flowed into my mind in the poignant minutes that followed, 'a surrender may be pardoned.' Still he might have missed; and the Blue Krantz ravine was very near and the two wire fences were still uncut. However, the deed was done. Thereupon my captor lowered his rifle and beckoned to me to come across to him. I obeyed. I walked through the wire fences and across the line and stood by his side. He sprang off his horse and began firing in the direction of the bridge upon the retreating engine and a few straggling British figures. Then when the last had disappeared he remounted and at his side I tramped back towards the spot where I had left Captain Haldane and his company. I saw none of them. They were already prisoners. I noticed that it was raining hard. As I plodded through the high grass by the side of my captor a disquieting and timely reflection came into my mind. I had two clips of Mauser ammunition, each holding ten rounds, in two little breast pockets one on each side of my khaki coat. These cartridges were the same as I had used at Omdurman, and were the only kind supplied for the Mauser pistol. They were what are called 'soft-nosed bullets.' I had never given them a thought until now; and it was borne in upon me that they might be a very dangerous possession. I dropped the right-hand clip on the ground without being seen. I had got the left-hand clip in my hand and was about to drop it, when my captor looked down sharply and said in English 'What have you got there?'

'What is it?' I said, opening the palm of my hand, 'I picked it up.'

He took it, looked at it and threw it away. We continued to plod on until we reached the general gang of prisoners and found ourselves speedily in the midst of many hundreds of mounted Boers who streamed into view, in long columns of twos and threes, many holding umbrellas over their heads in the pouring rain.

*   *   *   *   *

Such is the episode of the armoured train and the story of my capture on November 15, 1899.

It was not until three years later, when the Boer Generals visited England to ask for some loan or assistance on behalf of their devastated country, that I was introduced at a private luncheon to their leader, General Botha. We talked of the war and I briefly told the story of my capture. Botha listened in silence; then he said, 'Don't you recognise me? I was that man. It was I who took you prisoner. I, myself,' and his bright eyes twinkled with pleasure. Botha in white shirt and frock coat looked very different in all save size and darkness of complexion from the wild war-time figure I had seen that rough day in Natal. But about the extraordinary fact there can be no doubt. He had entered upon the invasion of Natal as a burgher; his own disapproval of the war had excluded him from any high command at its outset. This was his first action. But as a simple private burgher serving in the ranks he had galloped on ahead and in front of the whole Boer forces in the ardour of pursuit. Thus we met.

Few men that I have known have interested me more than Louis Botha. An acquaintance formed in strange circumstances and upon an almost unbelievable introduction ripened into a friendship which I greatly valued. I saw in this grand, rugged figure, the Father of his country, the wise and profound statesman, the farmer-warrior, the crafty hunter of the wilderness, the deep, sure man of solitude.

In 1906 when, as newly-elected first Prime Minister of the Transvaal, he came to London to attend the Imperial Conference, a great banquet was given to the Dominion Prime Ministers in Westminster Hall. I was Under Secretary of State for the Colonies, and as the Boer Leader, so recently our enemy, passed up the hall to his place, he paused to say to my mother, who stood by my side, 'He and I have been out in all weathers.' It was surely true.

Space does not allow me here to recount the many important matters of public business in which I was, over a long period of years, brought in contact with this great man. To me it was that he first disclosed his romantic project of presenting the Cullinan Diamond—of purest water and at least twenty times the size of any other—to the King. It fell to my lot to expound the whole of the policy of giving self-government to the Transvaal and the Orange Free State and to conduct the Constitution Bills through the House of Commons. Afterwards at the Board of Trade and at the Admiralty I was in frequent contact with General Botha and his colleague Smuts, while they ruled their country with such signal skill during the fifteen years from 1906 to the end of the Great War.

Botha always felt he had a special call upon my attention. Whenever he visited Europe we saw each other many times, in council, at dinner, at home and in the public offices. His unerring instinct warned him of the approach of the great struggle. In 1913, when he returned from a visit to Germany where he had been taking the waters for a cure, he warned me most earnestly of the dangerous mood prevailing there. 'Mind you are ready,' he said. 'Do not trust those people. I know they are very dangerous. They mean you mischief. I hear things you would not hear. Mind you have all your ships ready. I can feel that there is danger in the air. And what is more,' he added, 'when the day comes I am going to be ready too. When they attack you, I am going to attack German South-West Africa and clear them out once and for all. I will be there to do my duty when the time comes. But you, with the Navy, mind you are not caught by surprise.'

Chance and romance continued to weave our fortunes together in a strange way. On the 28th or 29th of July, 1914, midway in the week of crisis which preceded the world explosion, I was walking away from the House of Commons after Question Time and met in Palace Yard one of the South African Ministers, Mr. de Graaf, a very able Dutchman whom I had known for a long time. 'What does it mean? What do you think is going to happen?' he asked. 'I think it will be war,' I replied, 'and I think Britain will be involved. Does Botha know how critical it is?' De Graaf went away looking very grave, and I thought no more of the incident; but it had its consequences.

That night De Graaf telegraphed to Botha saying 'Churchill thinks war certain and Great Britain involved' or words to that effect. Botha was away from the seat of government: he was in the northern Transvaal, and General Smuts was acting in his stead at Pretoria. The telegram was laid before Smuts. He looked at it, pushed it on one side, and continued working through his files of papers. Then when he had finished he looked at it again. 'There must be something in this,' he thought, 'or De Graaf would not have telegraphed;' and he repeated the telegram to the absent Prime Minister in the northern Transvaal. It reached General Botha many hours later, but it reached him in time. That very night he was to start by train for Delagoa Bay, and the next morning he was to embark for his return journey to Cape Town on board *a German ship*. But for this telegram, so he afterwards told me, he would have been actually at sea on a German vessel when war was declared. The Prime Minister, the all-powerful national leader of South Africa, would have been in the hands of the enemy at the very moment when large areas of the South African Union were trembling on the verge of rebellion. One cannot measure the evils which might have come upon South Africa had such a disaster taken place. Instantly on receiving the message General Botha cancelled all his plans and returned by special train to Pretoria, which he reached before the outbreak and in time.

His grand exertions in the war, the risks he ran, the steadfast courage which he showed, the great command he exercised over his people, the brilliant manner in which he over-ran German South-West Africa, his rugged animated counsels at the meetings of the Imperial War Cabinet in 1917, his statesmanship and noble bearing after the victory in the Peace Conference in Paris in 1919—all these are matters of history.

I was Secretary of State for War when he quitted England for the last time. He came to see me at the War Office to say good-bye. We talked long about the ups and downs of life and the tremendous and terrible events through which we had safely passed. Many high personages from many countries used in those days of victory to visit me at the War Office, but there was only one whom I myself conducted down the great staircase and put with my own hands into his waiting car. I never saw him again. His death followed speedily on his return to his own country, of which in Peace and War, in Sorrow and in Triumph, in Rebellion and in Reconciliation, he had been a veritable saviour.

*   *   *   *   *

This considerable digression will, I hope, be pardoned by the reader, and I make haste to return to the true path of chronology. As I sat drenched and miserable on the ground with the prisoners and some mortally-wounded men, I cursed, not only my luck, but my own decision. I could quite decently have gone off upon the engine. Indeed, I think, from what was said about the affair by the survivors, I might even have been extremely well received. I had needlessly and by many exertions involved myself in a useless and hopeless disaster. I had not helped anybody by attempting to return to the Company. I had only cut myself out of the whole of this exciting war with all its boundless possibilities of adventure and advancement. I meditated blankly upon the sour rewards of virtue. Yet this misfortune, could I have foreseen the future, was to lay the foundations of my later life. I was not to be done out of the campaign. I was not to languish as a prisoner. I was to escape, and by escaping was to gain a public reputation or notoriety which made me well-known henceforward among my countrymen, and made me acceptable as a candidate in a great many constituencies. I was also put in the position to earn the money which for many years assured my independence and the means of entering Parliament. Whereas if I had gone back on the engine, though I should perhaps have been praised and petted, I might well have been knocked on the head at Colenso a month later, as were several of my associates on Sir Redvers Buller's Staff.

But these events and possibilities were hidden from me, and it was in dudgeon that I ranged myself in the line of prisoners before the swiftly-erected tent of the Boer headquarters. My gloomy reflections took a sharper and a darker turn when I found myself picked out from the other captive officers and ordered to stand by myself apart. I had enough military law to know that a civilian in a half uniform who has taken an active and prominent part in a fight, even if he has not fired a shot himself, is liable to be shot at once by drumhead court martial. None of the armies in the Great War would have wasted ten minutes upon the business. I therefore stood solitary in the downpour, a prey to gnawing anxiety. I occupied myself in thinking out what answers I should make to the various short, sharp questions which might soon be addressed to me, and what sort of appearance I could keep up if I were soon and suddenly told that my hour had come. After about a quarter of an hour of this I was much relieved when, as a result of deliberations which were taking place inside the tent, I was curtly told to rejoin the others. Indeed I felt quite joyful when a few minutes later a Boer field cornet came out of the tent and said, 'We are not going to let you go, old chappie, although you are a correspondent. We don't catch the son of a lord every day.' I need really never have been alarmed. The Boers were the most humane people where white men were concerned. Kaffirs were a different story, but to the Boer mind the destruction of a white man's life, even in war, was a lamentable and shocking event. They were the most good-hearted enemy I have ever fought against in the four continents in which it has been my fortune to see active service.

So it was settled that we were all to march off under escort sixty miles to the Boer railhead at Elandslaagte and to be sent to Pretoria as prisoners of war.

CHAPTER XX

IN DURANCE VILE

Prisoner of War! That is the least unfortunate kind of prisoner to be, but it is nevertheless a melancholy state. You are in the power of your enemy. You owe your life to his humanity, and your daily bread to his compassion. You must obey his orders, go where he tells you, stay where you are bid, await his pleasure, possess your soul in patience. Meanwhile the war is going on, great events are in progress, fine opportunities for action and adventure are slipping away. Also the days are very long. Hours crawl like paralytic centipedes. Nothing amuses you. Reading is difficult, writing, impossible. Life is one long boredom from dawn till slumber.

Moreover, the whole atmosphere of prison, even the most easy and best regulated prison, is odious. Companions in this kind of misfortune quarrel about trifles and get the least possible pleasure from each other's society. If you have never been under restraint before and never known what it was to be a captive, you feel a sense of constant humiliation in being confined to a narrow space, fenced in by railings and wire, watched by armed men, and webbed about with a tangle of regulations and restrictions. I certainly hated every minute of my captivity more than I have ever hated any other period in my whole life. Luckily it was very short. Less than a month passed from the time when I yielded myself prisoner in Natal till I was at large again, hunted but free, in the vast sub-Continent of South Africa. Looking back on those days I have always felt the keenest pity for prisoners and captives. What it must mean for any man, especially an educated man, to be confined for years in a modern convict prison strains my imagination. Each day exactly like the one before, with the barren ashes of wasted life behind, and all the long years of bondage stretching out ahead. Therefore in after years, when I was Home Secretary and had all the prisons of England in my charge, I did my utmost consistent with public policy to introduce some sort of variety and indulgence into the life of their inmates, to give to educated minds books to feed on, to give to all periodical entertainments of some sort to look forward to and to look back upon, and to mitigate as far as is reasonable the hard lot which, if they have deserved, they must none the less endure. Although I loathed the business of one human being inflicting frightful and even capital punishment upon others, I comforted myself on some occasions of responsibility by the reflection that a death sentence was far more merciful than a life sentence.

Dark moods come easily across the mind of a prisoner. Of course if he is kept on very low diet, chained in a dungeon, deprived of light and plunged into solitude, his moods only matter to himself. But when you are young, well fed, high spirited, loosely guarded, able to conspire with others, these moods carry thought nearer to resolve, and resolve ever nearer to action.

It took us three days' journey by march and train to reach our place of confinement at Pretoria from the front. We tramped round the Boer lines besieging Ladysmith in sound of the cannon, friendly and hostile, until we reached Elandslaagte station. Here our little party—Captain Haldane, a very young lieutenant of the Dublins named Frankland,* and myself—with about fifty men, were put into the train, and we rumbled our way slowly for hundreds of miles into the heart of the enemy's country. We were joined at an early station by a trooper of the Imperial Light Horse who had

*An officer of great personal charm and ability. He was killed, as a Colonel, on the beaches of Gallipoli, April 25, 1915.

been captured that day when on patrol. This man, whose name was Brockie, was a South African Colonist. He passed himself off to the Boers as an officer, and as he spoke Dutch and Kaffir fluently and knew the country, we did not gainsay him. We thought he was the very man for us. We all arrived at Pretoria on November 18, 1899. The men were taken off to their cage on the race-course, and we four officers were confined in the State Model Schools. Throughout our journey we had repeatedly discussed in undertones, and as occasion offered, plans for escape, and had resolved to try our utmost to regain our freedom. Curiously enough three out of our four at different times and in different circumstances made their escape from the State Model Schools; and with one exception we were the only prisoners who ever succeeded in getting away from them.

In the State Model Schools we found all the officers who had been taken prisoner in the early fighting of the war, and principally at Nicholson's Nek. We new arrivals were all lodged in the same dormitory, and explored our abode with the utmost care. We thought of nothing else but freedom, and from morn till night we racked our brains to discover a way of escape. We soon discovered the many defects in the system by which we were held in custody. We had so much liberty within our bounds, and were so free from observation during the greater part of the day and night, that we could pursue our aim unceasingly. We had not been there a week before our original impulse to escape became merged in a far more ambitious design.[1]

Gradually we evolved in deep consultation a scheme of desperate and magnificent audacity. It arose naturally from the facts of the case. We were ourselves in the State Model Schools about sixty officer prisoners of war, and we had about ten or eleven British soldier servants. Our guard consisted of about forty 'Zarps' (South African Republic Police). Of this guard ten were permanently on sentry-go on the four

[1]See plan on page 269.

261

sides of the enclosure in the centre of which the school building stood. By day another ten were usually off duty and out
in the town; while the rest remained cleaning their equipment, smoking, playing cards and resting in their guard tent.
This guard tent was pitched in one corner of the quadrangu-
lar enclosure; and in it by night the whole thirty 'Zarps' not
on duty slept the sleep of the just.

If this guard could be overpowered and disarmed, a very
important step would have been taken. It became extremely
necessary at the outset to learn how they disposed themselves
for the night, what they did with their rifles and revolvers,
what proportion of them lay down in their accoutrements,
fully armed or armed at least with their revolvers. Careful
investigations were made both by day and by night. In the
result it was ascertained that practically all the guard not
required for duty rolled themselves up in their blankets and
slept in two rows on either side of the marquee. Those who
were not wanted for sentry-go that night took off their boots
and most of their clothes. Even those who were expecting to
relieve their comrades in an hour or two took off their tunics,
their boots, and above all their belts. Their rifles and bandoliers were stacked and hung around the two tent-poles in
improvised racks. There were therefore periods in the night,
midway between the changes of the guard, when these thirty
men, sleeping without any protection other than the tent
wall, within fifty yards of sixty determined and athletic officers, were by no means so safe as they supposed.

The entrance of the guard tent was watched by a sentry.
Who shall say what is possible or impossible? In these spheres
of action one cannot tell without a trial. It did not seem impossible that this sentry might be engaged in conversation by a
couple of officers on some story or other. either about something alarming that had happened or of someone who was
suddenly ill, while at the same time two or three determined prisoners could enter the back of the guard tent by a
slit in the canvas, possess themselves of pistols or rifles from

the rack, and hold up the whole guard as they awoke from their slumbers. The armed sentry at the entrance would have to be seized in the moment of surprise. To master the guard without a shot being fired or an alarm given was a problem of extreme difficulty and hazard. All one could say about such an enterprise was that the history of war—and I must add, crime—contains many equally unexpected and audacious strokes. If this were achieved, it would only be the first step.

The ten armed sentries on duty were the second step. This phase was complicated by the fact that three of these men were posted outside the spiked railing of the enclosure. They were only a yard away from it, and would often stand leaning against it by day, chatting. But at night no such occasion would arise, and they were therefore ungetatable and outside the lions' den. All the rest were inside. Each of these ten men (three outside and seven in) was a proposition requiring a special study.

It did not follow that the enterprise would be wrecked if one or two of them got off and gave the alarm. Once the guard were overpowered and their rifles and pistols distributed, we should have become an armed force superior in numbers—and we believed superior also in discipline and intelligence—to any organized body of Boers who could or would be brought against us for at least half an hour. Much may happen in half an hour! It seemed obvious that about two o'clock in the morning, half-way through the middle watch, was the most favourable moment. If every British officer did exactly what he ought to do at the right moment, and if nothing miscarried, it seemed fair to hope that, making reasonable allowance for slips in minor matters, we might be masters of the State Model Schools.

The whole enclosure was brightly and even brilliantly lighted by electric lights on tall standards. But the wires on which these lights depended were discovered by us to pass through the dormitories we occupied in the State Model

School building. One of our number versed in such matters declared his ability to disconnect them at any moment and plunge the whole place in pitch darkness; and this in fact was momentarily done one might as an experiment. If this could be effected say a minute after the hold-up in the guard tent was signalled, the seizure of the sentries on duty, utterly bewildered at what was taking place, might not be so difficult as it seemed. Lastly, the gymnasium of the State Model Schools contained a good supply of dumb-bells. Who shall say that three men in the dark, armed with dumb-bells, desperate and knowing what they meant to do, are not a match for one man who, even though he is armed, is unsuspecting and ignorant of what is taking place? If once we could surprise the guard and overcome and disarm the majority of the sentries, if once we could have thirty officers armed with revolvers and thirty more armed with rifles in the heart of Pretoria, the enemy's capital, the first and by far the hardest phase in a great and romantic enterprise would have been achieved. What next?

A mile and a half away from the State Model Schools was the Pretoria race-course, and in this barbed wire enclosure upwards of two thousand British prisoners—soldiers and non-commissioned officers—were confined. We were in touch with these men and would be able to concert plans with them. Our channel of communication was a simple one. Some of the ten or eleven servants assigned to the officers in the State Model Schools from time to time gave cause for dissatisfaction, and were sent back to the race-course and replaced by others. Thus we knew regularly the feelings of these two thousand British soldiers and the conditions under which they were confined. We learned that they were extremely discontented. Their life was monotonous, their rations short, their accommodation poor. They were hungry and resentful. On one occasion they had surged up towards the guard at the entrance, and although no bloodshed had taken place, we knew that the Boers had been much exercised by the problem of keeping so many men in check. Our information told us that there were only about one hundred and twenty 'Zarps' with two machine-guns in charge of this large prisoners' cage. Such a force, if fully prepared, could no doubt have quenched any mutiny in blood. But suppose at the moment when the prisoners rose, the race-course guard was attacked from behind by sixty armed officers! Suppose the machine-guns were rushed from the rear! Suppose the whole two thousand, acting on a definite plan, attacked from the front! Who shall say that in the confusion and the night numbers and design would not have prevailed? If this were so, the second phase of the enterprise would in its turn have attained success. What then?

In the whole of Pretoria there were not five hundred men capable of bearing arms; and these for the most part were well-to-do burghers who had obtained exemption from the front, men unfit to go on commando, officials of the Government, clerks in the Government offices, etc. These were nominally formed into a town guard and had had rifles served out to them. Beyond this, organisation did not run. If the first step could have been taken, the second would have been far easier, and the third easier still. In imagination we saw ourselves masters of the enemy's capital. The forts were held only by caretakers. Everyone else was at the front. The guns of the forts all faced outwards. They were not defended in any effectual way from an attack from the rear. Had we been successful in obtaining control of the town, the occupation of the forts would have been easy, would have followed in fact as a natural consequence. The nearest British army was three hundred miles away. But if all had gone well, we should by a wave of the wand have been in possession of the enemy's fortified capital, with an adequate force and plenty of food and ammunition for a defence at least as long as that of Mafeking.

The whole of this would have taken place between dusk and dawn. How long should we have had before we were attacked? We thought that several days might certainly be secured. We should hold the central railway junction of the South African Republic. Here the railways north, east, and south were joined together. We could send a train down each of these lines as far as was prudent—perhaps forty or fifty miles, perhaps more—and then come back blowing up every bridge and culvert behind us. In the time thus gained the defence of the town could be effectually organised. Suppose this thing happened! Suppose the Boer armies woke up to find their capital was in the hands of the masses of prisoners of war whom they had so incautiously accumulated there without an adequate garrison! How many men would they have to detach to besiege it? The kind of fighting in which the Boers excelled required the open country. They never succeeded during the whole war in reducing any strong places. Kimberley, Mafeking, Ladysmith are examples. Wherever they came up against trenches and fixed positions, they had recoiled. The theatre in which they were so formidable was the illimitable veldt. If we got Pretoria we could hold it for months. And what a feat of arms! President Kruger and his Government would be prisoners in our hands. He had talked of 'staggering humanity.' But here indeed was something to stagger him.

Perhaps with these cards in our hands we could negotiate an honourable peace, and end the struggle by a friendly and fair arrangement which would save the armies marching and fighting. It was a great dream. It occupied our thoughts for many days. Some ardent spirits went so far as to stitch together a Union Jack for use 'on the day.' But all remained a dream. The two or three senior officers who were prisoners with us, on being apprised of our plans, pronounced decidedly against them; and I shall certainly not claim that they were wrong. One is reminded of the comic opera. The villain impressively announces: 'Twelve thousand armed muleteers are ready to sack the town.' 'Why don't they do it?' he is asked. 'The Police won't let them.' Yes, there was the rub. Ten men awake and armed may be a small obstacle to a great scheme, but in this case, as in so many others, they were decisive. We abandoned our collective designs and concentrated upon individual plans of escape.

CHAPTER XXI

I ESCAPE FROM THE BOERS—I

During the first three weeks of my captivity, although I was a party to all plans of revolt or escape, I was engaged in arguing with the Boer Authorities that they should release me as a Press Correspondent. They replied that I had forfeited my non-combatant status by the part I had taken in the armoured train fight. I contended that I had not fired a shot and had been taken unarmed. This was strictly true. But the Natal newspapers had been captured by the Boers. These contained glowing accounts of my activities, and attributed the escape of the engine and the wounded entirely to me. General Joubert therefore intimated that even if I had not fired a shot myself, I had injured the Boer operations by freeing the engine, and that I must therefore be treated as a prisoner-of-war. As soon as I learned of this decision, in the first week of December, I resolved to escape.

I shall transcribe what I wrote at the time where I cannot improve upon it.

'The State Model Schools stood in the midst of a quadrangle, and were surrounded on two sides by an iron grille and on two by a corrugated-iron fence about ten feet high. These boundaries offered little obstacle to anyone who possessed the activity of youth, but the fact that they were guarded on the inside by sentries, fifty yards apart, armed with rifle and revolver, made them a well-nigh insuperable barrier. No walls are so hard to pierce as living walls.

'After anxious reflection and continual watching, it was discovered by several of the prisoners that when the sentries along the eastern side walked about on their beats they were at certain moments unable to see the top of a few yards of the wall near the small circular lavatory office which can be

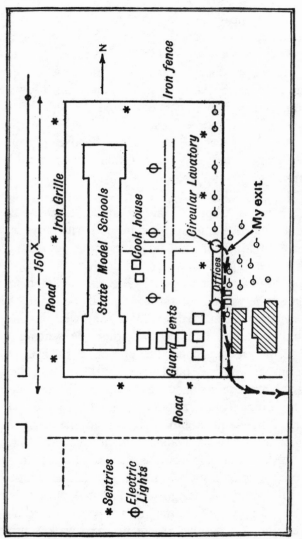

PLAN OF STATE MODEL SCHOOLS

seen on the plan. The electric lights in the middle of the quadrangle brilliantly lighted the whole place, but the eastern wall was in shadow. The first thing was therefore to pass the two sentries near the office. It was necessary to hit off the exact moment when both their backs should be turned together. After the wall was scaled we should be in the garden of the villa next door. There the plan came to an end. Everything after this was vague and uncertain. How to get out of the garden, how to pass unnoticed through the streets, how to evade the patrols that surrounded the town, and above all how to cover the two hundred and eighty miles to the Portuguese frontier, were questions which would arise at a later stage.'

'Together with Captain Haldane and Lieutenant Brockie I made an abortive attempt, not pushed with any decision, on December 11. There was no difficulty in getting into the circular office. But to climb out of it over the wall was a hazard of the sharpest character. Anyone doing so must at the moment he was on the top of the wall be plainly visible to the sentries fifteen yards away, if they were in the right place and happened to look! Whether the sentries would challenge or fire depended entirely upon their individual dispositions, and no one could tell what they would do. Nevertheless I was determined that nothing should stop my taking the plunge the next day. As the 12th wore away my fears crystallized more and more into desperation. In the evening, after my two friends had made an attempt, but had not found the moment propitious, I strolled across the quadrangle and secreted myself in the circular office. Through an aperture in the metal casing of which it was built I watched the sentries. For some time they remained stolid and obstructive. Then all of a sudden one turned and walked up to his comrade, and they began to talk. Their backs were turned.'

'Now or never! I stood on a ledge, seized the top of the wall with my hands, and drew myself up. Twice I let myself down again in sickly hesitation, and then with a third resolve scrambled up and over. My waistcoat got entangled with the ornamental metal-work on the top. I had to pause for an appreciable moment to extricate myself. In this posture I had one parting glimpse of the sentries still talking with their backs turned fifteen yards away. One of them was lighting his cigarette, and I remember the glow on the inside of his hands as a distinct impression which my mind recorded. Then I lowered myself lightly down into the adjoining garden and crouched among the shrubs. I was free! The first step had been taken, and it was irrevocable. It now remained to await the arrival of my comrades. The bushes in the garden gave a good deal of cover, and in the moonlight their shadows fell dark on the ground. I lay here for an hour in great impatience and anxiety. People were continually moving about in the garden, and once a man came and apparently looked straight at me only a few yards away. Where were the others? Why did they not make the attempt?'

'Suddenly I heard a voice from within the quadrangle say, quite loud, "All up." I crawled back to the wall. Two officers were walking up and down inside, jabbering Latin words, laughing and talking all manner of nonsense—amid which I caught my name. I risked a cough. One of the officers immediately began to chatter alone. The other said, slowly and clearly, "They cannot get out. The sentry suspects. It's all up. Can you get back again?" But now all my fears fell from me at once. To go back was impossible. I could not hope to climb the wall unnoticed. There was no helpful ledge on the outside. Fate pointed onwards. Besides, I said to myself, "Of course, I shall be recaptured, but I will at least have a run for my money." I said to the officers, "I shall go on alone."

'Now I was in the right mood for these undertakings—failure being almost certain, no odds against success affected me. All risks were less than the certainty. A glance at the plan will show that the gate which led into the road was only a few yards from another sentry. I said to myself, *"Toujours de l'audace,"* put my hat on my head, strode into the middle of the garden, walked past the windows of the house without any attempt at concealment, and so went through the gate and turned to the left. I passed the sentry at less than five yards. Most of them knew me by sight. Whether he looked at me or not I do not know, for I never turned my head. I restrained with the utmost difficulty an impulse to run. But after walking a hundred yards and hearing no challenge, I knew that the second obstacle had been surmounted. I was at large in Pretoria.

'I walked on leisurely through the night, humming a tune and choosing the middle of the road. The streets were full of burghers, but they paid no attention to me. Gradually I reached the suburbs, and on a little bridge I sat down to reflect and consider. I was in the heart of the enemy's country. I knew no one to whom I could apply for succour. Nearly three hundred miles stretched between me and Delagoa Bay. My escape must be known at dawn. Pursuit would be immediate. Yet all exits were barred. The town was picketed, the country was patrolled, the trains were searched, the line was guarded. I wore a civilian brown flannel suit. I had seventy-five pounds in my pocket and four slabs of chocolate, but the compass and the map which might have guided me, the opium tablets and meat lozenges which should have sustained me, were in my friends' pockets in the State Model Schools. Worst of all, I could not speak a word of Dutch or Kaffir, and how was I to get food or direction?

'But when hope had departed, fear had gone as well. I formed a plan. I would find the Delagoa Bay Railway. Without map or compass, I must follow that in spite of the pickets. I looked at the stars. Orion shone brightly. Scarcely a year before he had guided me when lost in the desert to the banks of the Nile. He had given me water. Now he should lead to freedom. I could not endure the want of either.

'After walking south for half a mile I struck the railroad.

Was it the line to Delagoa Bay or the Pietersburg branch? If it were the former, it should run east. But, so far as I could see, this line ran northwards. Still, it might be only winding its way out among the hills. I resolved to follow it. The night was delicious. A cool breeze fanned my face, and a wild feeling of exhilaration took hold of me. At any rate, I was free, if only for an hour. That was something. The fascination of the adventure grew. Unless the stars in their courses fought for me, I could not escape. Where, then, was the need of caution? I marched briskly along the line. Here and there the lights of a picket fire gleamed. Every bridge had its watchers. But I passed them all, making very short *détours* at the dangerous places, and really taking scarcely any precautions. Perhaps that was the reason I succeeded.

'As I walked I extended my plan. I could not march three hundred miles to the frontier. I would board a train in motion and hide under the seats, on the roof, on the couplings—anywhere. I thought of Paul Bultitude's escape from school in *Vice Versa*. I saw myself emerging from under the seat, and bribing or persuading some fat first-class passenger to help me. What train should I take? The first, of course. After walking for two hours I perceived the signal lights of a station. I left the line, and circling round it, hid in the ditch by the track about two hundred yards beyond the platform. I argued that the train would stop at the station and that it would not have got up too much speed by the time it reached me. An hour passed. I began to grow impatient. Suddenly I heard the whistle and the approaching rattle. Then the great yellow headlights of the engine flashed into view. The train waited five minutes at the station, and started again with much noise and steaming. I crouched by the track. I rehearsed the act in my mind. I must wait until the engine had passed, otherwise I should be seen. Then I must make a dash for the carriages.

'The train started slowly, but gathered speed sooner than I had expected. The flaring lights drew swiftly near. The rattle became a roar. The dark mass hung for a second above me. The engine-driver silhouetted against his furnace glow, the black profile of the engine, the clouds of steam rushed past. Then I hurled myself on the trucks, clutched at something, missed, clutched again, missed again, grasped some sort of hand-hold, was swung off my feet—my toes bumping on the line, and with a struggle seated myself on the couplings of the fifth truck from the front of the train. It was a goods train, and the trucks were full of sacks, soft sacks covered with coal-dust. They were in fact bags filled with empty coal bags going back to their colliery. I crawled on top and burrowed in among them. In five minutes I was completely buried. The sacks were warm and comfortable. Perhaps the engine-driver had seen me rush up to the train and would give the alarm at the next station; on the other hand, perhaps not. Where was the train going to? Where would it be unloaded? Would it be searched? Was it on the Delagoa Bay line? What should I do in the morning? Ah, never mind that. Sufficient for the night was the luck thereof. Fresh plans for fresh contingencies. I resolved to sleep, nor can I imagine a more pleasing lullaby than the clatter of the train that carries an escaping prisoner at twenty miles an hour away from the enemy's capital.

'How long I slept I do not know, but I woke up suddenly with all feelings of exhilaration gone, and only the consciousness of oppressive difficulties heavy on me. I must leave the train before daybreak, so that I could drink at a pool and find some hiding-place while it was still dark. I would not run the risk of being unloaded with the coal bags. Another night I would board another train. I crawled from my cosy hiding-place among the sacks and sat again on the couplings. The train was running at a fair speed, but I felt it was time to leave it. I took hold of the iron handle at the back of the truck, pulled strongly with my left hand, and sprang. My feet struck the ground in two gigantic strides, and the next instant I was sprawling in the ditch considerably shaken but unhurt. The train, my faithful ally of the night, hurried on its journey.

'It was still dark. I was in the middle of a wide valley, surrounded by low hills, and carpeted with high grass drenched in dew. I searched for water in the nearest gully, and soon found a clear pool. I was very thirsty, but long after I had quenched my thirst I continued to drink, that I might have sufficient for the whole day.

'Presently the dawn began to break, and the sky to the east grew yellow and red, slashed across with heavy black clouds. I saw with relief that the railway ran steadily towards the sunrise. I had taken the right line, after all.

'Having drunk my fill, I set out for the hills, among which I hoped to find some hiding-place, and as it became broad daylight I entered a small grove of trees which grew on the side of a deep ravine. Here I resolved to wait till dusk. I had one consolation: no one in the world knew where I was —I did not know myself. It was now four o'clock. Fourteen hours lay between me and the night. My impatience to proceed while I was still strong doubled their length. At first it was terribly cold, but by degrees the sun gained power, and by ten o'clock the heat was oppressive. My sole companion was a gigantic vulture, who manifested an extravagant interest in my condition, and made hideous and ominous gurglings from time to time. From my lofty position I commanded a view of the whole valley. A little tin-roofed town lay three miles to the westward. Scattered farmsteads, each with a clump of trees, relieved the monotony of the undulating ground. At the foot of the hill stood a Kaffir kraal, and the figures of its inhabitants dotted the patches of cultivation or surrounded the droves of goats and cows which fed on the pasture. . . . During the day I ate one slab of chocolate, which, with the heat, produced a violent thirst. The pool was hardly half a mile away, but I dared not leave the shelter of the little wood, for I could see the figures of white men riding or walking occasionally across the valley, and once a Boer came and fired two shots at birds close to my hiding-place. But no one discovered me.

'The elation and the excitement of the previous night had burnt away, and a chilling reaction followed. I was very hungry, for I had had no dinner before starting, and chocolate, though it sustains, does not satisfy. I had scarcely slept, but yet my heart beat so fiercely and I was so nervous and perplexed about the future that I could not rest. I thought of all the chances that lay against me; I dreaded and detested more than words can express the prospect of being caught and dragged back to Pretoria. I found no comfort in any of the philosophical ideas which some men parade in their hours of ease and strength and safety. They seemed only fair-weather friends. I realised with awful force that no exercise of my own feeble wit and strength could save me from my enemies, and that without the assistance of that High Power which interferes in the eternal sequence of causes and effects more often than we are always prone to admit, I could never succeed. I prayed long and earnestly for help and guidance. My prayer, as it seems to me, was swiftly and wonderfully answered.'

I wrote these lines many years ago while the impression of the adventure was strong upon me. Then I could tell no more. To have done so would have compromised the liberty and perhaps the lives of those who had helped me. For many years these reasons have disappeared. The time has come when I can relate the events which followed, and which changed my nearly hopeless position into one of superior advantage.

During the day I had watched the railway with attention. I saw two or three trains pass along it each way. I argued that the same number would pass at night. I resolved to board one of these. I thought I could improve on my procedure of the previous evening. I had observed how slowly the trains, particularly long goods-trains, climbed some of the steep gradients. Sometimes they were hardly going at a foot's pace. It would probably be easy to choose a point where the line was not only on an up grade but also on a curve. Thus I could board some truck on the convex side of the train when both the engine and the guard's van were bent away, and when consequently neither the engine-driver nor the guard would see me. This plan seemed to me in every respect sound. I saw myself leaving the train again before dawn, having been carried forward another sixty or seventy miles during the night. That would be scarcely one hundred and fifty miles from the frontier. And why should not the process be repeated? Where was the flaw? I could not see it. With three long bounds on three successive nights I could be in Portuguese territory. Meanwhile I still had two or three slabs of chocolate and a pocketful of crumbled biscuit —enough, that is to say, to keep body and soul together at a pinch without running the awful risk of recapture entailed by accosting a single human being. In this mood I watched with increasing impatience the arrival of darkness.

The long day reached its close at last. The western clouds flushed into fire; the shadows of the hills stretched out across the valley; a ponderous Boer wagon with its long team crawled slowly along the track towards the township; the Kaffirs collected their herds and drew them round their kraal; the daylight died, and soon it was quite dark. Then, and not until then, I set forth. I hurried to the railway line, scrambling along through the boulders and high grass and pausing on my way to drink at a stream of sweet cold water. I made my way to the place where I had seen the trains crawling so slowly up the slope, and soon found a point where the curve of the track fulfilled all the conditions of my plan. Here, behind a little bush, I sat down and waited hopefully. An hour passed; two hours passed; three hours —and yet no train. Six hours had now elapsed since the last, whose time I had carefully noted, had gone by. Surely one was due. Another hour slipped away. Still no train! My plan began to crumble and my hopes to ooze out of me. After all, was it not quite possible that no trains ran on this part of the

line during the dark hours? This was in fact the case, and I
might well have continued to wait in vain till daylight. However, between twelve and one in the morning I lost patience
and started along the track, resolved to cover at any rate ten
or fifteen miles of my journey. I did not make much progress. Every bridge was guarded by armed men; every few
miles were huts. At intervals there were stations with tin-
roofed villages clustering around them. All the veldt was
bathed in the bright rays of the full moon, and to avoid
these dangerous places I had to make wide circuits and even
to creep along the ground. Leaving the railroad I fell into
bogs and swamps, brushed through high grass dripping with
dew, and waded across the streams over which the bridges
carried the railway. I was soon drenched to the waist. I had
been able to take very little exercise during my month's imprisonment, and I was quickly tired with walking and with
want of food and sleep. Presently I approached a station. It
was a mere platform in the veldt, with two or three buildings and huts around it. But laid up on the sidings, obviously
for the night, were three long goods-trains. Evidently the
flow of traffic over the railway was uneven. These three
trains, motionless in the moonlight, confirmed my fears that
traffic was not maintained by night on this part of the line.
Where, then, was my plan which in the afternoon had looked
so fine and sure?

It now occurred to me that I might board one of these
stationary trains immediately, and hiding amid its freight
be carried forward during the next day—and night too if all
were well. On the other hand, where were they going to?
Where would they stop? Where would they be unloaded?
Once I entered a wagon my lot would be cast. I might find
myself ignominiously unloaded and recaptured at Witbank
or Middleburg, or at any station in the long two hundred
miles which separated me from the frontier. It was necessary
at all costs before taking such a step to find out where these
trains were going. To do this I must penetrate the station.

examine the labels on the trucks or on the merchandise, and see if I could extract any certain guidance from them. I crept up to the platform and got between two of the long trains on the siding. I was proceeding to examine the markings on the trucks when loud voices rapidly approaching on the outside of the trains filled me with fear. Several Kaffirs were laughing and shouting in their unmodulated tones, and I heard, as I thought, a European voice arguing or ordering. At any rate, it was enough for me. I retreated between the two trains to the extreme end of the siding, and slipped stealthily but rapidly into the grass of the illimitable plain.

There was nothing for it but to plod on—but in an increasingly purposeless and hopeless manner. I felt very miserable when I looked around and saw here and there the lights of houses and thought of the warmth and comfort within them, but knew that they meant only danger to me. Far off on the moonlit horizon there presently began to shine the row of six or eight big lights which marked either Witbank or Middleburg station. Out in the darkness to my left gleamed two or three fires. I was sure they were not the lights of houses, but how far off they were or what they were I could not be certain. The idea formed in my mind that they were the fires of a Kaffir kraal. Then I began to think that the best use I could make of my remaining strength would be to go to these Kaffirs. I had heard that they hated the Boers and were friendly to the British. At any rate, they would probably not arrest me. They might give me food and a dry corner to sleep in. Although I could not speak a word of their language, yet I thought perhaps they might understand the value of a British bank-note. They might even be induced to help me. A guide, a pony —but, above all, rest, warmth, and food—such were the promptings which dominated my mind. So I set out towards the fires.

I must have walked a mile or so in this resolve before a realisation of its weakness and imprudence took possession of

me. Then I turned back again to the railway line and retraced my steps perhaps half the distance. Then I stopped
and sat down, completely baffled, destitute of any idea what
to do or where to turn. Suddenly without the slightest reason all my doubts disappeared. It was certainly by no process
of logic that they were dispelled. I just felt quite clear that
I would go to the Kaffir kraal. I had sometimes in former
years held a 'Planchette' pencil and written while others had
touched my wrist or hand. I acted in exactly the same unconscious or subconscious manner now.

I walked on rapidly towards the fires, which I had in the
first instance thought were not more than a couple of miles
from the railway line. I soon found they were much farther
away than that. After about an hour or an hour and a half
they still seemed almost as far off as ever. But I persevered,
and presently between two and three o'clock in the morning
I perceived that they were not the fires of a Kaffir kraal. The
angular outline of buildings began to draw out against them,
and soon I saw that I was approaching a group of houses
around the mouth of a coal-mine. The wheel which worked
the winding gear was plainly visible, and I could see that the
fires which had led me so far were from the furnaces of the
engines. Hard by, surrounded by one or two slighter structures, stood a small but substantial stone house two storeys
high.

I halted in the wilderness to survey this scene and to re-
volve my action. It was still possible to turn back. But in
that direction I saw nothing but the prospect of further futile
wanderings terminated by hunger, fever, discovery, or surrender. On the other hand, here in front was a chance. I had
heard it said before I escaped that in the mining district of
Witbank and Middleburg there were a certain number of
English residents who had been suffered to remain in the
country in order to keep the mines working. Had I been led
to one of these? What did this house which frowned dark
and inscrutable upon me contain? A Briton or a Boer; a

friend or a foe? Nor did this exhaust the possibilities. I had my seventy-five pounds in English notes in my pocket. If I revealed my identity, I thought that I could give reasonable assurance of a thousand. I might find some indifferent neutral-minded person who out of good nature or for a large sum of money would aid me in my bitter and desperate need. Certainly I would try to make what bargain I could now—now while I still had the strength to plead my cause and perhaps to extricate myself if the results were adverse. Still the odds were heavy against me, and it was with faltering and reluctant steps that I walked out of the shimmering gloom of the veldt into the light of the furnace fires, advanced towards the silent house, and struck with my fist upon the door.

There was a pause. Then I knocked again. And almost immediately a light sprang up above and an upper window opened.

'*Wer ist da?*' cried a man's voice.

I felt the shock of disappointment and consternation to my fingers.

'I want help; I have had an accident,' I replied.

Some muttering followed. Then I heard steps descending the stairs, the bolt of the door was drawn, the lock was turned. It was opened abruptly, and in the darkness of the passage a tall man hastily attired, with a pale face and dark moustache, stood before me.

'What do you want?' he said, this time in English.

I had now to think of something to say. I wanted above all to get into parley with this man, to get matters in such a state that instead of raising an alarm and summoning others he would discuss things quietly.

'I am a burgher,' I began. 'I have had an accident. I was going to join my commando at Komati Poort. I have fallen off the train. We were skylarking. I have been unconscious for hours. I think I have dislocated my shoulder.'

It is astonishing how one thinks of these things. This

story leapt out as if I had learnt it by heart. Yet I had not the slightest idea what I was going to say or what the next sentence would be.

The stranger regarded me intently, and after some hesitation said at length, 'Well, come in.' He retreated a little into the darkness of the passage, threw open a door on one side of it, and pointed with his left hand into a dark room. I walked past him and entered, wondering if it was to be my prison. He followed, struck a light, lit a lamp, and set it on the table at the far side of which I stood. I was in a small room, evidently a dining-room and office in one. I noticed besides the large table, a roll desk, two or three chairs, and one of those machines for making soda-water, consisting of two glass globes set one above the other and encased in thin wire-netting. On his end of the table my host had laid a revolver, which he had hitherto presumably been holding in his right hand.

'I think I'd like to know a little more about this railway accident of yours,' he said, after a considerable pause.

'I think,' I replied, 'I had better tell you the truth.'

'I think you had,' he said, slowly.

So I took the plunge and threw all I had upon the board.

'I am Winston Churchill, War Correspondent of the *Morning Post*. I escaped last night from Pretoria. I am making my way to the frontier.' (Making my way!) 'I have plenty of money. Will you help me?'

There was another long pause. My companion rose from the table slowly and locked the door. After this act, which struck me as unpromising, and was certainly ambiguous, he advanced upon me and suddenly held out his hand.

'Thank God you have come here! It is the only house for twenty miles where you would not have been handed over. But we are all British here, and we will see you through.'

It is easier to recall across the gulf of years the spasm of relief which swept over me, than it is to describe it. A moment before I had thought myself trapped; and now friends, food, resources, aid were all at my disposal. I felt like a drowning man pulled out of the water and informed he has won the Derby!

My host now introduced himself as Mr. John Howard, manager of the Transvaal Collieries. He had become a naturalised burgher of the Transvaal some years before the war. But out of consideration for his British race and some inducements which he had offered to the local Field Cornet, he had not been called up to fight against the British. Instead he had been allowed to remain with one or two others on the mine, keeping it pumped out and in good order until coal-cutting could be resumed. He had with him at the mine-head, besides his secretary, who was British, an engine-man from Lancashire and two Scottish miners. All these four were British subjects and had been allowed to remain only upon giving their parole to observe strict neutrality. He himself as burgher of the Transvaal Republic would be guilty of treason in harbouring me, and liable to be shot if caught at the time or found out later on.

'Never mind,' he said, 'we will fix it up somehow.' And added, 'The Field Cornet was round here this afternoon asking about you. They have got the hue and cry out all along the line and all over the district.'

I said that I did not wish to compromise him.

Let him give me food, a pistol, a guide, and if possible a pony, and I would make my own way to the sea, marching by night across country far away from the railway line or any habitation.

He would not hear of it. He would fix up something. But he enjoined the utmost caution. Spies were everywhere. He had two Dutch servant-maids actually sleeping in the house. There were many Kaffirs employed about the mine premises and on the pumping-machinery of the mine. Surveying these dangers he became very thoughtful.

Then: 'But you are famishing.'

I did not contradict him. In a moment he had bustled off

into the kitchen, telling me meanwhile to help myself from a whisky bottle and the soda-water machine which I have already mentioned. He returned after an interval with the best part of a cold leg of mutton and various other delecta- ble commodities, and, leaving me to do full justice to these, quitted the room and let himself out of the house by a back door.

Nearly an hour passed before Mr. Howard returned. In this period my physical well-being had been brought into harmony with the improvement in my prospects. I felt con- fident of success and equal to anything.

'It's all right,' said Mr. Howard. 'I have seen the men, and they are all for it. We must put you down the pit to- night, and there you will have to stay till we can see how to get you out of the country. One difficulty,' he said, 'will be the *skoff* (food). The Dutch girl sees every mouthful I eat. The cook will want to know what has happened to her leg of mutton. I shall have to think it all out during the night. You must get down the pit at once. We'll make you com- fortable enough.'

Accordingly, just as the dawn was breaking, I followed my host across a little yard into the enclosure in which stood the winding-wheel of the mine. Here a stout man, intro- duced as Mr. Dewsnap, of Oldham, locked my hand in a grip of crushing vigour.

'They'll all vote for you next time,' he whispered.

A door was opened and I entered the cage. Down we shot into the bowels of the earth. At the bottom of the mine were the two Scottish miners with lanterns and a big bundle which afterwards proved to be a mattress and blankets. We walked for some time through the pitchy labyrinth, with frequent turns, twists, and alterations of level, and finally stopped in a sort of chamber where the air was cool and fresh. Here my guide set down his bundle, and Mr. Howard handed me a couple of candles, a bottle of whisky, and a box of cigars.

'There's no difficulty about these,' he said. 'I keep them

under lock and key. Now we must plan how to feed you to-morrow.'

'Don't you move from here, whatever happens,' was the parting injunction. 'There will be Kaffirs about the mine after daylight, but we shall be on the look-out that none of them wanders this way. None of them has seen anything so far.'

My four friends trooped off with their lanterns, and I was left alone. Viewed from the velvety darkness of the pit, life seemed bathed in rosy light. After the perplexity and even despair through which I had passed I counted upon freedom as certain. Instead of a humiliating recapture and long months of monotonous imprisonment, probably in the common jail, I saw myself once more rejoining the Army with a real exploit to my credit, and in that full enjoyment of freedom and keen pursuit of adventure dear to the heart of youth. In this comfortable mood, and speeded by intense fatigue, I soon slept the sleep of the weary—but of the triumphant.

CHAPTER XXII

I ESCAPE FROM THE BOERS—II

I DO not know how many hours I slept, but the following afternoon must have been far advanced when I found myself thoroughly awake. I put out my hand for the candle, but could feel it nowhere. I did not know what pitfalls these mining-galleries might contain, so I thought it better to lie quiet on my mattress and await developments. Several hours passed before the faint gleam of a lantern showed that someone was coming. It proved to be Mr. Howard himself, armed with a chicken and other good things. He also brought several books. He asked me why I had not lighted my candle. I said I couldn't find it.

'Didn't you put it under the mattress?' he asked.

'No.'

'Then the rats must have got it.'

He told me there were swarms of rats in the mine, that some years ago he had introduced a particular kind of white rat, which was an excellent scavenger, and that these had multiplied and thriven exceedingly. He told me he had been to the house of an English doctor twenty miles away to get the chicken. He was worried at the attitude of the two Dutch servants, who were very inquisitive about the depredations upon the leg of mutton for which I had been responsible. If he could not get another chicken cooked for the next day, he would have to take double helpings on his own plate and slip the surplus into a parcel for me while the servant was out of the room. He said that inquiries were being made for me all over the district by the Boers, and that the Pretoria Government was making a tremendous fuss about my escape. The fact that there were a number of English remaining in the Middleburg mining region indicated it as a likely place for me to have turned to, and all persons of English origin were more or less suspect.

I again expressed my willingness to go on alone with a Kaffir guide and a pony, but this he utterly refused to entertain. It would take a lot of planning, he said, to get me out of the country, and I might have to stay in the mine for quite a long time.

'Here,' he said, 'you are absolutely safe. Mac' (by which he meant one of the Scottish miners) 'knows all the disused workings and places that no one else would dream of. There is one place here where the water actually touches the roof for a foot or two. If they searched the mine, Mac would dive under that with you into the workings cut off beyond the water. No one would ever think of looking there. We have frightened the Kaffirs with tales of ghosts, and anyhow, we are watching their movements continually.'

He stayed with me while I dined, and then departed, leaving me, among other things, half-a-dozen candles which, duly warned, I tucked under my pillow and mattress.

I slept again for a long time, and woke suddenly with a feeling of movement about me. Something seemed to be pulling at my pillow. I put out my hand quickly. There was a perfect scurry. The rats were at the candles. I rescued the candles in time, and lighted one. Luckily for me, I have no horror of rats as such, and being reassured by their evident timidity, I was not particularly uneasy. All the same, the three days I passed in the mine were not among the most pleasant which my memory re-illumines. The patter of little feet and a perceptible sense of stir and scurry were continuous. Once I was waked up from a doze by one actually galloping across me. On the candle being lighted these beings became invisible.

The next day—if you can call it day—arrived in due course. This was December 14, and the third day since I had escaped from the State Model Schools. It was relieved by a visit from the two Scottish miners, with whom I had a long

confabulation. I then learned, to my surprise, that the mine
was only about two hundred feet deep.

There were parts of it, said Mac, where one could see the
daylight up a disused shaft. Would I like to take a turn
around the old workings and have a glimmer? We passed an
hour or two wandering round and up and down these sub-
terranean galleries, and spent a quarter of an hour near the
bottom of the shaft, where, grey and faint, the light of the
sun and of the upper world was discerned. On this promenade I saw numbers of rats. They seemed rather nice little
beasts, quite white, with dark eyes which I was assured in the
daylight were a bright pink. Three years afterwards a British
officer on duty in the district wrote to me that he had heard
my statement at a lecture about the white rats and their pink
eyes, and thought it was the limit of mendacity. He had
taken the trouble to visit the mine and see for himself, and
he proceeded to apologise for having doubted my truthful-
ness.

On the 15th Mr. Howard announced that the hue and cry
seemed to be dying away. No trace of the fugitive had been
discovered throughout the mining district. The talk among
the Boer officials was now that I must be hiding at the house
of some British sympathiser in Pretoria. They did not believe that it was possible I could have got out of the town.
In these circumstances he thought that I might come up and
have a walk on the veldt that night, and that if all was quiet
the next morning I might shift my quarters to the back room
of the office. On the one hand he seemed reassured, and on
the other increasingly excited by the adventure. Accordingly,
I had a fine stroll in the glorious fresh air and moonlight,
and thereafter, anticipating slightly our programme, I took
up my quarters behind packing-cases in the inner room of
the office. Here I remained for three more days, walking
each night on the endless plain with Mr. Howard or his as-
sistant.

On the 16th, the fifth day of escape, Mr. Howard informed me he had made a plan to get me out of the country. The mine was connected with the railway by a branch line. In the neighbourhood of the mine there lived a Dutchman, Burgener by name, who was sending a consignment of wool to Delagoa Bay on the 19th. This gentleman was well disposed to the British. He had been approached by Mr. Howard, had been made a party to our secret, and was willing to assist. Mr. Burgener's wool was packed in great bales and would fill two or three large trucks. These trucks were to be loaded at the mine's siding. The bales could be so packed as to leave a small place in the centre of the truck in which I could be concealed. A tarpaulin would be fastened over each truck after it had been loaded, and it was very unlikely indeed that, if the fastenings were found intact, it would be removed at the frontier. Did I agree to take this chance?

I was more worried about this than almost anything that had happened to me so far in my adventure. When by extraordinary chance one has gained some great advantage or prize and actually had it in one's possession and been enjoying it for several days, the idea of losing it becomes almost insupportable. I had really come to count upon freedom as a certainty, and the idea of having to put myself in a position in which I should be perfectly helpless, without a move of any kind, absolutely at the caprice of a searching party at the frontier, was profoundly harassing. Rather than face this ordeal I would much have preferred to start off on the veldt with a pony and a guide, and far from the haunts of man to make my way march by march beyond the wide territories of the Boer Republic. However, in the end I accepted the proposal of my generous rescuer, and arrangements were made accordingly.

I should have been still more anxious if I could have read some of the telegrams which were reaching English newspapers. For instance:

Pretoria, December 13.—Though Mr. Churchill's escape

was cleverly executed there is little chance of his being able to cross the border.

Pretoria, December 14.—It is reported that Mr. Winston Churchill has been captured at the border railway station of Komati Poort.

Lourenço Marques, December 16.—It is reported that Mr. Churchill has been captured at Waterval Boven.

London, December 16.—With reference to the escape from Pretoria of Mr. Winston Churchill, fears are expressed that he may be captured again before long and if so may probably be shot;

or if I had read the description of myself and the reward for my recapture which were now widely distributed or posted along the railway line. I am glad I knew nothing of all this.

The afternoon of the 18th dragged slowly away. I remember that I spent the greater part of it reading Stevenson's *Kidnapped*. Those thrilling pages which describe the escape of David Balfour and Alan Breck in the glens awakened sensations with which I was only too familiar. To be a fugitive, to be a hunted man, to be 'wanted,' is a mental experience by itself. The risks of the battlefield, the hazards of the bullet or the shell are one thing. Having the police after you is another. The need for concealment and deception breeds an actual sense of guilt very undermining to morale. Feeling that at any moment the officers of the law may present themselves or any stranger may ask the questions, 'Who are you?' 'Where do you come from?' 'Where are you going?'—to which questions no satisfactory answer could be given—gnawed the structure of self-confidence. I dreaded in every fibre the ordeal which awaited me at Komati Poort and which I must impotently and passively endure if I was to make good my escape from the enemy.

In this mood I was startled by the sound of rifle-shots close at hand, one after another at irregular intervals. A

£25.—.—

(vijf en twintig pond stg.)
*belooning uitgeloofd door
de Sub-Commissie van Wijk V
voor den Specialen Constabel
dezer wijk, die den ontvluchte
Krijgsgevangene
Churchill
levend of dood te dezer kantore
aflevert.—*

Namens de Sub-Comm.
Wijk V
Oudde Haas
Sec.

Translation.

£25

(Twenty-five Pounds stg.) REWARD is offered by the
Sub-Commission of the fifth division, on behalf of the Special Constable
of the said division, to anyone who brings the escaped prisoner of war

CHURCHILL,

dead or alive to this office.

For the Sub-Commission of the fifth division,
(Signed) LODK. de HAAS, Sec.

NOTE.—The Original Reward for the arrest of Winston Churchill on his escape from Pretoria, posted on the Government House at
Pretoria, brought to England by the Hon. Henry Masham, and is now the property of W. R. Burton.

sinister explanation flashed through my mind. The Boers had come! Howard and his handful of Englishmen were in open rebellion in the heart of the enemy's country! I had been strictly enjoined upon no account to leave my hiding-place behind the packing-cases in any circumstances whatever, and I accordingly remained there in great anxiety. Presently it became clear that the worst had not happened. The sounds of voices and presently of laughter came from the office. Evidently a conversation amicable, sociable in its character was in progress. I resumed my companionship with Alan Breck. At last the voices died away, and then after an interval my door was opened and Mr. Howard's pale, sombre face appeared, suffused by a broad grin. He relocked the door behind him and walked delicately towards me, evidently in high glee.

'The Field Cornet has been here,' he said. 'No, he was not looking for you. He says they caught you at Waterval Boven yesterday. But I didn't want him messing about, so I challenged him to a rifle match at bottles. He won two pounds off me and has gone away delighted.

'It is all fixed up for to-night,' he added.

'What do I do?' I asked.

'Nothing. You simply follow me when I come for you.'

At two o'clock on the morning of the 19th I awaited, fully dressed, the signal. The door opened. My host appeared. He beckoned. Not a word was spoken on either side. He led the way through the front office to the siding where three large bogie trucks stood. Three figures, evidently Dewsnap and the miners, were strolling about in different directions in the moonlight. A gang of Kaffirs were busy lifting an enormous bale into the rearmost truck. Howard strolled along to the first truck and walked across the line past the end of it. As he did so he pointed with his left hand. I nipped on to the buffers and saw before me a hole between the wool bales and the end of the truck, just wide enough to squeeze into. From this there led a narrow tunnel formed of wool bales into the centre of the truck. Here was a space wide enough to lie in, high enough to sit up in. In this I took up my abode.

Three or four hours later, when gleams of daylight had reached me through the interstices of my shelter and through chinks in the boards of the floorings of the truck, the noise of an approaching engine was heard. Then came the bumping and banging of coupling up. And again, after a further pause, we started rumbling off on our journey into the unknown.

I now took stock of my new abode and of the resources in munitions and supplies with which it was furnished. First there was a revolver. This was a moral support, though it was not easy to see in what way it could helpfully be applied to any problem I was likely to have to solve. Secondly, there were two roast chickens, some slices of meat, a loaf of bread, a melon, and three bottles of cold tea. The journey to the sea was not expected to take more than sixteen hours, but no one could tell what delay might occur to ordinary commercial traffic in time of war.

There was plenty of light now in the recess in which I was confined. There were many crevices in the boards composing the sides and floor of the truck, and through these the light found its way between the wool bales. Working along the tunnel to the end of the truck, I found a chink which must have been nearly an eighth of an inch in width, and through which it was possible to gain a partial view of the outer world. To check the progress of the journey I had learnt by heart beforehand the names of all the stations on the route. I can remember many of them to-day: Witbank, Middelburg, Bergendal, Belfast, Dalmanutha, Machadodorp, Waterval Boven, Waterval Onder, Elands, Nooidgedacht, and so on to Komati Poort. We had by now reached the first of these. At this point the branch line from the mine joined the railway. Here, after two or three hours' delay and shunting, we were evidently coupled up to a regular train, and soon started off at a superior and very satisfactory pace.

All day long we travelled eastward through the Transvaal, and when darkness fell we were laid up for the night at a station which, according to my reckoning, was Waterval Boven. We had accomplished nearly half of our journey. But how long should we wait on this siding? It might be for days; it would certainly be until the next morning. During all the dragging hours of the day I had lain on the floor of the truck occupying my mind as best I could, painting bright pictures of the pleasures of freedom, of the excitement of rejoining the army, of the triumph of a successful escape— but haunted also perpetually by anxieties about the search at the frontier, an ordeal inevitable and constantly approaching. Now another apprehension laid hold upon me. I wanted to go to sleep. Indeed, I did not think I could possibly keep awake. But if I slept I might snore! And if I snored while the train was at rest in the silent siding, I might be heard. And if I were heard! I decided in principle that it was only prudent to abstain from sleep, and shortly afterwards fell into a blissful slumber from which I was awakened the next morning by the banging and jerking of the train as the engine was again coupled to it.

Between Waterval Boven and Waterval Onder there is a very steep descent which the locomotive accomplishes by means of a rack and pinion. We ground our way down this at three or four miles an hour, and this feature made my reckoning certain that the next station was, in fact, Waterval Onder. All this day, too, we rattled through the enemy's country, and late in the afternoon we reached the dreaded Komati Poort. Peeping through my chink, I could see this was a considerable place, with numerous tracks of rails and several trains standing on them. Numbers of people were moving about. There were many voices and much shouting and whistling. After a preliminary inspection of the scene I retreated, as the train pulled up, into the very centre of my fastness, and covering myself up with a piece of sacking lay flat on the floor of the truck and awaited developments with a beating heart. 294

Three or four hours passed, and I did not know whether we had been searched or not. Several times people had passed up and down the train talking in Dutch. But the tarpaulins had not been removed, and no special examination seemed to have been made of the truck. Meanwhile darkness had come on, and I had to resign myself to an indefinite continuance of my uncertainties. It was tantalizing to be held so long in jeopardy after all these hundreds of miles had been accomplished, and I was now within a few hundred yards of the frontier. Again I wondered about the dangers of snoring. But in the end I slept without mishap.

We were still stationary when I awoke. Perhaps they were searching the train so thoroughly that there was consequently a great delay! Alternatively, perhaps we were forgotten on the siding and would be left there for days or weeks. I was greatly tempted to peer out, but I resisted. At last, at eleven o'clock, we were coupled up, and almost immediately started. If I had been right in thinking that the station in which we had passed the night was Komati Poort, I was already in Portuguese territory. But perhaps I had made a mistake. Perhaps I had miscounted. Perhaps there was still another station before the frontier. Perhaps the search still impended. But all these doubts were dispelled when the train arrived at the next station. I peered through my chink and saw the uniform caps of the Portuguese officials on the platform and the name Resana Garcia painted on a board. I restrained all expression of my joy until we moved on again. Then, as we rumbled and banged along, I pushed my head out of the tarpaulin and sang and shouted and crowed at the top of my voice. Indeed, I was so carried away by thankfulness and delight that I fired my revolver two or three times in the air as a *feu de joie*. None of these follies led to any evil results.

It was late in the afternoon when we reached Lourenço Marques. My train ran into a goods yard, and a crowd of Kaffirs advanced to unload it. I thought the moment had now come for me to quit my hiding-place, in which I had passed nearly three anxious and uncomfortable days. I had already thrown out every vestige of food and had removed all traces of my occupation. I now slipped out at the end of the truck between the couplings, and mingling unnoticed with the Kaffirs and loafers in the yard—which my slovenly and unkempt appearance well fitted me to do—I strolled my way towards the gates and found myself in the streets of Lourenço Marques.

Burgener was waiting outside the gates. We exchanged glances. He turned and walked off into the town, and I followed twenty yards behind. We walked through several streets and turned a number of corners. Presently he stopped and stood for a moment gazing up at the roof of the opposite house. I looked in the same direction, and there—blest vision!—I saw floating the gay colours of the Union Jack. It was the British Consulate.

The secretary of the British Consul evidently did not expect my arrival.

'Be off,' he said. 'The Consul cannot see you to-day. Come to his office at nine to-morrow, if you want anything.'

At this I became so angry, and repeated so loudly that I insisted on seeing the Consul personally at once, that that gentleman himself looked out of the window and finally came down to the door and asked me my name. From that moment every resource of hospitality and welcome was at my disposal. A hot bath, clean clothing, an excellent dinner, means of telegraphing—all I could want.

I devoured the file of newspapers which was placed before me. Great events had taken place since I had climbed the wall of the States Model Schools. The Black Week of the Boer War had descended on the British Army. General Gatacre at Stormberg, Lord Methuen at Magersfontein, and Sir Redvers Buller at Colenso, had all suffered staggering defeats, and casualties on a scale unknown to England since the Crimean War. All this made me eager to rejoin the army, and the Consul himself was no less anxious to get me out of Lourenço Marques, which was full of Boers and Boer sympathizers. Happily the weekly steamer was leaving for Durban that very evening; in fact, it might almost be said it ran in connection with my train. On this steamer I decided to embark.

The news of my arrival had spread like wildfire through the town, and while we were at dinner the Consul was at first disturbed to see a group of strange figures in the garden. These, however, turned out to be Englishmen fully armed who had hurried up to the Consulate determined to resist any attempt at my recapture. Under the escort of these patriotic gentlemen I marched safely through the streets to the quay, and at about ten o'clock was on salt water in the steamship *Induna*.

I reached Durban to find myself a popular hero. I was received as if I had won a great victory. The harbour was decorated with flags. Bands and crowds thronged the quays. The Admiral, the General, the Mayor pressed on board to grasp my hand. I was nearly torn to pieces by enthusiastic kindness. Whirled along on the shoulders of the crowd, I was carried to the steps of the town hall, where nothing would content them but a speech, which after a becoming reluctance I was induced to deliver. Sheaves of telegrams from all parts of the world poured in upon me, and I started that night for the Army in a blaze of triumph.

Here, too, I was received with the greatest goodwill. I took up my quarters in the very plate-layer's hut within one hundred yards of which I had a little more than a month before been taken prisoner, and there with the rude plenty of the Natal campaign celebrated by a dinner to many friends my good fortune and Christmas Eve.

CHAPTER XXIII

BACK TO THE ARMY

I FOUND that during the weeks I had been a prisoner of war my name had resounded at home. The part I had played in the armoured train had been exaggerated by the railway men and the wounded who had come back safely on the engine. The tale was transmitted to England with many crude or picturesque additions by the Press correspondents gathered at Estcourt. The papers had therefore been filled with extravagant praise of my behaviour. The news of my escape coming on the top of all this, after nine days' suspense and rumours of recapture, provoked another outburst of public eulogy. Youth seeks Adventure. Journalism requires Advertisement. Certainly I had found both. I became for the time quite famous. The British nation was smarting under a series of military reverses such as are so often necessary to evoke the exercise of its strength, and the news of my outwitting the Boers was received with enormous and no doubt disproportionate satisfaction. This produced the inevitable reaction, and an undercurrent of disparagement, equally undeserved, began to mingle with the gushing tributes. For instance *Truth* of November 23:

'. . . The train was upset and Mr. Churchill is described as having rallied the force by calling out "Be men! be men!" But what can the officers have been doing who were in command of the detachment? Again, were the men showing signs of behaving otherwise than as men? Would officers in command on the battlefield permit a journalist to "rally" those who were under their orders?'

The *Phœnix* (now extinct), November 23:

'That Mr. Winston Churchill saved the life of a wounded man in an armoured train is very likely. Possibly he also seized a rifle and fired at a Boer. But the question occurs what was he doing in the armoured train? He had no right there whatever. He is not now a soldier, although he once held a commission in the Fourth Hussars, and I hear that he no longer represents the *Morning Post*. Either, then, whoever commanded this ill-fated armoured train overstepped his duty in allowing Mr. Churchill to be a passenger by the train, or Mr. Churchill took the unwarrantable liberty of going without permission, thereby adding to the already weighty responsibilities of the officer in command.' . . . The *Phœnix* continued in a fairly cold-blooded spirit, considering that I was a fellow-countryman still in the hands of the enemy and whose case was undetermined: 'It is to be sincerely hoped that Mr. Churchill will not be shot. At the same time the Boer General cannot be blamed should he order his execution. A non-combatant has no right to carry arms. In the Franco-Prussian War all non-combatants who carried arms were promptly executed, when they were caught; and we can hardly expect the Boers to be more humane than were the highly civilized French and Germans.' . . .

The *Daily Nation* (also extinct) of December 16:

'Mr. Churchill's escape is not regarded in military circles as either a brilliant or honourable exploit. He was captured as a combatant, and of course placed under the same parole as the officers taken prisoners. He has however chosen to disregard an honourable undertaking, and it would not be surprising if the Pretoria authorities adopted more strenuous measures to prevent such conduct.' . . .

Finally the *Westminster Gazette* of December 26:

'Mr. Winston Churchill is once more free. With his accustomed ingenuity he has managed to escape from Pretoria; and the Government there is busy trying to find out how the escape was managed. So far, so good. But whilst it was perfectly within the rules of the game to get free, we confess that we hardly understand the application which Mr. Churchill is reported to have made to General Joubert asking to be released on the ground that he was a newspaper correspondent and had taken "no part in the fighting." We rubbed our eyes when we read this—have we not read glowing (and apparently authentic) accounts of Mr. Churchill's heroic exploits in the armoured train affair? General Joubert, apparently, rubbed his eyes too. He replied that Mr. Churchill—unknown to him personally—was detained because all the Natal papers attributed the escape of the armoured train to his bravery and exertion. But since this seemed to be a mistake, the General would take the correspondent's word that he was a non-combatant, and sent an order for his release—which arrived half a day after Mr. Churchill had escaped. Mr. Churchill's non-combatancy is indeed a mystery, but one thing is clear—that he cannot have the best of both worlds. His letter to General Joubert absolutely disposes of that probable V.C. with which numerous correspondents have decorated him.'

When these comments were sent me I could not but think them ungenerous. I had been in no way responsible for the tales which the railway men and the wounded from the armoured train had told, nor for the form in which these statements had been transmitted to England; and still less for the wide publicity accorded to them there. I was a prisoner and perforce silent. The reader of these pages will understand why I accompanied Captain Haldane on his ill-starred reconnaissance, and exactly the part I had taken in the fight, and can therefore judge for himself how far my claim to be a non-combatant was valid. Whether General Joubert had actually reversed his previous decision to hold me as a prisoner of war or not, I do not know, but it is certainly an odd coincidence that this order should only have been given publicity *after* I had escaped from the State Model Schools. The statement that I had broken my parole or any honourable understanding in escaping was of course untrue. No parole was extended to any of the prisoners of war, and we were all kept as I have described in strict confinement under armed guard. The lie once started, however, persisted in the alleys of political controversy, and I have been forced to extort damages and public apologies by prosecutions for libel on at least four separate occasions. At the time I thought the Pro-Boers were a spiteful lot.

Criticism was also excited in military and society circles by a telegram which I sent to the *Morning Post* from Durban.

'Reviewing the whole situation,' I wrote, 'it is foolish not to recognize that we are fighting a formidable and terrible adversary. The high qualities of the burghers increase their efficiency. The Government, though vilely corrupt, devote their whole energies to military operations.

'We must face the facts. The individual Boer, mounted in suitable country, is worth from three to five regular soldiers. The power of modern rifles is so tremendous that frontal attacks must often be repulsed. The extraordinary mobility of the enemy protects his flanks. The only way of treating the problem is either to get men equal in character and intelligence as riflemen, or, failing the individual, huge masses of troops. The advance of an army of 80,000 men in force, covered by 150 guns in line, would be an operation beyond the Boer's capacity to grapple with, but columns of 15,000 are only strong enough to suffer loss. It is a perilous policy to dribble out reinforcements and to fritter away armies.

'The Republics must weaken, like the Confederate States, through attrition. We should show no hurry, but we should collect overwhelming masses of troops. It would be much cheaper in the end to send more than necessary. There is plenty of work here for a quarter of a million men, and South Africa is well worth the cost in blood and money. More irregular corps are wanted. Are the gentlemen of England all foxhunting? Why not an English Light Horse? For the sake of our manhood, our devoted colonists, and our dead soldiers, we must persevere with the war.'

These unpalatable truths were resented. The assertion that 'the individual Boer mounted in suitable country was worth from three to five regular soldiers' was held derogatory to the Army. The estimate of a quarter of a million men being necessary was condemned as absurd. Quoth the *Morning Leader*: 'We have received no confirmation of the statement that Lord Lansdowne has, pending the arrival of Lord Roberts, appointed Mr. Winston Churchill to command the troops in South Africa, with General Sir Redvers Buller, V.C., as his Chief of Staff.' Unhappily this was sarcasm. The old colonels and generals at the 'Buck and Dodder Club' were furious. Some of them sent me a cable saying, 'Best friends here hope you will not continue making further ass of yourself.' However, my 'infantile' opinions were speedily vindicated by events. Ten thousand Imperial Yeomanry and gentlemen volunteers of every kind were sent to reinforce the professional army, and more than a quarter of a million British soldiers, or five times the total Boer forces, stood on South African soil before success was won. I might therefore console myself from the Bible: 'Better a poor and a wise child than an old and foolish king. . . .'

Meanwhile the disasters of the 'Black Week' had aroused the British nation and the Administration responded to their mood. Mr. Balfour, deemed by his critics a ladylike, dilèttante dialectician, proved himself in the face of this crisis the mainspring of the Imperial Government. Sir Redvers Buller —though this we did not know till long afterwards—had been so upset by his repulse at Colenso on December 15 and his casualty list of eleven hundred—then thought a terrible loss—that he had sent a panic-stricken dispatch to the War Office and pusillanimous orders to Sir George White. He advised the defender of Ladysmith to fire off his ammunition and make the best terms of surrender he could. He cabled to the War Office on December 15: 'I do not think I am now strong enough to relieve White.' This cable arrived at a week-end, and of the Ministers only Mr. Balfour was in London. He replied curtly, 'If you cannot relieve Ladysmith, hand your command over to Sir Francis Clery and return home.' White also sent a chilling reply saying that he had no intention of surrendering. Meanwhile, some days earlier the German Emperor, in a curiously friendly mood, had sent the British Military Attaché in Berlin to England with a personal message for Queen Victoria, saying: 'I cannot sit on the safety valve for ever. My people demand intervention. You must get a victory. I advise you to send out Lord Roberts and Lord Kitchener.' Whether upon this suggestion or otherwise, Lord Roberts was, on December 16, appointed to the chief command, with Lord Kitchener as Chief of Staff. Reinforcements, comprising the entire British Army outside India with powerful volunteer additions from home and the colonies, were set in motion towards South Africa. Buller, strongly reinforced, was assigned the command in Natal with orders to persevere in the relief of Ladysmith, while the main army, marshalled on a far larger scale than originally contemplated, was to advance northwards from the Cape Colony to relieve Kimberley and capture Bloemfontein.

Buller was by no means overjoyed at his task. He knew the strength of the enemy's positions on the heights beyond the Tugela, and since the shock he had sustained at Colenso, he even exaggerated the high qualities of the Boers. After one of his series of unsuccessful attempts to force the Tugela, he unbosomed himself to me in terms of the utmost candour. 'Here I am,' he exclaimed, 'condemned to fight in Natal, which all my judgment has told me to avoid, and to try to advance along the line worst of all suited to our troops.'

He now bent himself stubbornly to his unwelcome lot. I have no doubt that at his age he no longer possessed the military capacity, or the mental and physical vigour, or the resource and ruthlessness, which his duty required. Nevertheless he continued to command the confidence of his soldiers and remained the idol of the British public.

I am doubtful whether the fact that a man has gained the Victoria Cross for bravery as a young officer fits him to command an army twenty or thirty years later. I have noticed more than one serious misfortune which arose from such assumptions. Age, easy living, heaviness of body, many years of promotion and success in time of peace, dissipate the vital forces indispensable to intense action. During the long peace the State should always have ready a few naval and military officers of middle rank and under forty. These officers should be specially trained and tested. They should be moved from one command to another and given opportunities to take important decisions. They should be brought into the Council of Defence and cross-examined on their opinions. As they grow older they should be replaced by other men of similar age. 'Blind old Dandolos' are rare. Lord Roberts was an exception.

* * * * *

After Sir Redvers Buller had examined me at length upon the conditions prevailing in the Transvaal, and after I had given him whatever information I had been able to collect from the somewhat scanty view-point of my chink between the boards of the railway truck, he said to me:

'You have done very well. Is there anything we can do for you?'

I replied at once that I should like a commission in one of the irregular corps which were being improvised on all sides. The General, whom I had not seen since our voyage had ended, but whom, of course, I had known off and on during the four years I had served in the Army, appeared somewhat disconcerted at this, and after a considerable pause inquired:

'What about poor old Borthwick?' meaning thereby Sir Algernon Borthwick, afterwards Lord Glenesk, proprietor of the *Morning Post* newspaper. I replied that I was under a definite contract with him as war correspondent and could not possibly relinquish this engagement. The situation therefore raised considerable issues. In the various little wars of the previous few years it had been customary for military officers on leave to act as war correspondents, and even for officers actually serving to undertake this double duty. This had been considered to be a great abuse, and no doubt it was open to many objections. No one had been more criticised in this connection than myself for my dual rôle both on the Indian frontier and up the Nile. After the Nile Expedition the War Office had definitely and finally decided that no soldier could be a correspondent and no correspondent could be a soldier. Here then was the new rule in all its inviolate sanctity, and to make an exception to it on my account above all others—I who had been the chief cause of it—was a very hard proposition. Sir Redvers Buller, long Adjutant-General at the War Office, a man of the world, but also a representative of the strictest military school, found it very awkward. He took two or three tours round the room, eyeing me in a droll manner. Then at last he said:

'All right. You can have a commission in Bungo's[1] regiment. You will have to do as much as you can for both jobs. But,' he added, 'you will get no pay for ours.'

To this irregular arrangement I made haste to agree.

* * * * *

Behold me, then, restored to the Army with a lieutenant's commission in the South African Light Horse. This regiment of six squadrons and over 700 mounted men with a battery of galloping Colt machine-guns had been raised in the Cape Colony by Colonel Julian Byng, a Captain of the 10th Hussars and an officer from whom great things were rightly expected. He made me his assistant-adjutant, and let me go where I liked when the regiment was not actually fighting. Nothing could suit me better. I stitched my badges of rank to my khaki coat and stuck the long plume of feathers from the tail of the *sakabulu* bird in my hat, and lived from day to day in perfect happiness.

The S.A.L.H. formed a part of Lord Dundonald's cav-

[1]Colonel Byng, now Lord Byng of Vimy.

alry brigade, and the small group of officers and friends who inspired and directed this force nearly all attained eminence in the great European War. Byng, Birdwood and Hubert Gough all became Army Commanders. Barnes, Solly Flood, Tom Bridges and several others commanded Divisions. We messed together around the same camp fire or slept under the same wagons during the whole of the Natal fighting, and were the best of friends. The soldiers were of very varied origin, but first-rate fighting men. The S.A.L.H. were mostly South Africans, with a high proportion of hard-bitten adventurers from all quarters of the world, including a Confederate trooper from the American Civil War. Barnes' squadron of Imperial Light Horse were Outlanders from the Rand goldfields. Two squadrons of Natal Carabineers and Thorneycroft's Mounted Infantry were high-class farmers and colonists of the invaded province, and the two companies of British mounted infantry were as good as could be found in the Army. The Colonists, of course, especially the Outlanders and the men from Natal, were filled with a bitterness against the enemy which regular soldiers in those days considered unprofessional; but all worked cordially together.

CHAPTER XXIV

SPION KOP

THIS is not the place to re-tell at any length the story of the Relief of Ladysmith: but a brief account is needed.[1] Sir Redvers Buller abandoned his plan of forcing the Tugela at Colenso and advancing directly along the railway line. Having been reinforced till his army consisted of 19,000 infantry, 3,000 cavalry and 60 guns, he proceeded to attempt to turn the Boer right flank and to cross the Tugela about 25 miles upstream from Colenso. On January 11 Dundonald's cavalry brigade by a rapid march seized the heights overlooking Potgieter's and Trichardt's Drifts or fords; and on the following day all his infantry, leaving their tents standing and covered by our screen of cavalry outposts along the river, marched by easy stages by night to Trichardt's Drift. At daybreak on the 17th the whole of the cavalry crossed this ford without serious opposition, and continually reaching out their left hand reached by nightfall the neighbourhood of Acton Homes after a sharp and successful fight with about 200 Boers. Meanwhile the leading infantry brigade, having with some difficulty crossed the deep ford, had established themselves among the underfeatures of Spion Kop mountain and covered the throwing of two pontoon bridges. The bridges were completed during the morning, and the 2nd Division under Sir Charles Warren with an extra Brigade and most of the artillery of the Army crossed safely during the night. The morning of the 18th therefore saw nearly 16,000 troops safely across the Tugela, and their cavalry not very far from the open ground which lies beyond Acton Homes and offers two easy marches into Ladysmith. It was the general belief among the fighting troops, including the experienced Colonials, that a continuance of the left-

[1]Here the reader should look at the map on page 317.

handed movement of the cavalry would have turned the whole line of heights west of Spion Kop mountain, and that the relief of Ladysmith could be effected by mere persistence in the movement so prosperously launched.

Buller, on the other hand, and his staff were not without reason fearful of their communications. They were making in fact a lengthy flank march around the right of a most mobile enemy. One British brigade held the crossings about Colenso, another, Lyttelton's, was established opposite Potgieter's Drift. The main army was drawn up with its right resting on the base of Spion Kop mountain with the cavalry stretched out still farther to the left. But this front of 30 miles was by no means continuous. At any moment two or three thousand Boers could have crossed the river in the intervals between the watching brigades, and riding south might have interrupted the trailing line of communications along which all supplies had to be carried. The nightmare which haunted the Commander-in-Chief was of being cut off from the railway and encircled like Sir George White in Ladysmith without even an entrenched camp or adequate supplies to stand a siege. These dangers were rendered real by the leisureliness which marred all Buller's movements. While we therefore in the cavalry were eager to press on in our wide turning movement, Buller felt it vital to shorten the route and for this purpose to pivot on Spion Kop mountain. Accordingly on the night of the 23–24th an infantry brigade and Thorneycroft's regiment (dismounted) were sent to seize Spion Kop. The attack was successful. The few Boers on the mountain fled and morning saw General Woodgate's brigade established on the summit, while the rest of the army lay drawn out in the foothills and ridges to the westward.

Meanwhile the Boers had watched for six days the incredibly slow and ponderous movements of the British. Buller had sauntered and Warren had crawled. The enemy had had time to make entirely new dispositions and entrenchments. They were able to spare from the investment of Ladysmith about 7,000 mounted men and perhaps a dozen guns and Pom-poms. When, however, they found our cavalry aggressively threatening Acton Homes, a panic ensued, and large numbers of burghers, not only individually but by commandos, began to trek northwards. The spectacle of the British in occupation of Spion Kop caused surprise rather than alarm. General Schalk-Burger, gathering by his personal exertions about 1,500 men, mostly of the Ermelo and Pretoria Commandos, began within an hour of the morning fog lifting a fierce rifle counter-attack upon Spion Kop, and at the same time directed upon it from all angles the fire of his few but excellently-served and widely-spread guns.

Spion Kop is a rocky hill—almost a mountain—rising 1,400 feet above the river with a flat top about as large as Trafalgar Square. Into this confined area 2,000 British infantry were packed. There was not much cover, and they had not been able to dig more than very shallow trenches before the attack began. The Boer assailants very quickly established a superiority in the rifle duel. Shrapnel converging from a half-circle lashed the crowded troops. It would have been easier for the British to advance than to hold the summit. A thrust forward down all the slopes of Spion Kop accompanied by the advance of the whole army against the positions immediately in their front would certainly at this time have been successful. Instead of this, the brigade on the top of Spion Kop was left to bear its punishment throughout the long hours of the South African summer day. The general was killed at the beginning of the action, and losses, terrible in proportion to the numbers engaged, were suffered by the brigade. With equal difficulty and constancy the summit was held till nightfall; but at least 1,000 officers and men, or half the force exposed to the fire, were killed or wounded in this cramped space. In a desperate effort to relieve the situation Lyttleton sent two battalions across the river at Potgieter's Drift. These fine troops—the 60th Rifles and the

Cameronians—climbed the hill from the other side and actually established themselves on two nipples called the Twin Peaks, which were indeed decisive points, had their capture been used with resolution by the Commander-in-Chief. The rest of the army looked on, and night fell with the British sorely stricken, but still in possession of all the decisive positions.

I had marched with the cavalry to the Tugela, passed a precarious week expecting attack on our thin-spun outpost line, crossed the river at Trichardt's Drift early on the morning of the 17th, and taken part in the skirmish at Acton Homes on that evening. This was an inspiriting affair. The Boers thought they were going to outflank our brigade and lay an ambush for it, while two of our squadrons galloping concealed along the low ground by the river performed the same office for them. The enemy rode into a spoon-shaped hollow quite carelessly in pairs, and we opened fire on them from three sides and eventually got about half, including 30 prisoners, our losses being only four or five. Of course both cavalry brigades ought to have been allowed to go on the next day and engage the enemy freely, thus drawing him away from the front of the infantry. However, peremptory orders were issued for all the cavalry to come back into close touch with the left of the infantry. In this position three days later (20th) we attacked the line of heights beyond Venter's Spruit. We trotted to the stream under shell fire, left our horses in its hollows, and climbed the steep slopes on foot, driving back the Boer outposts. Following sound tactics we advanced up the salients, stormed Child's Kopje, and reached the general crest line with barely a score of casualties. These hills are however table-topped, and the Boers, whose instinct for war was better than the drill-books, had a line of trenches and rifle-pits about 300 yards back from the edge of the table. They saluted with a storm of bullets every man or head that showed, and no advance was possible across this bare grass glacis. We therefore hung on along the edge of the table until we were relieved after dark by the infantry.

The next day was for us a day of rest, but on the morning of the 24th when we awoke, all eyes were directed to the top of Spion Kop mountain which frowned upon our right. We were told it had been captured in the night by our troops, and that the Boers were counter-attacking was evident from the ceaseless crown of shrapnel shells bursting around the summit. After luncheon I rode with a companion to Three Tree Hill to see what was going on. Here were six field batteries and a battery of howitzers, an enormously powerful force in such a war; but they did not know what to fire at. They could not find the scattered Boer guns which all the time were bombarding Spion Kop, and no other targets were visible. We decided to ascend the mountain. Leaving our horses at its foot we climbed from one enormous boulder to another up its rear arête, starting near Wright's farm. The severity of the action was evident. Streams of wounded, some carried or accompanied by as many as four or five unwounded soldiers, trickled and even flowed down the hill, at the foot of which two hospital villages of tents and waggons were rapidly growing. At the edge of the table-top was a reserve battalion quite intact, and another brigadier who seemed to have nothing to do. Here we learned that after General Woodgate had been killed, Colonel Thorneycroft had been placed in command of all the troops on the summit and was fighting desperately. The brigadier had received orders not to supersede him. The white flag had already gone up once and the Boers had advanced to take the surrender of several companies, but Thorneycroft had arrived in a fury, had beaten down the flag, and heavy firing had been resumed at close quarters by both sides. To our right we could see the Twin Peaks, on which tiny figures moved from time to time. It was generally assumed they were the enemy. If so they were well posted and would soon compromise the retreat of the force. They were in fact our friends, the Cameronians from Potgieter's Drift. We crawled forward a short way on to the plateau, but the fire was much too hot for mere sight-seeing. We decided we would go and report the situation to the Staff.

It was sunset when we reached the headquarters of the 2nd Division. Sir Charles Warren was an officer 59 years old, and aged for his years. Sixteen years before he had commanded an expedition to Bechuanaland. He had been seconded from the army to become Chief Commissioner of the Metropolitan Police. He was now resuscitated to a most active and responsible position. He seemed worried. He had had no communication with the summit for several hours. Our tidings did not cheer him. His Staff Officer said, 'We have been very anxious all day, but the worst should be over now. We will send up fresh troops, dig in all night, and hold the position with a much smaller force to-morrow. Go now and tell this to Colonel Thorneycroft.' I asked for a written message, and the officer complied with this request.

So I climbed the mountain again, this time in pitch darkness. I passed through the reserve battalion still untouched and walked out on to the top of the plateau. The firing had died away and only occasional bullets sang through the air. The ground was thickly dotted with killed and wounded and I wandered about for some time before I found Colonel Thorneycroft. I saluted, congratulated him on becoming Brigadier-General, and handed him my note. 'Precious lot of brigadier there'll be to-morrow,' he said. 'I ordered a general retirement an hour ago.' He read the note. 'There is nothing definite in this,' he said impatiently. 'Reinforcements indeed! There are too many men here already. What is the general plan?' I said, 'Had I not better go and tell Sir Charles Warren before you retire from the hill? I am sure he meant you to hold on.' 'No,' he said, 'I have made up my mind. The retirement is already in progress. We have given up a lot of ground. We may be cut off at any moment,' and then, with great emphasis, 'Better six good battalions safely off the hill to-night than a bloody mop-up in the morning.' As he had no aide-de-camp or staff officer and was exhausted morally and physically by the ordeal through which he had passed, I continued at his side while for an hour or more the long files of men trooped in the darkness down the hill.

All was quiet now, and we were I think almost the last to leave the scene. As we passed through a few stunted trees dark figures appeared close at hand. 'Boers,' said Thorneycroft in a whisper; 'I knew they'd cut us off.' We drew our revolvers. Of course they were our own men. As we quitted the plateau a hundred yards farther on, we came upon the reserve battalion still fresh and unused. Colonel Thorneycroft gazed at the clustering soldiers for a minute or two as if once again balancing the decision, but the entire plateau was now evacuated and for all we knew re-occupied by the enemy, and shaking his head he resumed the descent. When half an hour later we had nearly reached the bottom of the mountain, we met a long column of men with picks and shovels. The sapper officer at their head had a shrouded lantern. 'I have a message for Colonel Thorneycroft,' he said. 'Read it,' said Thorneycroft to me. I tore the envelope. The message was short. 'We are sending,' it said in effect, '400 sappers and a fresh battalion. Entrench yourselves strongly by morning,' but Colonel Thorneycroft, brandishing his walking-stick, ordered the relieving troops to countermarch and we all trooped down together. The night was very dark, and it took me an hour to find the way through the broken ground to Warren's headquarters. The general was asleep. I put my hand on his shoulder and woke him up. 'Colonel Thorneycroft is here, sir.' He took it all very calmly. He was a charming old gentleman. I was genuinely sorry for him. I was also sorry for the army.

Colonel Thorneycroft erred gravely in retiring against his orders from the position he had so nobly held by the sacrifices of his troops. His extraordinary personal bravery throughout the day and the fact that his resolution had alone prevented a fatal surrender more than once during the action were held to condone and cover a military crime. It was certainly not for those who had left him so long without definite orders or any contact to lay the blame on him. A young active divisional general, having made all plans for the relief, would have joined him on the summit at nightfall and settled everything in person. A cruel misfortune would thus have been averted.

The Boers had also suffered heavy losses in the fight and had been grievously disheartened by their failure to take the hill. They were actually in retreat when Louis Botha—private two months before, now in chief command—coming from Ladysmith, turned them round and led them on to the table-top. All were appalled by the carnage. The shallow trenches were choked with dead and wounded. Nearly a hundred officers had fallen. Having re-occupied the position Botha sent forthwith a flag of truce inviting us to tend and gather our wounded and bury the dead. The 25th passed in complete silence. During the 25th and 26th our enormous wagon train rumbled back across the bridges, and on the night of the 26th the whole of the fighting troops recrossed the river. I have never understood why the Boers did not shell the bridges. As it was we passed unmolested, and Sir Redvers Buller was able to proclaim that he had effected his retreat 'without the loss of a man or a pound of stores.' That was all there was to show for the operations of a whole army corps for sixteen days at a cost of about eighteen hundred casualties.

Buller's next effort was directed against the ridges running eastward of Spion Kop to the bluffs of Doorn Kloof. The army had received drafts and reinforcements. The artillery had increased to nearly 100 guns, including a number of 50-pounder long-range naval guns. The plan was complicated, but can be simply explained. A bridge had been thrown across the river at Potgieter's Drift. An infantry brigade supported by the bulk of the artillery was to threaten the centre of the Boer position. While the enemy's eyes were supposed to be riveted upon this, three other brigades were to move to a point two miles downstream, where a second bridge would be rapidly thrown. One of these brigades was to attack the Vaal Krantz ridge upon its left, the others were to attack the Doorn Kloof position. The two cavalry brigades, the regulars and our own with a battery of horse artillery, were then to gallop towards Klip Poort through the hoped-for gap opened by these outward-wheeling attacks. We heard these proposals, when in deep secrecy they were confided to us the night before, with some concern. In fact when from Spearman's Hill we surveyed with telescopes the broken ground, interspersed with hummocks and watercourses and dotted with scrub and boulders, into which we were to be launched *on horseback*, we expected very rough treatment. However, the matter was not one on which we were invited to express an opinion.

The action began with a tremendous bombardment by our heavy artillery mounted on Zwaart Kop, and as our long cavalry columns filed slowly down the tracks from Spearman's Hill towards the river the spectacle was striking. The enemy's positions on the Vaal Krantz ridge smoked like volcanoes under the bursting shells. I had obtained a commission in the S.A.L.H. for my brother, who was just nineteen. He had arrived only two days before, and we rode down the hill together. Lyttelton's brigade crossed the second bridge, deployed to its left, and attacked the eastern end of the Vaal Krantz position. When they could get no farther they dug themselves in. It was now the turn of the second brigade; but there seemed great reluctance to launch this into the very difficult ground beyond the lower bridge. A battalion was soon involved in heavy fighting and the movement of the rest of the brigade was suspended. So about four o'clock in the afternoon we were told we should not be wanted till the next day. We bivouacked at the foot of the Heights, disturbed only by an occasional hostile shell. Although all our transport was only five miles back, we had nothing but what was necessary for our intended gallop through the gap, if gap there were. The night was chilly. Colonel Byng and I shared a blanket. When he turned over I was in the cold. When I turned over I pulled the blanket off him and he objected. He was the Colonel. It was not a good arrangement. I was glad when morning came.

Meanwhile General Lyttelton and his riflemen had dug themselves deeply in upon their ridge. They expected to be heavily shelled at daylight, and they were not disappointed. However, they had burrowed so well that they endured the whole day's bombardment and beat off several rifle attacks with less than two hundred casualties. We watched them all day in our bivouac with a composure tempered only by the thought that the hour for our gallop would soon come. It never came. That very night Lyttelton's brigade was withdrawn across the river. The pontoon bridges were lifted, and our whole army, having lost about 500 men, marched by leisurely stages back to the camps at Chieveley and Frere whence we had started to relieve Ladysmith nearly a month before. Meanwhile the garrison was on starvation rations and was fast devouring its horses and mules. Sir George White declared that he could hold out for another six weeks. He had however no longer any mobility to co-operate with us. He could just sit still and starve as slowly as possible. The outlook was therefore bleak.

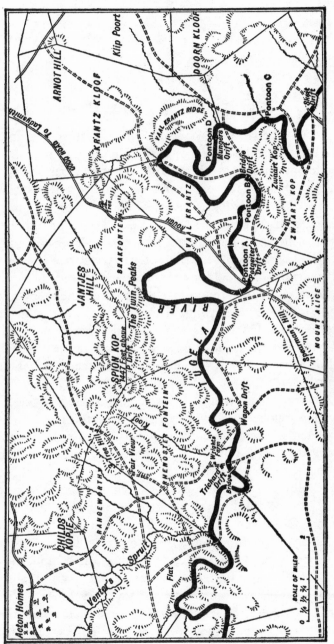

AROUND SPION KOP

CHAPTER XXV

THE RELIEF OF LADYSMITH

IN spite of the vexatious course of the war, the two months' fighting for the relief of Ladysmith make one of the most happy memories of my life. Although our irregular cavalry brigade was engaged with the enemy on at least three days out of five, our losses except in Thorneycroft's regiment at Spion Kop were never severe. We had one skirmish after another with casualties running from half a dozen to a score. I saw all there was to see. Day after day we rode out in the early morning on one flank or another and played about with the Boers, galloped around or clambered up the rocky hills, caught glimpses of darting, fleeting horsemen in the distance, heard a few bullets whistle, had a few careful shots and came safe home to a good dinner and cheery, keenly-intelligent companions. Meanwhile I dispatched a continual stream of letters and cables to *The Morning Post*, and learned from them that all I wrote commanded a wide and influential public. I knew all the generals and other swells, had access to everyone, and was everywhere well received. We lived in great comfort in the open air, with cool nights and bright sunshine, with plenty of meat, chickens and beer. The excellent Natal newspapers often got into the firing line about noon and always awaited us on our return in the evening. One lived entirely in the present with something happening all the time. Care-free, no regrets for the past, no fears for the future; no expense, no duns, no complications, and all the time my salary was safely piling up at home! When a prisoner I had thought it my duty to write from Pretoria to *The Morning Post* releasing them from their contract, as it seemed they would get no more value out of me. They did not accept my offer; but before I knew this,

I was already free. My relations with them continued to be of the best; and one could not serve better employers.

It was a great joy to me to have my brother Jack with me, and I looked forward to showing him round and doing for him the honours of war. This pleasure was however soon cut short. On February 12 we made a reconnaissance 6 or 7 miles to the east of the railway line and occupied for some hours a large wooded eminence known to the army as Hussar Hill. Buller and the Headquarters staff, it seemed, wished to examine this ground. Using our whole brigade we drove away the Boer pickets and patrols, set up an outpost line of our own, and enabled the general to see what he wanted. As the morning passed, the rifle fire became more lively, and when the time came to go home the Boers followed on our tail and we had some loss in disengaging ourselves.

After quitting Hussar Hill and putting at a gallop a mile between us and the enemy, our squadrons reined into a walk and rode slowly homewards up a long smooth grass slope. I was by now a fairly experienced young officer and I could often feel danger impending from this quarter or from that, as you might feel a light breeze on your cheek or neck. When one rode for instance within rifle shot of some hill or water-course about which we did not know enough, I used to feel a draughty sensation. On this occasion as I looked back over my shoulder from time to time at Hussar Hill or surveyed the large brown masses of our rearmost squadrons riding so placidly home across the rolling veldt, I remarked to my companion, 'We are still much too near those fellows.' The words were hardly out of my mouth when a shot rang out, followed by the rattle of magazine fire from two or three hundred Mauser rifles. A hail of bullets whistled among our squadrons, emptying a few saddles and bringing down a few horses. Instinctively our whole cavalcade spread out into open order and scampered over the crest now nearly two hundred yards away. Here we leapt off our horses, which were hurried into cover, threw ourselves on the grass, and returned the fire with an answering roar and rattle.

If the Boers had been a little quicker and had caught us a quarter of a mile farther back we should have paid dearly for the liberty we had taken: but the range was now over 2,000 yards; we were prone, almost as invisible as the enemy, and very little harm was done. Jack was lying by my side. All of a sudden he jumped and wriggled back a yard or two from the line. He had been shot in the calf, in this his very first skirmish, by a bullet which must have passed uncommonly near his head. I helped him from the firing line and saw him into an ambulance. The fusillade soon ceased and I rode on to the field hospital to make sure he was properly treated. The British army doctors were in those days very jealous of their military rank; so I saluted the surgeon, addressed him as 'Major,' had a few words with him about the skirmish, and then mentioned my brother's wound. The gallant doctor was in the best of tempers, promised chloroform, no pain, and every attention, and was certainly as good as his word.

But now here was a curious coincidence. While I had been busy in South Africa my mother had not been idle at home. She had raised a fund, captivated an American millionaire, obtained a ship, equipped it as a hospital with a full staff of nurses and every comfort. After a stormy voyage she had arrived at Durban and eagerly awaited a consignment of wounded. She received her younger son as the very first casualty treated on board the hospital ship *Maine*. I took a few days' leave to go and see her, and lived on board as on a yacht. So here we were all happily reunited after six months of varied experiences. The greatest swell in Durban was Captain Percy Scott, commander of the armoured cruiser *Terrible*. He lavished his courtesies upon us and showed us all the wonders of his vessel; he named the 4.7-inch gun that he had mounted on a railway truck after my mother, and even eventually organised a visit for her to the front to see it fire. Altogether there was an air of grace and amenity about this war singularly lacking fifteen years later on the Western Front.

Buller now began his fourth attempt to relieve Ladysmith. The garrison was in dire straits, and for all of us, relievers and besieged, it was kill or cure. The enemy's main positions were upon the bluffs and heights along the Tugela.[1] After flowing under the broken railway bridge at Colenso, the river takes a deep bend towards Ladysmith. The tongue of land encircled by the river included on our left (as we faced the enemy) Hlangwane Hill, assaulted by the South African Light Horse on December 15; in the centre, a long grassy plateau called the Green Hill, and on the far right, two densely-wooded and mountainous ridges named respectively Cingolo and Monte Cristo. Thus the Boer right had the river in its front and their left and centre had the river in its rear. It was now decided to make a wide turning movement, and try to surprise and seize these commanding ridges which constituted the true left flank of the enemy. If we were successful two infantry divisions sustained by all the artillery would assault the central plateau, and thence by a continued right-handed attack capture Hlangwane Hill itself. The conquest of this hill would render the Boer positions around Colenso untenable, and would open the passage of the river. This was a sound and indeed fairly obvious plan and there was no reason why it should not have been followed from the very beginning. Buller had not happened to think of it before. At Colenso, although assured that Hlangwane was on *his* side of the river, he had not believed it. He only gradually accepted the fact. That was all.

On the 15th the whole army marched from its camps along the railway to Hussar Hill and deployed for attack. Everything however depended upon our being able to capture Cingolo and Monte Cristo. This task was entrusted to Colonel Byng and our regiment, supported by an infantry

[1]See map on page 325.

brigade. It proved surprisingly easy. We marched by devious paths through the night and at dawn on the 18th climbed the southern slopes of Cingolo. We surprised and drove in the handful of Boers who alone were watching these key positions. During that day and the next in conjunction with the infantry we chased them off Cingolo, across the *nek* or saddle which joined the two ridges, and became masters of the whole of Monte Cristo. From this commanding height we overlooked all the Boer positions beyond the Tugela, and saw Ladysmith lying at our feet only six miles away. Meanwhile the main infantry and artillery attack on the sand-bag redoubts and entrenchments of the Green Hills had been entirely successful. The enemy, handled properly by envelopment and resolute attack, and disquieted by having a river in his rear, made but little resistance. By the night of the 20th the whole of the Boer positions south of the Tugela, including the rugged hill of Hlangwane, were in the British grip. The Boers evacuated Colenso and everywhere withdrew to their main line of defence across the river. So far so good.

We had only to continue this right-handed movement to succeed, for Monte Cristo actually dominated the Boer trenches at Barton's Hill beyond the river; and Barton's Hill, if taken, exposed the neighbouring eminence, and so on. But now Buller, urged it was said by Warren, made a mistake difficult to pardon after all the schooling he had received at the expense of his troops. Throwing a pontoon bridge near Colenso, he drew in his right, abandoned the commanding position, and began to advance by his left, along the railway line. In the course of the next two days he got his army thoroughly clumped-up in the maze of hills and spurs beyond Colenso. In these unfavourable conditions, without any turning movement, he assaulted the long-prepared, deeply-entrenched Boer position before Pieters. The purblind viciousness of these manœuvres was apparent to many. When I talked on the night of the 22nd with a high officer on the Headquarters' Staff, afterwards well known as Colonel Repington, he said bluntly, 'I don't like the situation. We have come down off our high ground. We have taken all the big guns off the big hills. We are getting ourselves cramped among these kopjes in the valley of the Tugela. It will be like being in the Coliseum and shot at by every row of seats!' So indeed it proved. The Boers, who had despaired of resisting our wide turning movement, and many of whom had already begun to trek northwards, returned in large numbers when they saw the British army once again thrusting its head obstinately into a trap.

Heavy confused fighting with many casualties among the low kopjes by the Tugela occupied the night of the 22nd/23rd. The assault of the Pieters position could not begin till the next evening. As the cavalry could play no part, I rode across the river and worked my way forward to a rocky spur where I found General Lyttelton[1] crouching behind a stone watching the fight. He was quite alone, and seemed glad to see me. The infantry, General Hart's Irish Brigade leading, filed and wound along the railway line, losing a lot of men at exposed points and gradually completing their deployment for their left-handed assault. The Pieters position consisted of three rounded peaks easily attackable from right to left, and probably impregnable from left to right. It was four o'clock when the Irish Brigade began to toil up the steep sides of what is now called Inniskilling Hill, and sunset approached before the assault was delivered by the Inniskilling and Dublin Fusiliers. The spectacle was tragic. Through our glasses we could see the Boers' heads and slouch hats in miniature silhouette, wreathed and obscured by shell-bursts, against the evening sky. Up the bare grassy slopes slowly climbed the brown figures and glinting bayonets of the Irishmen, and the rattle of intense musketry drummed in our ears. The climbing figures dwindled; they ceased to move; they vanished into the darkening hillside. Out of twelve

[1]Afterwards Sir Neville Lyttelton.

hundred men who assaulted, both colonels, three majors, twenty officers and six hundred soldiers had fallen, killed or wounded. The repulse was complete.

Sir Redvers Buller now allowed himself to be persuaded to resume the right-handed movement, and to deploy again upon a widely-extended front. It took three days to extricate the army from the tangle into which he had so needlessly plunged it. For two of these days hundreds of wounded lying on Inniskilling Hill suffered a cruel ordeal. The plight of these poor men between the firing lines without aid or water, waving pitiful strips of linen in mute appeal, was hard to witness. On the 26th Buller sought an armistice. The Boers refused a formal truce, but invited doctors and stretcher-bearers to come without fear and collect the wounded and bury the dead. At nightfall, this task being completed, firing was resumed.

February 27 was the anniversary of Majuba, and on this day the Natal army delivered its final attack. All the big guns were now back again on the big hills, and the Brigades, having passed the river by the Boer bridge which was undamaged, attacked the Boer position from the right. First Barton's Hill was stormed. This drew with it the capture of Railway Hill; and lastly the dreaded position of the Inniskilling Hill, already half turned and to some extent commanded, was carried by the bayonet. The last row of hills between us and Ladysmith had fallen. Mounting in haste we galloped to the river, hoping to pursue. The Commander-in-Chief met us at the bridge and sternly ordered us back. 'Damn pursuit!' were said to be the historic words he uttered on this occasion. As one might say 'Damn reward for sacrifices! Damn the recovery of debts overdue! Damn the prize which eases future struggles!'

The next morning, advancing in leisurely fashion, we crossed the river, wended up and across the battle-scarred heights, and debouched upon the open plain which led to Ladysmith six miles away. The Boers were in full retreat;

the shears were up over their big gun on Bulwana Hill, and the dust of the wagon-trains trekking northward rose from many quarters of the horizon. The order 'Damn pursuit!' still held. It was freely said that the Commander-in-Chief had remarked 'Better leave them alone now they are going off.' All day we chafed and fumed, and it was not until eve-

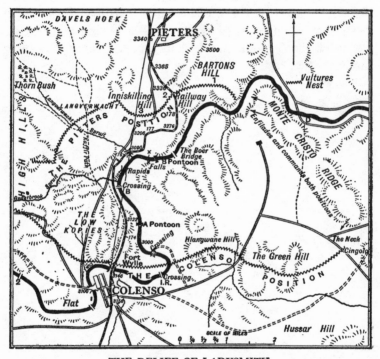

THE RELIEF OF LADYSMITH

ning that two squadrons of the S.A.L.H. were allowed to brush through the crumbling rearguards and ride into Lady-smith. I rode with these two squadrons, and galloped across the scrub-dotted plain, fired at only by a couple of Boer guns. Suddenly from the brushwood up rose gaunt figures waving hands of welcome. On we pressed, and at the head of a battered street of tin roofed houses met Sir George

White on horseback, faultlessly attired. Then we all rode together into the long beleaguered, almost starved-out, Ladysmith. It was a thrilling moment.

I dined with the Headquarters staff that night. Ian Hamilton, Rawlinson, Hedworth Lambton, were warm in their
welcome. Jealously preserved bottles of champagne were uncorked. I looked for horseflesh, but the last trek-ox had been
slain in honour of the occasion. Our pallid and emaciated
hosts showed subdued contentment. But having travelled so
far and by such rough and devious routes, I rejoiced to be in
Ladysmith at last.

CHAPTER XXVI

IN THE ORANGE FREE STATE

LORD ROBERTS had been a great friend of my father's. Lord Randolph Churchill had insisted as Secretary of State for India in 1885 in placing him at the head of the Indian Army, thrusting on one side for this purpose the claims of Lord Wolseley himself. They had continued friends until my father's death ten years later; and I as a child had often met the General and could pride myself on several fascinating conversations with him. He was always very kind to youth, tolerant of its precocity and exuberance, and gifted naturally with every art that could captivate its allegiance. I certainly felt as a young officer that here at any rate in the higher ranks of the Army was an august friend upon whose countenance I could rely.

While we in Natal were rejoicing in a success all the sweeter for so many disappointments, the news had already arrived that Roberts advancing northwards from the Cape Colony into the Orange Free State, had relieved Kimberley and had surrounded and captured the Boer Army under Cronje in the considerable fighting of Paardeberg. It seemed as if by a wave of the wand the whole war situation had been transformed and the black week of November 1899 had been replaced by the universal successes of February 1900. All this dramatic change in the main aspect of the war redounded in the public mind to the credit of Lord Roberts. This wonderful little man, it was said, had suddenly appeared upon the scene; and as if by enchantment, the clouds had rolled away and the sun shone once again brightly on the British armies in every part of the immense sub-continent.

In consequence of their reverses the Boers abandoned the invasion of Natal. They withdrew with their usual extraordinary celerity through the Drakensbergs back into their own territory. Dragging their heavy guns with them and all their stores, they melted away in the course of a fortnight and abandoned the whole of the colony of Natal to the Imperial troops. It was evident that a long delay would of necessity have to intervene before these ponderous forces—never more ponderous than under Buller—could be set in motion, repair the damaged railway, transport their immense quantities of supplies, and cover the 150 miles which separated Ladysmith from the Transvaal frontiers.

I now became impatient to get into the decisive and main theatre of the war. On the free and easy footing which had been accorded me by the Natal Army authorities since my escape from Pretoria, it was not difficult for me to obtain indefinite leave of absence from the South African Light Horse, and without resigning my commission to transfer my activities as a correspondent to Lord Roberts's army, at that time in occupation of Bloemfontein. I packed my kit-bag, descended the Natal Railway, sailed from Durban to Port Elizabeth, traversed the railways of the Cape Colony, and arrived in due course at the sumptuous Mount Nelson Hotel at Cape Town. Meanwhile the *Morning Post,* who regarded me as their principal correspondent, made the necessary application for me to be accredited to Lord Roberts's army. I expected the formalities would take several days, and these I passed very pleasantly interviewing the leading South African and Dutch politicians in the South African capital.

Hitherto I had been regarded as a Jingo bent upon the ruthless prosecution of the war, and was therefore vilified by the pro-Boers. I was now to get into trouble with the Tories. The evacuation of Natal by the invaders exposed all those who had joined, aided or sympathised with them to retribution. A wave of indignation swept through the colony.

The first thoughts of the British Government on the other hand now that they had won were to let bygones be bygones. An Under Secretary, Lord Wolverton, was allowed to make a speech in this sense. All my instincts acclaimed this magnanimity. On March 24 I had telegraphed from Ladysmith:

In spite of the feelings of the loyal colonists who have fought so gallantly for the Empire, I earnestly hope and urge that a generous and forgiving policy be followed. If the military operations are prosecuted furiously and tirelessly there will be neither necessity nor excuse for giving rebels who surrender a 'lesson.' The wise and right course is to beat down all who resist, even to the last man, but not to withhold forgiveness and even friendship from any who wish to surrender. The Dutch farmers who have joined the enemy are only traitors in the legal sense. That they obeyed the natural instinct of their blood to join the men of their own race, though no justification, is an excuse. Certainly their conduct is morally less reprehensible than that of Englishmen who are regular burghers of the Republics, and who are fighting as fiercely as proper belligerents against their own countrymen.

Yet even these Englishmen would deserve some tolerance were they not legally protected by their citizenship. The Dutch traitor is less black than the renegade British-born burgher, but both are the results of our own mistakes and crimes in Africa in former years. On purely practical grounds it is most important to differentiate between rebels who want to surrender and rebels who are caught fighting. Every influence should be brought to bear to weaken the enemy and make him submit. On the one hand are mighty armies advancing irresistibly, slaying and smiting with all the fearful engines of war; on the other, the quiet farm with wife and children safe under the protection of a government as merciful as it is strong. The policy which will hold these two pictures ever before the eyes of the Republican soldiers is truly 'thorough,' and therein lies the shortest road to 'peace with honour.'

This message was very ill received in England. A vindictive spirit, unhelpful but not unnatural, ruled. The Government had rallied to the nation; the Under Secretary had been suppressed; and I bore the brunt of Conservative anger. Even the *Morning Post,* while printing my messages, sorrowfully disagreed with my view. The Natal newspapers were loud-voiced in condemnation. I replied that it was not the first time that victorious gladiators had been surprised to see thumbs turned down in the Imperial box.

Sir Alfred Milner was far more undei standing, and spoke to me with kindliness and comprehension. His A.D.C. the Duke of Westminster, had organised a pack of hounds for his chief's diversion and exercise. We hunted jackal beneath Table Mountain, and lunched after a jolly gallop sitting among the scrub.

The High Commissioner said, 'I thought they would be upset, especially in Natal, by your message when I saw it. Of course all these people have got to live together. They must forgive and forget, and make a common country. But now passions are running too high. People who have had their friends or relations killed, or whose homes have been invaded, will not hear of clemency till they calm down. I understand your feelings, but it does no good to ·express them now.' I was impressed by hearing these calm, detached, broad-minded opinions from the lips of one so widely portrayed as the embodiment of rigid uncompromising subjugation. In the event, for all the fierce words, the treatment accorded to rebels and traitors by the British Government was indulgent in the extreme.

Here I must confess that all through my life I have found myself in disagreement alternately with both the historic English parties. I have always urged fighting wars and other contentions with might and main till overwhelming victory, and then offering the hand of friendship to the vanquished. Thus I have always been against the Pacifists during the quarrel, and against the Jingoes at its close. Many years after this South African incident, Lord Birkenhead mentioned to me a Latin quotation which seems to embody this idea extremely well. *'Parcere subjectis et debellare superbos,'* which he translated finely 'Spare the conquered and war down the proud.' I seem to have come very near achieving this thought by my own untutored reflections. The Romans have often forestalled many of my best ideas, and I must concede to them the patent rights in this maxim. Never indeed was it more apt than in South Africa. Wherever we departed from it, we suffered; wherever we followed it, we triumphed.

And not only in South Africa. I thought we ought to have conquered the Irish and then given them Home Rule: that we ought to have starved out the Germans, and then revictualled their country; and that after smashing the General Strike, we should have met the grievances of the miners. I always get into trouble because so few people take this line. I was once asked to devise an inscription for a monument in France. I wrote, 'In war, Resolution. In defeat, Defiance. In victory, Magnanimity. In peace, Goodwill.' The inscription was not accepted. It is all the fault of the human brain being made in two lobes, only one of which does any thinking, so that we are all right-handed or left-handed; whereas if we were properly constructed we should use our right and left hands with equal force and skill according to circumstances. As it is, those who can win a war well can rarely make a good peace, and those who could make a good peace would never have won the war. It would perhaps be pressing the argument too far to suggest that I could do both.

*   *   *   *   *

After several days had passed agreeably at Cape Town I began to wonder why no pass had reached me to proceed to

Bloemfontein. When more than a week had elapsed without any response to the regular application which had been made, I realised that some obstacle had arisen. I could not imagine what this obstacle could be. In all my writings from Natal I had laboured ceaselessly to maintain confidence at home and put the best appearance possible upon the many reverses and 'regrettable incidents' which had marked the operations in Natal. War Correspondents were considerable people in those days of small wars, and I was at that time one of the best-known writers among them and serving one of the most influential newspapers. I racked my brain and searched my conscience to discover any reasonable cause for the now obvious obstruction with which I was confronted.

Luckily I had at Lord Roberts's Headquarters two good and powerful friends. He had sent for Ian Hamilton, his former Aide-de-Camp and trusted friend, as soon as Lady-smith was relieved. General Nicholson—'Old Nick' of Lock-hart's Staff in Tirah—held a high position at Headquarters. These two had been to Roberts through many years of peace and war a part of what Marshal Foch in later years was accustomed to describe as '*ma famille militaire.*' Both were in the highest favour and had at all times the freest access to the Commander-in-Chief. In spite of certain differences of age and rank, I could count on them almost upon a footing of equal friendship. To these officers therefore I had recourse. They informed me by telegram that the obstacle was none other than the Commander-in-Chief himself. Lord Kitchener, it appeared, had been offended by some passages in *The River War,* and Lord Roberts felt that it might be resented by his Chief of Staff if I were attached as correspondent to the main portion of the army. But there was, they said, an additional cause of offence which had very seriously affected Lord Roberts's mind. In a letter to the *Morning Post* written from Natal, I had criticised severely the inadequacy of a sermon preached to the troops on the eve of battle by a Church of England Army Chaplain. The Commander-in-Chief regarded this as a very unjust reflection on the spiritual ministrations of these devoted officials. He was, my friends said, 'extremely stiff.' They were trying their best to soften him and believed that in a few days they would succeed. Meanwhile there was nothing for it but to wait.

I now recalled very clearly the incident of the Army Chaplain's sermon and what I had written about it. It was the Sunday between Spion Kop and Vaal Krantz. The men of a whole brigade, expecting to be seriously engaged on the next day or the day after, had gathered for Service in a little grassy valley near the Tugela and just out of gunshot of the enemy's lines. At this moment when all hearts, even the most indifferent, were especially apt to receive the consolations of religion, and when a fine appeal might have carried its message to deep and permanent results, we had been treated to a ridiculous discourse on the peculiar and unconvincing tactics by which the Israelites were said to have procured the downfall of the walls of Jericho. My comment, caustic perhaps, but surely not undeserved, had been: 'As I listened to these foolish sentences I thought of the gallant and venerable figure of Father Brindle in the Omdurman campaign,[1] and wondered whether Rome would again seize the opportunity which Canterbury disdained.' These strictures had, it appeared, caused commotion in the Established Church. Great indignation had been expressed, and following thereupon had been a veritable crusade. Several of the most eloquent divines, vacating their pulpits, had volunteered for the Front and were at this moment swiftly journeying to South Africa to bring a needed reinforcement to the well-meant exertions of the Army Chaplains Corps. But though the result had been so effective and as we may trust beneficent, the cause remained an offence. Lord Roberts, a deeply religious man, all his life a soldier, felt that the Military Chaplains' Department had suffered unmerited asper-

[1] A well-known and honoured figure in the British Army in this period; and afterwards Bishop of Nottingham.

sion, and the mere fact that outside assistance had now been proffered only seemed to aggravate the sting. In these circumstances my prospects for several days seemed very gloomy, and I languished disconsolately amid the Capuan delights of the Mount Nelson Hotel.

However, in the end my friends prevailed. My pass was granted and I was free to proceed to Bloemfontein, with the proviso however that before taking up my duties as War Correspondent I should receive an admonition from the Military Secretary to the Commander-in-Chief against reckless and uncharitable criticism. This was good enough for me, and I started on the long railway journey that same night. I was welcomed very cordially by my two distinguished friends, whose influence and authority were such as to bear down all opposition from subordinates. I received in due course, and with pious resignation, the lecture of the Military Secretary, and from that moment had entire liberty to move where I would, and, subject to mild censorship, write what I chose. But Lord Roberts maintained an air of inflexible aloofness. Although he knew that every day I was with people who were his closest assistants and friends, and although he knew that I knew how much my activities were a subject of discussion at his table even amid the press of great events, he never received me nor offered the slightest sign of recognition. When one morning in the market place at Bloemfontein amid a crowd of officers I suddenly found myself quite unexpectedly within a few yards of him, he acknowledged my salute only as that of a stranger.

There was so much interest and excitement in everyday life, that there was little time to worry unduly about the displeasure even of so great a personage and so honoured a friend. Equipped by the *Morning Post* on a munificent scale with whatever good horses and transport were necessary, I moved rapidly this way and that from column to column, wherever there was a chance of fighting. Riding sometimes quite alone across wide stretches of doubtful country, I would arrive at the rear-guard of a British column, actually lapped about by the enemy in the enormous plains, stay with them for three or four days if the General was well disposed, and then dart back across a landscape charged with silent menace, to keep up a continuous stream of letters and telegrams to my newspaper.

After the relief of Ladysmith and their defeat in the Free State, many of the Boers thought the war was over and made haste to return to their farms. The Republics sought peace by negotiation, observing quaintly that as the British had 'now recovered their prestige' this should be possible. Of course no one would entertain such an idea. The Imperial Government pointed to the injuries they had received from the Boer invasions, and sternly replied that they would make known their terms for the future settlement of South Africa from Pretoria. Meanwhile thousands of Boers in the Free State had returned to their homes and taken an oath of neutrality. Had it been possible for Lord Roberts to continue his advance without delay to Pretoria, it is possible that all resistance, at any rate south of the Vaal River, would have come to an end. But the army must first gather supplies. The principal railway bridges had been destroyed, and their repair by temporary structures involved reduced freights. The daily supply of the army drew so heavily upon the traffic, that supplies only accumulated at the rate of one day in four. It was evident therefore that several weeks must pass before the advance could be resumed. Meanwhile the resolute leaders of the Boers pulled themselves together and embarked upon a second effort, which though made with smaller resources, was far more prolonged and costly to us than their original invasion. The period of partisan warfare had begun. The first step was to recall to the commandos the burghers who had precipitately made separate peace for themselves. By threats and violence, oaths of neutrality notwithstanding, thousands of these were again forced to take up arms. The British denounced this treacherous behaviour, and although no one was executed for violating his oath, a new element of bitterness henceforward mingled in the struggle.

I learned that the war so far had not been kind to General Brabazon. He had come out in charge of a regular cavalry brigade, but in the waiting, wearing operations before Colesburg he had fallen out with General French. French was the younger and more forceful personality. Old 'Brab' did not find it easy to adapt himself to the new conditions of war. He thought of 'how we did it in Afganistan in '78, or at Suakim in '84,' when French was only a subaltern. But French was now his Commanding General, and the lessons of 1878 and 1884 were obsolete and fading memories. To these inconveniences Brabazon added the dangers of a free and mocking tongue. His comments, not only on French's tactics but on his youthful morals, were recounted in a jaunty vein. Tales were told to Headquarters. French struck back. Brabazon lost his regular brigade and emerged at the head of the ten thousand Imperial Yeomanry now gradually arriving in South Africa. This looked at first like promotion and was so represented to Brabazon. It proved to be a veritable 'Irishman's rise.' The ten thousand yeomanry arrived only to be dispersed over the whole theatre of war. One single brigade of these despised amateurs was all my poor friend could retain. With these he was now working in the region south-east of Bloemfontein. I resolved to join him.

I put my horses and wagon in a truck and trained south to Edenburg. I trekked thence through a disturbed district in drenching rain on the morning of April 17. I travelled prosperously, and on the night of the 19th overtook the British column eleven miles from Dewetsdorp. It was the 8th Division, the last division of our regular army scraped together from our fortresses all over the Empire. It was commanded by Sir Leslie Rundle, later unkindly nicknamed 'Sir Leisurely Trundle,' whom I had known up the Nile. Brabazon's brigade was scouting on ahead. Rundle was affable and hospitable; and early the next morning I rode on to join Brabazon. He was delighted to see me, told me his grievances, and entertained me vastly with stories and criticisms of French, as well as of the war and the world in general. We abode together for some days.

Very soon we began to approach the hills around Dewetsdorp. The distant patter of musketry broke the silence, and our patrols came scurrying back. Now ensued some of the most comical operations I have ever witnessed. Brabazon's yeomanry soon occupied the nearest hills, and a brisk skirmish developed with the Boers, who were apparently in some strength on the grass ridges before the town. Three or four enemy guns began to fire. Word was sent back to Rundle, and in the evening he arrived with his two brigades. I was admitted to the council. Brabazon was all for battle. All preparations were made for a regular attack next day. However, very early in the morning the leading Brigadier, Sir Herbert Chermside, made representations to our chief commander upon the gravity of the enterprise. In 1878—twenty-two years before—Chermside had been in the Russo-Turkish war. He therefore spoke with high authority. He declared that the Boers now held positions as formidable as those of Plevna, and that it would be imprudent without gathering every man and gun to launch an assault which might cost thousands of lives. It was therefore resolved to await the arrival of a third brigade under General Barr-Campbell, containing two battalions of Guards, who were already on the march from the railway and should arrive by night. So we passed a pleasant day skirmishing with the Boers, and as soon as evening fell another long column of infantry arrived. We now had nearly eleven thousand men and eighteen guns. All the dispositions were made for battle the next day. On the same evening however forty men of the Berkshire regiment, going out in the darkness to fetch water from a handy spring, unluckily missed their way and walked into the Boer lines instead of our own. This incident produced a sinister impression upon our Commander, and he telegraphed to Lord Roberts for orders. All the Generals at this time had received the most severe warnings against incurring casualties. Frontal attacks were virtually prohibited. Everything was to be done by kindness and manœuvre: instructions admirable in theory, paralysing in effect!

At daybreak when the whole force was drawn up for attack and our yeomanry awaited the signal to ride round the enemy's left flank, suddenly there arrived a staff officer with the news that the battle was again put off for that day at least. This was too much for Brabazon. He rode towards me wagging his head, and with a droll expression emitted suddenly in a loud voice and before everyone the words 'Bob Acres.' Whether the staff officer was so spiteful as to repeat this indiscretion, I cannot tell.

To appease Brabazon and also to do something or other, the cavalry were allowed to reconnoitre and test the left of the enemy's so-called 'Plevna.' And here I had a most exciting adventure.

Lest my memory should embroider the tale, I transcribe the words I wrote that same evening.

The brigade, which included the Mounted Infantry, and was about a thousand strong, moved southward behind the outpost line, and making a rapid and wide circuit, soon came on the enemy's left flank. . . . The ground fell steeply towards a flat basin, from the middle of which rose a most prominent and peculiar kopje. Invisible behind this was Dewetsdorp. Round it stood Boers, some mounted, some on foot, to the number of about two hundred.

Our rapid advance, almost into the heart of their position, had disturbed and alarmed them. They were doubtful whether this was reconnaissance or actual attack. They determined to make certain by making an attempt to outflank the outflanking Cavalry; and no sooner had our long-range rifle fire compelled them to take cover behind the hill than a new force, as it seemed, of two hundred rode into the open, and passing across our front at a distance of perhaps 2,000 yards, made for a white stone kopje on our right.

Angus McNeill, who had commanded Montmorency's Scouts since that officer had been killed, ran up to the General: 'Sir, may we head them off? I think we can just do it.' The scouts pricked up their ears. The General reflected. 'All right,' he said, 'you may try.'

'Mount, mount, mount, the scouts!' cried their impetuous officer, scrambling into his saddle. Then, to me, 'Come with us, we'll give you a show now—first-class.'

A few days before, in an unguarded moment, I had promised to follow the fortunes of the scouts for a day. I looked at the Boers: they were nearer to the white stone kopje than we, but on the other hand they had the hill to climb, and were probably worse mounted. It might be done, and if it were done—I thought of the affair of Acton Homes—how dearly they would have to pay in that open plain. So, in the interests of the *Morning Post*, I got on my horse and we all started—forty or fifty scouts, McNeill and I, as fast as we could, by hard spurring, make the horses go.

It was from the very beginning a race, and recognised as such by both sides. As we converged I saw the five leading Boers, better mounted than their comrades, outpacing the others in a desperate resolve to secure the coign of vantage. I said, 'We can't do it'; but no one would admit defeat or leave the matter undecided. The rest is exceedingly simple.

We arrived at a wire fence 100 yards—to be accurate, 120 yards—from the crest of the kopje, dismounted, and, cutting the wire, were about to seize the precious rocks when —as I had seen them in the railway cutting at Frere, grim, hairy, and terrible—the heads and shoulders of a dozen Boers appeared; and how many more must be close behind them?

There was a queer, almost inexplicable, pause, or perhaps there was no pause at all; but I seem to remember much happening. First the Boers—one fellow with a long, drooping, black beard, and a chocolate-coloured coat, another with a red scarf round his neck. Two scouts cutting the wire fence stolidly. One man taking aim across his horse, and McNeill's voice, quite steady: 'Too late; back to the other kopje. Gallop!'

Then the musketry crashed out, and the 'swish' and 'whirr' of the bullets filled the air. I put my foot in the stirrup. The horse, terrified at the firing, plunged wildly. I tried to spring into the saddle; it turned under the animal's belly. He broke away, and galloped madly away. Most of the scouts were already 200 yards off. I was alone, dismounted, within the closest range, and a mile at least from cover of any kind.

One consolation I had—my pistol. I could not be hunted down unarmed in the open as I had been before. But a disabling wound was the brightest prospect. I turned, and, for the second time in this war, ran for my life on foot from the Boer marksmen, and I thought to myself, 'Here at last I take it.' Suddenly, as I ran, I saw a scout. He came from the left, across my front; a tall man, with skull and crossbones badge, and on a pale horse. Death in Revelation, but life to me!

I shouted to him as he passed: 'Give me a stirrup.' To my surprise he stopped at once. 'Yes. Get up,' he said shortly. I ran to him, did not bungle in the business of mounting, and in a moment found myself behind him on the saddle.

Then we rode. I put my arms round him to catch a grip of the mane. My hand became soaked with blood. The horse was hard hit; but, gallant beast, he extended himself nobly. The pursuing bullets piped and whistled—for the range was growing longer—overhead.

'Don't be frightened,' said my rescuer; 'they won't hit you.' Then, as I did not reply, 'My poor horse, oh, my poor —— horse; shot with an explosive bullet. The devils! But their hour will come. Oh, my poor horse!'

I said, 'Never mind, you've saved my life.' 'Ah,' he rejoined, 'but it's the horse I'm thinking about.' That was the whole of our conversation.[1]

Judging from the number of bullets I heard I did not expect to be hit after the first 500 yards were covered, for a galloping horse is a difficult target, and the Boers were breathless and excited. But it was with a feeling of relief that I turned the corner of the further kopje and found I had thrown double sixes again.

When we returned to camp we learned that Lord Roberts, supposing that Rundle was 'held up by powerful forces', had set in motion from Bloemfontein another infantry division, and the whole of French's three brigades of cavalry in a wide sweeping movement against Dewetsdorp from the northwest. In two days this combination was complete, and the 2,500 Boers who for nearly ten days had wasted the energy of at least ten times their number of British troops slipped quietly away to the northward taking their prisoners with them. It was evident that the guerrilla phase would present a problem of its own.

I now attached myself to French's cavalry division and marched north with them. Here I found myself in a none too friendly atmosphere. It appeared that like a good many other Generals at this time, French disapproved of me. The hybrid combination of subaltern officer and widely-followed war correspondent was not unnaturally obnoxious to the military mind. But to these general prejudices was added a personal complication. I was known to be my old Colonel's partisan and close friend. I was therefore involved in the zone of these larger hostilities. Even Jack Milbanke, French's aide-de-camp, now recovered from his wound and newly decorated with the V.C., was unable to mitigate the antagonism that prevailed. Although I was often with

[1]Trooper Roberts received for his conduct on this occasion the Distinguished Conduct Medal.

French's column in march and skirmish, the General completely ignored my existence, and showed me no sign of courtesy or goodwill. I was sorry for this, because I greatly admired all I had heard of his skilful defence of the Coles-

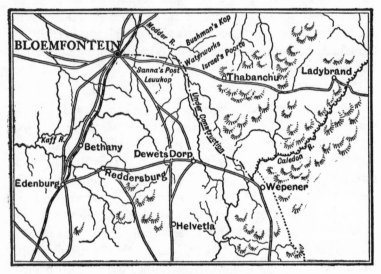

IN THE ORANGE FREE STATE

berg front, his dashing gallop through the Boer lines to the relief of Kimberley, and was naturally attracted by this gallant soldierly figure, upon whom fell at this moment the gleam of a growing fame. Thus during the South African war I never exchanged a word with the General who was afterwards to be one of my greatest friends and with whom I was for many years to work at grave matters in peace and war.

CHAPTER XXVII

JOHANNESBURG AND PRETORIA

IT was not until the beginning of May that Lord Roberts had replenished his magazines sufficiently to begin his march upon Johannesburg and Pretoria. Meanwhile the whole aspect of the war had degenerated, and no swift conclusion was in sight. The Army Headquarters had lain for two months in Bloemfontein, and great was the bustle before the advance. Lord Roberts at this time had upon his staff in one capacity or another, the Duke of Norfolk, the Duke of Westminster and the Duke of Marlborough. This had led to sarcastic paragraphs in the Radical newspapers, and the Commander-in-Chief—perhaps by nature unduly sensitive to public opinion—determined to shorten sail. He selected the Duke of Marlborough for retrenchment. My cousin was deeply distressed at the prospect of being left behind in the advance. Luckily, Ian Hamilton found himself with the rank of General entrusted with the command of a detached force of 16,000 men, at least 4,000 of whom were mounted, which was to move parallel to the main body at a distance of forty or fifty miles from its right or eastern flank. I had decided to march with this force, where I should be welcome and at home. I proposed by telegram to Hamilton that he should take Marlborough upon his staff. The General agreed, and Lord Roberts, who never liked to treat anyone unfairly, gave a cordial approval. I inspanned my four-horsed wagon, and we started upon a forty-mile march to overtake the flanking column. We came through the Boer-infested countryside defenceless but safely, and caught up our friends on the outskirts of Winburg. Henceforward all was well.

Then began a jolly march, occupying with halts about six weeks and covering in that period between four and five hundred miles. The wonderful air and climate of South Africa, the magnificent scale of its landscape, the life of unceasing movement and of continuous incident made an impression on my mind which even after a quarter of a century recurs with a sense of freshness and invigoration. Every day we saw new country. Every evening we bivouacked— for there were no tents—by the side of some new stream. We lived on flocks of sheep which we drove with us, and chickens which we hunted round the walls of deserted farms. My wagon had a raised floor of deal boards beneath which reposed two feet of the best tinned provisions and alcoholic stimulants which London could supply. We had every comfort, and all day long I scampered about the moving cavalry screens searching in the carelessness of youth for every scrap of adventure, experience or copy. Nearly every day as daylight broke and our widespread array of horse and foot began to move, the patter of rifle fire in front, on the flank, or more often at the heels of the rear-guard provided the exceptional thrills of active service. Sometimes, as at the passage of the Sand River, there were regular actions in which large bodies of troops were seen advancing against kopjes and ridges held by skilful, speedy and ubiquitous mounted Boers. Every few days a score of our men cut off, ambushed, or entrapped, made us conscious of the great fighting qualities of these rifle-armed horsemen of the wilderness who hung upon the movements of the British forces with sleuth-like vigilance and tenacity.

Lord Roberts, against the advice of his Intelligence Officer, believed that the enemy would retreat into the Western rather than the Eastern Transvaal. Accordingly, as we approached the frontiers of the Transvaal, Sir Ian Hamilton's column was shifted from the right of the main army to the left. We crossed the central line of railway at America siding and marched to the fords of the Vaal River. In this disposition we were so placed as to turn the western flank of the Johannesburg district and so compel its evacuation by

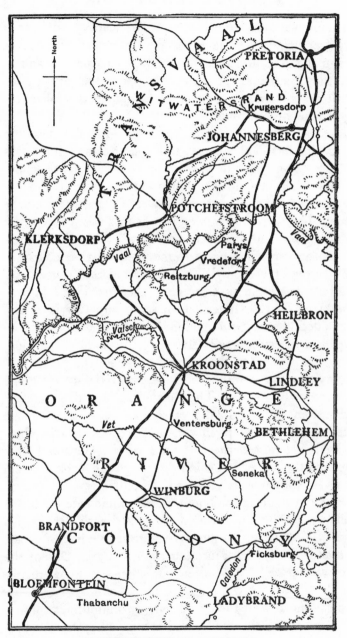

BLOEMFONTEIN TO PRETORIA

the enemy without requiring the main army to deliver a costly frontal attack. The Boers were alive to the purpose of this manœuvre, and although ready to evacuate Johannesburg, they sent a strong force to oppose the advance of Hamilton's column at a point called Florida on the Johannesburg-Potchefstroom route.

Here on June 1, 1900, on the very ground where the Jameson raiders had surrendered four years before, was fought what in those days was considered a sharp action. The Boers, buried amid the jagged outcropping rocks of the ridges, defied bombardment and had to be dislodged by the bayonet. The Gordon Highlanders, with a loss of nearly a hundred killed and wounded, performed this arduous task, while at the same time French's mounted forces tried rather feebly to turn the enemy's right flank and rear. I had myself a fortunate escape in this fight. After the ridge had been taken by the Highlanders, General Smith-Dorrien, who commanded one of Sir Ian Hamilton's brigades, wished to bring his artillery immediately on to the captured position, and as time was short, determined to choose the place himself. Inviting me to follow him, he cantered forward alone across the rolling slopes. The Boers had, according to their usual custom, lighted the dry grass, and long lines of smoke blotted out the landscape in various directions. In these baffling veils we missed the left flank of the Gordon Highlanders on the ridge, and coming through the smoke curtain with its line of flame, found ourselves only a few score yards distant from the enemy. There was an immediate explosion of rifle fire. The air all around us cracked with a whip-lash sound of close-range bullets. We tugged our horses' heads round and plunged back into our smoke-curtain. One of the horses was grazed by a bullet, but otherwise we were uninjured.

On the morrow of the action, Sir Ian Hamilton's column lay across the main road to the west of Johannesburg. Twenty miles away to the south of the city was the point

where Lord Roberts's headquarters should now have arrived. No means of communication existed between the two
forces. Johannesburg was still in the hands of the enemy,
and to go back southward by the way we had come meant
a detour of nearly eighty miles round rough hill ranges.
Mounted men were sent forthwith along this circuitous
route. A more speedy means of communication with the
Commander-in-Chief was at that juncture extremely important. Civilians who came out of the city and entered our
lines gave conflicting accounts of the conditions inside. The
Boers were clearing out, but they were still there. A young
Frenchman who seemed extremely well-informed assured
me that it would be quite easy to bicycle through the city in
plain clothes. The chances against being stopped and questioned in the closing hours of an evacuation were remote. He
offered to lend me a bicycle and guide me himself. I decided to make the attempt. Sir Ian Hamilton gave me his
dispatch, and I had also my own telegrams for the *Morning
Post*. We started in the afternoon and bicycled straight down
the main road into the city. As we passed our farthest outpost lines I experienced a distinct sensation of adventure. We
were soon in the streets of Johannesburg. Darkness was already falling. But numbers of people were about, and at once
I saw among them armed and mounted Boers. They were
still in possession of the city, and we were inside their lines.
According to all the laws of war my situation, if arrested,
would have been disagreeable. I was an officer holding a
commission in the South African Light Horse, disguised in
plain clothes and secretly within the enemy's lines. No court-
martial that ever sat in Europe would have had much difficulty in disposing of such a case. On all these matters I was
quite well informed.

We had to walk our bicycles up a long steep street, and
while thus engaged we heard behind us the overtaking approach of a slowly-trotting horseman. To alter our pace
would have been fatal. We continued to plod along, in ap-

347

pearance unconcerned, exchanging a word from time to time as we had agreed in French. In a few moments the horseman was alongside. He reined his horse into a walk and scrutinised us attentively. I looked up at him, and our eyes met. He had his rifle slung on his back, his pistol in his holster, and three bandoliers of cartridges. His horse was heavily loaded with his belongings. We continued thus to progress three abreast for what seemed to me an uncommonly long time, and then our unwelcome companion, touching his horse with a spur, drew again into his trippling trot and left us behind. It was too soon to rejoice. At any moment we might come upon the Boer picket line—if such a line existed—opposite Lord Roberts's troops; and our intention was to bicycle along the road without the slightest attempt at concealment. However, we found no Boer picket line nor, I regret to say, any British picket line. As the streets of Johannesburg began to melt into the country we met the first British soldiers of Lord Roberts's forces. They were quite unarmed and strolling forward into the city in search of food, or even drink. We asked where the army was. They indicated that it was close by. We advised them not to go farther into the town or they would be taken prisoners or shot.

'What's that, guv'nor?' said one of them, suddenly becoming interested in this odd possibility.

On being told that we had passed armed Boers only a mile farther back, these warriors desisted from their foray and turned off to examine some small neighbouring houses. My companion and I bicycled along the main road till we found the headquarters of Lord Roberts's leading division. From here we were directed to the General Headquarters nearly ten miles farther south. It was quite dark when at last we reached them. An aide-de-camp whom I knew came to the door.

'Where do you spring from?'

'We have come from Ian Hamilton. I have brought a dispatch for the Commander-in-Chief.'

'Splendid!' he said. 'We have been longing for news.'

He disappeared. My business was with the Press Censor, for whom I had a heavy sheaf of telegrams full of earliest and exclusive information. But before I could find this official the aide-de-camp reappeared.

'Lord Roberts wants you to come in at once.'

The Commander-in-Chief was at dinner with about a dozen officers of his Headquarter Staff. He jumped up from his chair as I entered, and with a most cordial air advanced towards me holding out his hand.

'How did you come?' he asked.

'We came along the main road through the city, sir.'

'Through Johannesburg? Our reports are that it is still occupied by the enemy.'

'There are a few, sir,' I said, 'but they are clearing out.'

'Did you see any of them?'

'Yes, we saw several, sir.'

His eye twinkled. Lord Roberts had very remarkable eyes, full of light. I remember being struck by this at the moment.

'Did you see Hamilton's action yesterday?' was his next question.

'Yes, sir.'

'Tell me all about it.'

Then, while being most hospitably entertained, I gave a full account of the doings of General Hamilton's force to my father's old friend and now once again my own.

*　　*　　*　　*　　*

Pretoria capitulated four days later. Enormous spans of oxen had dragged two 9.5-inch howitzers, the cow-guns as they were called, all these hundreds of miles to bombard the forts; but they were never needed after all. Nevertheless my re-entry of the Boer capital was exciting. Early on the morning of the 5th Marlborough and I rode out together and soon reached the head of an infantry column already in the

349

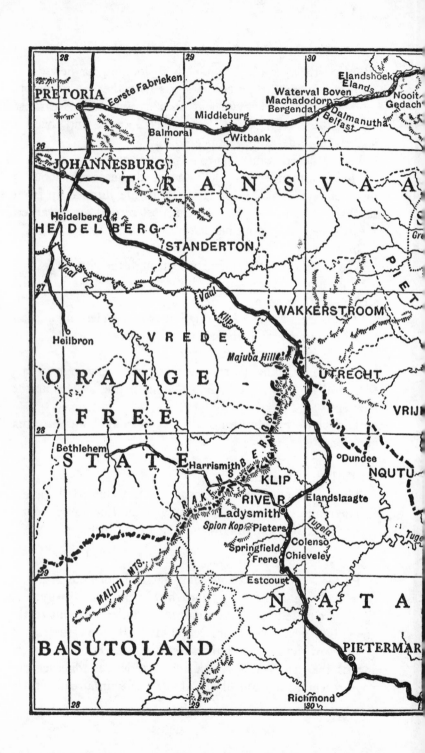

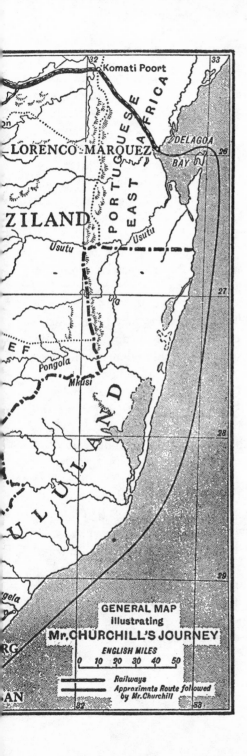

GENERAL MAP
illustrating
Mr. CHURCHILL'S JOURNEY

ENGLISH MILES

0   10   20   30   40   50

——————— Railways
—+—+—+—+— Approximate Route followed
                by Mr. Churchill

outskirts of the town. There were no military precautions, and we arrived, a large group of officers, at the closed gates of the railway level crossing. Quite slowly there now steamed past our eyes a long train drawn by two engines and crammed with armed Boers whose rifles bristled from every window. We gazed at each other dumbfounded at three yards' distance. A single shot would have precipitated a horrible carnage on both sides. Although sorry that the train should escape, it was with unfeigned relief that we saw the last carriage glide away past our noses.

Then Marlborough and I cantered into the town. We knew that the officer prisoners had been removed from the State Model Schools, and we asked our way to the new cage where it was hoped they were still confined. We feared they had been carried off—perhaps in the very last train. But as we rounded a corner, there was the prison camp, a long tin building surrounded by a dense wire entanglement. I raised my hat and cheered. The cry was instantly answered from within. What followed resembled the end of an Adelphi melodrama. We were only two, and before us stood the armed Boer guard with their rifles at the 'ready.' Marlborough, resplendent in the red tabs of the staff, called on the Commandant to surrender forthwith, adding by a happy thought that he would give a receipt for the rifles. The prisoners rushed out of the house into the yard, some in uniform, some in flannels, hatless or coatless, but all violently excited. The sentries threw down their rifles, the gates were flung open, and while the last of the guard (they numbered 52 in all) stood uncertain what to do, the long-penned-up officers surrounded them and seized their weapons. Someone produced a Union Jack, the Transvaal emblem was torn down, and amidst wild cheers from our captive friends the first British flag was hoisted over Pretoria. Time: 8.47, June 5. Tableau!

*   *   *   *   *

I had one more adventure in South Africa. After taking part a fortnight later in the action of Diamond Hill, fought to drive the Boers farther away from Pretoria, I decided to return home. Our operations were at an end. The war had become a guerrilla and promised to be shapeless and indefinite. A general election could not long be delayed. With the consent of the authorities I resumed my full civilian status and took the train for Cape Town.

All went well till we reached the neighbourhood beyond Kopjes Station, about 100 miles south of Johannesburg. In the first light of morning I was breakfasting with West-minister, who was travelling on some commission for Lord Roberts, when suddenly the train stopped with a jerk. We got out on to the line, and at the same moment there arrived almost at our feet a shell from a small Boer gun. It burst with a startling bang, throwing up clods from the embankment. A hundred yards ahead of us a temporary wooden bridge was in flames. The train was enormously long, and crowded with soldiers from a score of regiments, who for one reason or another were being sent south or home. No one was in command. The soldiers began to get out of the carriages in confusion. I saw no officers. Kopjes Station, where there was a fortified camp surmounted by two 5-inch guns, was three miles back. My memories of the armoured train made me extremely sensitive about our line of retreat. I had no wish to repeat the experiences of November 15; I therefore ran along the railway line to the engine, climbed into the cab, and ordered the engine-driver to blow his whistle to make the men re-entrain, and steam back instantly to Kopjes Station. He obeyed. While I was standing on the foot-plate to make sure the soldiers had got back into the train, I saw, less than a hundred yards away in the dry water-course under the burning bridge, a cluster of dark figures. These were the last Boers I was to see as enemies. I fitted the wooden stock to the Mauser pistol and fired six or seven times at them. They scattered without firing back. Then the

353

engine started, and we were soon all safely within the entrenchment at Kopjes Station. Here we learned that a fierce action was proceeding at Honing Spruit, a station farther down the line. The train before ours had been held up, and was at that moment being attacked by a considerable Boer force with artillery. The line had been broken in front of our train, no doubt to prevent reinforcements coming to their aid. However, with a loss of 60 or 70 men our friends at Honing Spruit managed to hold out till the next day when help arrived from the south and the Boers retreated. As it would take several days to repair the line, we borrowed horses and marched all night from Kopjes Station with a troop of Australian Lancers, coming through without misadventure. I thought for many years that the 2-inch Creusot shell which had burst so near us on the embankment was the last projectile I should ever see fired in anger. This expectation however proved unfounded.

CHAPTER XXVIII

THE KHAKI ELECTION

MOST people in England thought that the war was over now that Pretoria was taken and above all when Mafeking was relieved. They were encouraged in this by Lord Roberts's speeches. They gave themselves up to rejoicings. But the Government knew better. They had allowed themselves to be drawn on by the tides of success into an arbitrary and dangerous position. There was to be no negotiation with the Boer Republics. They were simply to be blotted out. If the Boers liked to come in and surrender either singly or under their generals, they would get very good treatment, and ultimately, after enough English had settled in the conquered territory to make it safe, they would be given self-government as in other British colonies. Otherwise they would be hunted down or caught even to the very last man. As Lord Milner put it some time later on, 'in a certain sense the war would never be ended'; it would just fade away. The guerrilla phase would be ended by the armies; and after that, brigandage in the mountains and the back-veldt would be put down by armed police.

This was an error destined to cost us dear. There were still many thousands of wild, fierce, dauntless men under leaders like Botha, Smuts, De Wet, De la Rey and Hertzog who now fought on in their vast country not for victory, but for honour. The flames of partisan warfare broke out again and again behind the armies in regions completely pacified. Even the Cape Colony was rekindled by Smuts into a fire which smouldered or blazed for two destructive years and was extinguished only by formal negotiation. This long-drawn struggle bred shocking evils. The roving enemy wore no uniforms of their own; they mingled with the population, lodged and were succoured in farmhouses whose owners had taken the oath of neutrality, and sprang into being, now here now there, to make some formidable and bloody attack upon an unwary column or isolated post. To cope with all this the British military authorities found it necessary to clear whole districts of their inhabitants and gather the population into concentration camps. As the railways were continually cut, it was difficult to supply these camps with all the necessaries of life. Disease broke out and several thousands of women and children died. The policy of burning farms whose owners had broken their oath, far from quelling the fighting Boers, only rendered them desperate. The British on their side were incensed against the rebels, oath-breakers, and Boers who wore captured British uniforms (mainly because they had no other clothes, but sometimes as a treacherous strategem). However, very few persons were executed. Kitchener shot with impartial rigour a British officer and some colonial troopers convicted long after their offence of having killed some Boer prisoners; and to the very end the Boer commandos did not hesitate to send their wounded into the British field hospitals. Thus humanity and civilisation were never wholly banished, and both sides preserved amid frightful reciprocal injuries some mutual respect during two harsh years of waste and devastation. All this however lay in the future.

I received the warmest of welcomes on returning home. Oldham almost without distinction of party accorded me a triumph. I entered the town in state in a procession of ten landaus, and drove through streets crowded with enthusiastic operatives and mill-girls. I described my escape to a tremendous meeting in the Theatre Royal. As our forces had now occupied the Witbank Colliery district, and those who had aided me were safe under British protection, I was free for the first time to tell the whole story. When I mentioned the name of Mr. Dewsnap, the Oldham engineer who had wound me down the mine, the audience shouted: 'His wife's in the gallery.' There was general jubilation.

This harmony was inevitably to be marred. The Conservative leaders determined to appeal to the country before the enthusiasm of victory died down. They had already been in office for five years. A General Election must come in eighteen months, and the opportunity was too good to be thrown away. Indeed they could not have carried out the policy of annexing the Boer Republics and of suppressing all opposition by force of arms without parley, except in a new Parliament and with a new majority. Early in September therefore Parliament was dissolved. We had the same kind of election as occurred in a far more violent form after the Great War in December 1918. All the Liberals, even those who had most loyally supported the war measures, including some who had lost their sons, were lapped in a general condemnation as 'Pro-Boers.' Mr. Chamberlain uttered the slogan, 'Every seat lost to the Government is a seat gained to the Boers' and Conservatives generally followed in his wake. The Liberal and Radical masses, however, believing in the lull of the war that the fighting was over, rallied stubbornly to their party organisations. The election was well contested all over the country. The Conservatives in those days had a large permanent majority of the English electorate. The prevailing wave of opinion was with them, and Lord Salisbury and his colleagues were returned with a scarcely diminished majority of 134 over all opponents, including the 80 Irish Nationalists. His majority in the main island was overwhelming.

I stood in the van of this victory. In those days our wise and prudent law spread a general election over nearly six weeks. Instead of all the electors voting blindly on one day, and only learning the next morning what they had done, national issues were really fought out. A rough but earnest and searching national discussion took place in which leading men on both sides played a part. The electorate of a constituency was not unmanageable in numbers. A candidate could address all his supporters who wished to hear him. A great speech by an eminent personage would often turn a constituency or even a city. Speeches of well-known and experienced statesmen were fully reported in all the newspapers and studied by wide political classes. Thus by a process of rugged argument the national decision was reached in measured steps.

In those days of hammer and anvil politics, the earliest election results were awaited with intense interest. Oldham was almost the first constituency to poll. I fought on the platform that the war was just and necessary, that the Liberals had been wrong to oppose it, and in many ways had hampered its conduct; that it must be fought to an indisputable conclusion, and that thereafter there should be a generous settlement. I had a new colleague at my side, Mr. C. B. Crisp, a City of London merchant. Mr. Mawdsley was no more. He was a very heavy man. He had taken a bath in a china vessel which had broken under his weight, inflicting injuries to which he eventually succumbed. My opponents, Mr. Emmott and Mr. Runciman, had both adopted in the main Lord Rosebery's attitude towards the war; that is to say, they supported the country in the conflict, but alleged gross incompetence in its conduct by the Conservative Party. The Liberals, it appeared, would have made quite a different set of mistakes. As a second string, they suggested that the Liberals would have shown such tact in their diplomacy that war might possibly have been avoided altogether, and all its objects—like making President Kruger give way—have been achieved without shedding blood. All this of course rested on mere assertion. I rejoined that however the negotiations had been conducted, they had broken down because the Boers invaded British territory; and that however ill the war had been waged, we had now repulsed the invaders and taken both their capitals. The Conservative Party throughout the country also argued that this was a special election on the sole national issue of the justice of the war and to win a complete

victory; and that ordinary class, sectarian, and party differences ought to be set aside by patriotic men. This at the time
was my sincere belief.

Mr. Chamberlain himself came to speak for me. There
was more enthusiasm over him at this moment than after
the Great War for Mr. Lloyd George and Sir Douglas Haig
combined. There was at the same time a tremendous opposition; but antagonism had not wholly excluded admiration
from their breasts. We drove to our great meeting together
in an open carriage. Our friends had filled the theatre; our
opponents thronged its approaches. At the door of the theatre our carriage was jammed tight for some minutes in an
immense hostile crowd, all groaning and booing at the tops
of their voices, and grinning with the excitement of seeing a
famous fellow-citizen whom it was their right and duty to
oppose. I watched my honoured guest with close attention.
He loved the roar of the multitude, and with my father
could always say 'I have never feared the English democracy.' The blood mantled in his cheek, and his eye as it
caught mine twinkled with pure enjoyment. I must explain
that in those days we had a real political democracy led by a
hierarchy of statesmen, and not a fluid mass distracted by
newspapers. There was a structure in which statesmen, electors and the press all played their part. Inside the meeting
we were all surprised at Mr. Chamberlain's restraint. His
soft purring voice and reasoned incisive sentences, for most
of which he had a careful note, made a remarkable impression. He spoke for over an hour; but what pleased the audience most was that, having made a mistake in some fact or
figure to the prejudice of his opponents, he went back and
corrected it, observing that he must not be unfair. All this
was before the liquefaction of the British political system
had set in.

When we came to count the votes, of which there were
nearly 30,000, it was evident that the Liberals and Labour-
ists formed the stronger party in Oldham. Mr. Emmott

headed the poll. However, it appeared that about 200 Liberals who had voted for him had given their second votes to me out of personal goodwill and war feeling. So I turned Mr. Runciman out of the second place and was elected to the House of Commons by the modest margin of 230 votes. I walked with my friends through the tumult to the Conservative Club. There I found already awaiting me the glowing congratulations of Lord Salisbury. The old Prime Minister must have been listening at the telephone, or very near it, for the result. Then from every part of the country flowed in a stream of joyous and laudatory messages. Henceforward I became a 'star turn' at the election. I was sought for from every part of the country. I had to speak in London the next night, and Mr. Chamberlain demanded the two following nights in the Birmingham area. I was on my way to fulfil these engagements, when my train was boarded by a messenger from Mr. Balfour informing me that he wished me to cancel my London engagement, to come back at once to Manchester and speak with him that afternoon, and to wind up the campaign in Stockport that night. I obeyed.

Mr. Balfour was addressing a considerable gathering when I arrived. The whole meeting rose and shouted at my entry. With his great air the Leader of the House of Commons presented me to the audience. After this I never addressed any but the greatest meetings. Five or six thousand electors —all men—brimming with interest, thoroughly acquainted with the main objects, crowded into the finest halls, with venerated pillars of the party and many-a-year members of Parliament sitting as supporters on the platform! Such henceforward in that election and indeed for nearly a generation were my experiences. I spent two days with Mr. Chamberlain at Highbury. He passed the whole of one of them in bed resting; but after I had been carried around in a special train to three meetings in the Midland area, he received me at supper in his most gleaming mood with a bottle of '34 port. For three weeks I had what seemed to me a triumphal progress through the country. The party managers selected the critical seats, and quite a lot of victories followed in my train. I was twenty-six. Was it wonderful that I should have thought I had arrived? But luckily life is not so easy as all that: otherwise we should get to the end too quickly.

There seemed however to be still two important steps to be taken. The first was to gather sufficient money to enable me to concentrate my attention upon politics without having to do any other work. The sales of *The River War* and of my two books of war correspondence from South Africa, together with the ten months' salary amounting to £2,500 from the *Morning Post*, had left me in possession of more than £4,000. An opportunity of increasing this reserve was now at hand. I had planned to lecture all the autumn and winter at home and in America. The English tour began as soon as the election was over. Having already spoken every night for five weeks, I had now to undergo two and a half months of similar labours interrupted only by the week's voyage across the ocean. The lectures in England were successful. Lord Wolseley presided over the first, and the greatest personages in the three kingdoms on both sides of politics took the chair as I moved from one city to another. All the largest halls were crowded with friendly audiences to whom, aided by a magic lantern, I unfolded my adventures and escape, all set in the general framework of the war. I hardly ever earned less than £100 a night and often much more. At the Philharmonic Hall in Liverpool I gathered over £300. Altogether in the month of November I banked safely over £4,500, having toured little more than half of Great Britain.

Parliament was to meet in the opening days of December, and I longed to take my seat in the House of Commons. I had however, instead, to cross the Atlantic to fulfil my engagements. A different atmosphere prevailed in the United States. I was surprised to find that many of these amiable and hospitable Americans who spoke the same language and seemed in essentials very like ourselves, were not nearly so excited about the South African War as we were at home. Moreover a great many of them thought the Boers were in the right; and the Irish everywhere showed themselves actively hostile. The audiences varied from place to place. At Baltimore only a few hundreds assembled in a hall which would have held 5,000. At Boston, on the other hand, an enormous pro-British demonstration was staged, and even the approaches to the Tremont Hall were thronged. The platform here was composed of 300 Americans in red uniforms belonging to an Anglo-American Society, and the aspect of the meeting was magnificent. In Chicago I encountered vociferous opposition. However, when I made a few jokes against myself, and paid a sincere tribute to the courage and humanity of the Boers, they were placated. On the whole I found it easy to make friends with American audiences. They were cool and critical, but also urbane and good-natured.

Throughout my journeyings I received the help of eminent Americans. Mr. Bourke Cockran, Mr. Chauncey Depew, and other leading politicians presided, and my opening lecture in New York was under the auspices of no less a personage than 'Mark Twain' himself. I was thrilled by this famous companion of my youth. He was now very old and snow-white, and combined with a noble air a most delightful style of conversation. Of course we argued about the war. After some interchanges I found myself beaten back to the citadel 'My country right or wrong.' 'Ah,' said the old gentleman, 'When the poor country is fighting for its life, I agree. But this was not your case.' I think however I did not displease him; for he was good enough at my request to sign every one of the thirty volumes of his works for my benefit; and in the first volume he inscribed the following maxim intended, I daresay, to convey a gentle admonition: 'To do good is noble; to teach others to do good is nobler, and no trouble.'

All this quiet tolerance changed when we crossed the

Canadian border. Here again were present the enthusiastic throngs to which I had so easily accustomed myself at home. Alas, I could only spend ten days in these inspiring scenes. In the middle of January I returned home and resumed my tour of our cities. I visited every one of them. When I spoke in the Ulster Hall, the venerable Lord Dufferin introduced me. No one could turn a compliment so well as he. I can hear him now saying with his old-fashioned pronunciation, 'And this young man—at an age when many of his contemporaries have hardly left their studies—has seen more active service than half the general *orficers* in Europe.' I had not thought of this before. It was good.

When my tour came to an end in the middle of February, I was exhausted. For more than five months I had spoken for an hour or more almost every night except Sundays, and often twice a day, and had travelled without ceasing, usually by night, rarely sleeping twice in the same bed. And this had followed a year of marching and fighting with rarely a roof or a bed at all. But the results were substantial. I had in my possession nearly £10,000. I was entirely independent and had no need to worry about the future, or for many years to work at anything but politics. I sent my £10,000 to my father's old friend, Sir Ernest Cassel, with the instruction 'Feed my sheep.' He fed the sheep with great prudence. They did not multiply fast, but they fattened steadily, and none of them ever died. Indeed from year to year they had a few lambs; but these were not numerous enough for me to live upon. I had every year to eat a sheep or two as well; so gradually my flock grew smaller, until in a few years it was almost entirely devoured. Nevertheless, while it lasted, I had no care.

CHAPTER XXIX

THE HOUSE OF COMMONS

PARLIAMENT reassembled late in February and plunged immediately into fierce debates. In those days the proceedings in the House of Commons were fully reported in the Press and closely followed by the electors. Crucial questions were often argued with sustained animation in three-day debates. During their course all the principal orators contended, and at their close the parties took decisive trials of strength. The House used to sit till midnight, and from 9.30 onwards was nearly always crowded. It was Mr. Balfour's practice as Leader to wind up almost every important debate, and the chiefs of the Opposition, having summed up in massive form their case from ten to eleven, heard a comprehensive reply from eleven to twelve. Anyone who tried to speak after the leaders had finished was invariably silenced by clamour.

It was an honour to take part in the deliberations of this famous assembly which for centuries had guided England through numberless perils forward on the path of empire. Though I had done nothing else for many months but address large audiences, it was with awe as well as eagerness that I braced myself for what I regarded as the supreme ordeal. As I had not been present at the short winter session, I had only taken my seat for four days before I rose to address the House. I need not recount the pains I had taken to prepare, nor the efforts I had made to hide the work of preparation. The question in debate, which raised the main issue of the war, was one upon which I felt myself competent to argue or advise. I listened to counsel from many friendly quarters. Some said 'It is too soon; wait for a few months till you know the House.' Others said 'It is your subject: do not miss the chance.' I was warned against offending the House by being too controversial on an occasion when everyone wished to show goodwill. I was warned against mere colourless platitude. But the best advice I got was from Mr. Henry Chaplin, who said to me in his rotund manner, 'Don't be hurried; unfold your case. If you have anything to say, the House will listen.'

I learned that a rising young Welshman, a pro-Boer, and one of our most important bugbears, named Lloyd George, who from below the gangway was making things very difficult for the leaders of the Liberal party, would probably be called about nine o'clock. He had a moderately phrased amendment on the paper, but whether he would move it was not certain. I gathered that I could, if I wished, have the opportunity of following him. In those days, and indeed for many years, I was unable to say anything (except a sentence in rejoinder), that I had not written out and committed to memory beforehand. I had never had the practice which comes to young men at the University of speaking in small debating societies impromptu upon all sorts of subjects. I had to try to foresee the situation and to have a number of variants ready to meet its possibilities. I therefore came with a quiverful of arrows of different patterns and sizes, some of which I hoped would hit the target. My concern was increased by the uncertainty about what Mr. Lloyd George would do. I hoped that the lines I had prepared would follow fairly well from what he would probably say.

The hour arrived. I sat in the corner seat above the gangway, immediately behind the Ministers, the same seat from which my father had made his speech of resignation and his terrible Piggott attack. On my left, a friendly counsellor, sat the long-experienced Parliamentarian, Mr. Thomas Gibson Bowles. Towards nine o'clock the House began to fill. Mr. Lloyd George spoke from the third bench below the gangway on the Opposition side, surrounded by a handful of Welshmen and Radicals, and backed by the Irish Nationalist

party. He announced forthwith that he did not intend to
move his amendment, but would instead speak on the main
question. Encouraged by the cheers of the 'Celtic fringes' he
soon became animated and even violent. I constructed in
succession sentence after sentence to hook on with after he
should sit down. Each of these poor couplings became in turn
obsolete. A sense of alarm and even despair crept across me.
I repressed it with an inward gasp. Then Mr. Bowles whispered 'You might say "instead of making his violent speech
without moving his moderate amendment, he had better
have moved his moderate amendment without making his
violent speech."' Manna in the wilderness was not more
welcome! It fell only just in time. To my surprise I heard
my opponent saying that he 'would curtail his remarks as he
was sure the House wished to hear a new member,' and with
this graceful gesture he suddenly resumed his seat.

I was up before I knew it, and reciting Tommy Bowles's
rescuing sentence. It won a general cheer. Courage returned.
I got through all right. The Irish—whom I had been taught
to detest—were a wonderful audience. They gave just the
opposition which would help, and said nothing they thought
would disturb. They did not seem the least offended when I
made a joke at their expense. But presently when I said 'the
Boers who are fighting in the field—*and if I were a Boer, I
hope I should be fighting in the field*—. . . .' I saw a
ruffle upon the Treasury bench below me. Mr. Chamberlain
said something to his neighbour which I could not hear. Afterwards George Wyndham told me it was 'That's the way
to throw away seats!' But I could already see the shore at no
great distance, and swam on vigorously till I could scramble
up the beach, breathless physically, dripping metaphorically,
but safe. Everyone was very kind. The usual restoratives
were applied, and I sat in a comfortable coma till I was strong
enough to go home. The general verdict was not unfavourable. Although many guessed I had learnt it all by heart,
this was pardoned because of the pains I had taken. The

House of Commons, though gravely changed, is still an august collective personality. It is always indulgent to those who are proud to be its servants.

After this debate I first made the acquaintance of Mr. Lloyd George. We were introduced at the Bar of the House of Commons. After compliments, he said 'Judging from your sentiments, you are standing against the Light.' I replied 'You take a singularly detached view of the British Empire.' Thus began an association which has persisted through many vicissitudes.

I only made two more really successful speeches from the Conservative benches in this Parliament, and both were in its earliest months. The War Office had appointed a certain General Colville to command a brigade at Gibraltar. Having done this they became dissatisfied about his conduct in some South African action fought nearly a year before, but the facts of which they had only just found out. They therefore dismissed him from his command. The Opposition championed the General and censured his belated punishment. There was a row at Question time, and a debate was fixed for the following week. Here was a country with which I was familiar, and I had plenty of time to choose the best defensive positions. The debate opened ill for the Government, and criticism was directed upon them from all sides. In those days it was a serious matter for an Administration, even with a large majority, to be notably worsted in debate. It was supposed to do harm to the party. Ministers were quite upset if they felt that Harcourt, Asquith, Morley or Grey had broken their front in any degree. I came in well on this, with what everybody thought was a debating speech; but it was only the result of a lucky anticipation of the course of the debate. In fact I defended the Government by arguments which appealed to the Opposition. The Conservatives were pleased and the Liberals complimentary. George Wyndham, now Irish Secretary, with whom I became increasingly intimate, told me that nice things were said in the highest ministerial circles. I really seemed to be finding my footing in the House.

Meanwhile however I found myself in marked reaction from the dominant views of the Conservative party. I was all for fighting the war, which had now flared up again in a desultory manner, to a victorious conclusion; and for that purpose I would have used far larger numbers, and also have organised troops of a higher quality than were actually employed. I would also have used Indian troops. At the same time I admired the dauntless resistance of the Boers, resented the abuse with which they were covered and hoped for an honourable peace which should bind these brave men and their leaders to us for ever. I thought farm-burning a hateful folly; I protested against the execution of Commandant Scheepers; I perhaps played some part behind the scenes in averting the execution of Commandant Kruitzinger. My divergences extended to a wider sphere. When the Secretary of State for War said 'It is by accident that we have become a military nation. We must endeavour to remain one,' I was offended. I thought we should finish the war by force and generosity, and then make haste to return to paths of peace, retrenchment and reform. Although I enjoyed the privilege of meeting in pleasant circles most of the Conservative leaders, and was always treated with extraordinary kindness and good nature by Mr. Balfour; although I often saw Mr. Chamberlain and heard him discuss affairs with the greatest freedom, I drifted steadily to the left. I found that Rosebery, Asquith and Grey and above all John Morley seemed to understand my point of view far better than my own chiefs. I was fascinated by the intellectual stature of these men and their broad and inspiring outlook upon public affairs, untrammelled as it was by the practical burden of events.

The reader must remember that not having been to a university, I had not been through any of those processes of youthful discussion by which opinion may be formed or reformed in happy irresponsibility. I was already a well-known public character. I—at least—attached great importance to everything I said, and certainly it was often widely published. I became anxious to make the Conservative party follow Liberal courses. I was in revolt against 'jingoism.' I had a sentimental view about the Boers. I found myself differing from both parties in various ways, and I was so untutored as to suppose that all I had to do was to think out what was right and express it fearlessly. I thought that loyalty in this outweighed all other loyalties. I did not understand the importance of party discipline and unity, and the sacrifices of opinion which may lawfully be made in their cause.

My third speech was a very serious affair. Mr. Brodrick, Secretary of State for War, had announced his scheme for reorganising the Army on a somewhat larger scale. He proposed to form all the existing forces, regulars, militia and volunteers, into six army corps by what would in the main be a paper transaction. I resolved to oppose this whenever the Army Estimates should be introduced. I took six weeks to prepare this speech, and learnt it so thoroughly off by heart that it hardly mattered where I began it or how I turned it. Two days were assigned for the discussion, and by good fortune and the favour of the Speaker I was called at eleven o'clock on the first day. I had one hour before a division after midnight was taken on some other subject. The House was therefore crowded in every part, and I was listened to throughout with the closest attention. I delivered what was in effect a general attack, not only upon the policy of the Government, but upon the mood and tendency of the Conservative party, urging peace, economy and reduction of armaments. The Conservatives treated me with startled consideration, while the Opposition of course cheered generously. As a speech it was certainly successful; but it marked a definite divergence of thought and sympathy from nearly all those who thronged the benches around me. I had sent it off to the *Morning Post* beforehand, and it was already in print. What would have happened if I had not been called, or had not got through with it, I cannot imagine. The worry and anxiety of manufacturing and letting off a set piece of this kind were harassing. I was much relieved when it was over. But certainly to have the whole House of Commons listening as they had seemed to me a tremendous event, and to repay both the effort and the consequences.

Meanwhile we had formed our small Parliamentary society nicknamed 'The Hooligans.' It consisted of Lord Percy, Lord Hugh Cecil, Mr. Ian Malcolm, Mr. Arthur Stanley and myself. We dined every Thursday in the House and always invited one distinguished guest. All the leading men on both sides came. Sometimes we entertained well-known strangers like Mr. W. J. Bryan. We even asked Lord Salisbury himself. But he replied by bidding us dine with him at Arlington Street. The Prime Minister was in the best of humours, and conversed majestically on every subject that was raised. As we walked out into the street Percy said to me, 'I wonder how it feels to have been Prime Minister for twenty years, and to be just about to die.' With Lord Salisbury much else was to pass away. His retirement and death marked the end of an epoch. The new century of storm and change had already embraced the British Empire in its fierce grip.

The world in which Lord Salisbury had reigned, the times and scenes with which these pages have dealt, the structure and character of the Conservative Party, the foundations of English governing society, all were soon to be separated from us by gulfs and chasms such as have rarely opened in so brief a space. Little could we foresee how strong would be the tides that would bear us forward or apart with resistless force; still less the awful convulsions which would shake the world and shiver into fragments the structures of the nineteenth century. However, Percy had a premonition of events he was not destined to see. When I walked with him in the autumn at Dunrobin, he explained to me the Irvingite religion. There had it appeared been twelve apostles sent to warn mankind; but their message had been disregarded. The last of them had died on the same day as Queen Victoria. Our chance of safety was therefore gone. He predicted with strange assurance an era of fearful wars and of terrors unmeasured and renewing. He used the word Armageddon, of which I had only previously heard mention in the Bible. It happened that the German Crown Prince was staying at Dunrobin. I could not help wondering whether this agreeable young man, our companion in pillow-fights and billiardtable fives, would play any part in the realisation of Percy's sombre prophecies.

In April 1902 a breeze arose in the House of Commons about a certain Mr. Cartwright. This man was a newspaper editor who had courageously published a letter criticising the treatment of Boer women and children in concentration camps. He had been tried for sedition and imprisoned for a year in South Africa. He had served his sentence and wished to come to England. The military authorities in South Africa refused him leave, and when Ministers were interrogated upon this in Parliament, the Under Secretary for War replied 'that it was undesirable to increase the number of persons in England who disseminated anti-British propaganda.' Thus an abuse of power was defended by the worst of reasons: for where else could anti-British propaganda be less harmful at this time than in Great Britain? John Morley moved an adjournment. In those days such a motion was discussed forthwith. All the Opposition leaders spoke with indignation, and I and another of our small group supported them from the Conservative benches. The matter was trumpery, but feeling ran high.

That night we were to have Mr. Chamberlain as our dinner guest. 'I am dining in very bad company,' he observed, surveying us with a challenging air. We explained how inept and arrogant the action of the Government had been. How could we be expected to support it? 'What is the use,' he replied, 'of supporting your own Government only when it is right? It is just when it is in this sort of pickle that you ought to have come to our aid.' However, as he mellowed, he became most gay and captivating. I never remember having heard him talk better. As he rose to leave he paused at the door, and turning said with much deliberation, 'You young gentlemen have entertained me royally, and in return I will give you a priceless secret. Tariffs! There are the politics of the future, and of the near future. Study them closely and make yourselves masters of them, and you will not regret your hospitality to me.'

He was quite right. Events were soon to arise in the fiscal sphere which were to plunge me into new struggles and absorb my thoughts and energies at least until September 1908, when I married and lived happily ever afterwards.